Barrier

Barrier

THE SEAM OF
THE ISRAELI-PALESTINIAN
CONFLICT

Isabel Kershner

First published 2005 by
PALGRAVE MACMILLAN™
175 Fifth Avenue, New York, N.Y. 10010 and
Houndmills, Basingstoke, Hampshire, England RG21 6XS.
Companies and representatives throughout the world.

PALGRAVE MACMILLAN is the global academic imprint of the Palgrave
Macmillan division of St. Martin's Press, LLC and of Palgrave Macmillan Ltd.
Macmillan® is a registered trademark in the United States, United Kingdom
and other countries. Palgrave is a registered trademark in the European Union
and other countries.

ISBN 1–4039–6801–2 hardback

Library of Congress Cataloging-in-Publication Data
Barrier: the seam of the Israeli-Palestinian conflict / Isabel Kershner.
    p.   cm.
  ISBN 1–4039–6801–2
  1. Arab-Israeli conflict—1993-   2. Israeli West Bank Barrier.   I. Title.

DS119.76.K37   2005
956.05'3—dc22

2005048701

A catalogue record for this book is available from the British Library.

Design by Letra Libre, Inc.

First edition: November 2005
10   9   8   7   6   5   4   3   2

Printed in the United States of America

For Hirsh, Gavriel, and Lev, with love

Contents

Photos

Acknowledgments

Whenever my editor at Palgrave Macmillan, David Pervin, worried about meeting deadlines on this project, I always assured him that this manuscript would be completed long before the security barrier was. At least on that score, I have not let him down. I thank David deeply for approaching me with the idea for this book in the first place and for guiding the whole creative process through from beginning to end with skill, tenacity, perceptiveness and even some humor.

I am grateful to my colleagues at *The Jerusalem Report*, particularly former chief editor David Horovitz and current chief editor Sharon Ashley, for giving me the space and time to write this book, for being ever encouraging and accommodating, and for allowing me to pursue my interests and obsessions. I thank all my peers at *The Jerusalem Report* who have covered for me and contributed to my education over the years. I am especially indebted to Gershom Gorenberg and Adi Covitz for their assistance.

Ehud Ya'ari has been a true mentor and a continual inspiration to me. Fellow journalist Khaled Abu Toameh has made an invaluable contribution to this project by opening up parts of the West Bank I could never have otherwise reached. The same applies to my colleague Saud Abu Ramadan in the Gaza Strip. Ehud Ya'ari, Sharon Ashley, and Hirsh Goodman all read the manuscript in its early stages and made some crucial comments and observations. Any errors in the text are my own.

Numerous others have offered their time and assistance, among them Marc Luria of Security Fence for Israel and Daniel Seidemann of Ir Amim in Jerusalem, Sani Meo in Ramallah, the staff of ECF in Tel Aviv, Monica Awad, Steffen Jensen, the IDF Spokesperson's Office, and the Israel-Palestine Center for Research and Information. I have drawn on the resources and publications of many organizations for purposes of research, including the IDF, B'Tselem, the PLO Negotiations Affairs Department and Negotiations Support Unit, the Association for Civil Rights in Israel, BIMKOM (Planners for Planning Rights), and the local and foreign media. Among the books I have used for reference are *Warrior* by Ariel Sharon, *Story of My Life* by Moshe Dayan (Hebrew), *Jerusalem* by Ze'ev Vilnai (Hebrew), *The Story of the Security Fence* by Yeshayahu Folman (Hebrew), *Intifada* by Ze'ev Schiff and Ehud Ya'ari, *Israel* by Martin Gilbert, and *Just Beyond Reach* by Gilead Sher (Hebrew).

My sincere thanks go to Esteban Alterman, photo editor of *The Jerusalem Report*, for the photographs he has contributed. For the use of the other photographs, credit goes to the Israeli Government Press Office, B'Tselem, and the PLO Negotiation Affairs Department. The maps were prepared by Avigdor Orgad.

Finally, this book would never have been written without the patience, unconditional love and support of my family. My parents, Harold and Doreen, have always provided me with the confidence and freedom to do things my own way. My adorable sons, Gavriel and Lev, make sure I always keep things in perspective and have given me lots of turns on the computer. They are glad to have me back. But after writing all these words, none seem adequate to express my gratitude to, and profound love for, my husband Hirsh. A respected journalist and author, Hirsh has believed in me from the day we met. Hirsh always says it takes a journalist to know one. His devotion and understanding have allowed me to aspire and grow. I could not wish for a kinder, more generous, wiser or more entertaining soul mate. May we, and everyone who inhabits this land, know peace.

Jerusalem 2005

1. *The Region.*

2. Israel, the West Bank, and Gaza Strip.

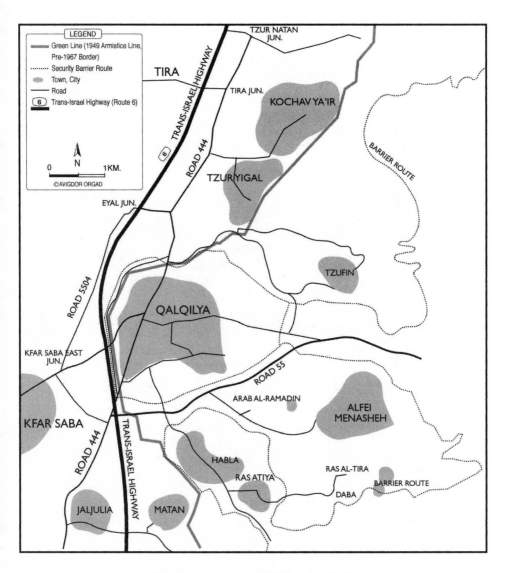

3. *Qalqilya area and the Alfei Menashe "Enclave."*

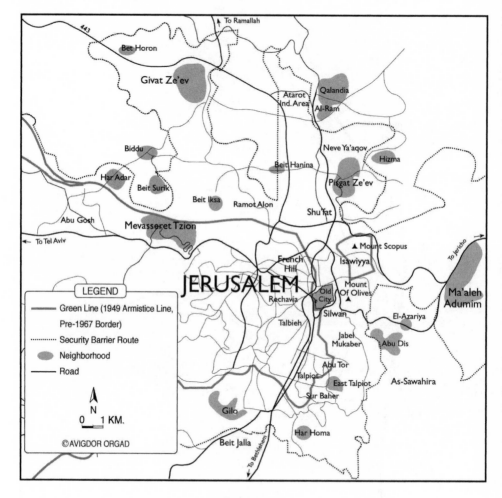

4. Jerusalem area.

5. *The Gaza Strip*

1

The Stolen Sunset

Sami Khadar leads as we clamber over a patch of long grass and thistles toward the base of the immense, glowering wall. Running for two kilometers along the 1949 armistice line, known as the Green Line, this curtain of concrete, part of Israel's new security barrier, divides the West Bank Palestinian city of Qalqilya from Israel's coastal plain, which lies a few meters away from us on the other side. Here, the Green Line, formerly an invisible boundary, has turned an ugly, depressing gray.

Khadar, a physically rounded, intellectual-looking 41-year-old with steel-framed spectacles, is sporting weekend stubble, this being Friday, the Muslim day of rest. He glances nervously in the direction of a steel-colored, cylindrical army watchtower built into the wall about 50 meters from where we are standing and points out the security cameras dotted at regular intervals along the top. "Are these people shooting or not?" he wonders aloud in Arabic-accented English, somewhat concerned for our safety and panting slightly from the minor exertion as we proceed gingerly across a narrow dirt path and up to the wall itself. "Why are these holes here?" he inquires, examining one of several hollow tubes that have been drilled through the otherwise opaque 8-meter high slabs, right above us. "Perhaps to let the wind through," he surmises. "It is the first time I see these holes."

The air tubes slant upwards from this side of the wall, presumably so that they cannot be used by local gunmen to shoot at the cars speeding along the ultra-modern Trans-Israel Highway, Israel's sleek north-south toll road that runs parallel to our dirt track on the other side of the barrier. If someone on the Israeli (western) side were to shoot through the tubes into Qalqilya, on the other hand, they would be aiming roughly at head height. Khadar stretches out a hand and touches the slightly corrugated surface of the wall, like a pilgrim arriving at a revered site. "It's soft," he says, meaning smooth.

Sami Khadar is the veterinarian at Qalqilya Zoo, the only zoo in the West Bank. Its cages, dingy and cramped, with bare concrete floors, have long served as a metaphor for this Palestinian city of 43,000, which now finds itself entrapped, surrounded by the security barrier from nearly all sides. Where the concrete wall ends, curving around at the corners a little before coming to an abrupt stop, the chain-link security fence picks up. The fence courses through the fields on the outskirts of Qalqilya, looping around it from the north and south and turning the city into a virtual enclave. There is one narrow opening in the fence to the east, like the neck of a bottle, where a bumpy two-lane road leads in and out of the West Bank. From the outside, Qalqilya, with its wall, guard towers, and fences, resembles a prison camp. "One man told me that my zoo is a small jail, and Qalqilya is a big jail," Khadar says, trying to raise a half-hearted smile.

For the Israelis, the barrier is less an expression of choice than a measure of last resort. Since the outbreak of the Al-Asqa intifada in September 2000, ceaseless infiltrations by Palestinian suicide bombers and gunmen had taken a terrible toll as they crossed the Green Line into Israel with what security officials decried as "unbearable ease." In more than four years of violence around 1,000 Israelis had lost their lives, two thirds of them civilians and over half of them—men, women, and children—killed inside the Green Line. (During the same period, over 3,300 Palestinians were killed in Israeli retaliatory raids, some 650 of them minors under the age of 18.) Qalqilya itself spawned one of the worst outrages of the intifada when, in June 2001, Sa'id Hassan Hutari, a 22-year-old resident of the town, blew himself up in the middle of a crowd at the entrance of the Dolphinarium discoteque in Tel Aviv. Twenty-one Israelis were killed, most of them teenage immigrants from the former Soviet Union who were waiting to get into the club.

The suicide bombers proved a particularly potent weapon. While they carried out only 0.5 percent of the total number of hostile acts against Israelis, they were responsible for more than 50 percent of the deaths. These human bombs would go off in buses, in cafés, and in shopping malls, their explosive belts and vests packed with nails, bolts, and ball bearings to maximize the numbers killed and maimed. They posed an existential threat to the Israeli way of life, with parents scared of going together to a restaurant

1. *If this barrier promises Israelis a sense of security, to the Palestinians it feels like a noose closing in: The wall at Qalqilya, November 2003. Credit: B'Tselem.*

or supermarket for fear of leaving behind orphans, and with children not knowing if the bus they were riding to school would ever arrive. The terrorists also posed a strategic threat, dictating a war policy and vetoing any chance for a resumption of political talks.

The Palestinian terror campaign peaked in March 2002, when a Passover-eve suicide bombing in Netanya's Park Hotel killed 30, bringing the number of Israeli dead to over 130 in that month alone. In response, the army launched Operation Defensive Shield, reinvading all the Palestinian cities of the West Bank in the biggest military campaign seen there since Israel conquered the territory in the 1967 war. At the same time, Prime Minister Ariel Sharon reluctantly gave in to mounting public pressure and brought the plans for the security barrier to the cabinet table for approval, setting in motion one of the most expensive and ambitious national infrastructure projects Israel has ever undertaken.

Once completed, the 600 kilometers of barrier twisting along the length of the West Bank will mostly consist of wire fence, with only five or six percent of the total route made up of solid concrete walls. In Hebrew the barrier is invariably referred to as "the fence," evoking images of orderly boundaries and good neighborliness. In Arabic the Palestinians have dubbed it "the wall," reflecting their utter rejection of what they see as a new blight on the landscape. The obvious allusions to Berlin are compounded by the fact that most of the concrete walls have gone up in densely populated Palestinian areas for all to see, rather than in the open countryside, generally because the concrete panels, which are 45 centimeters thick, take up less space than the fence apparatus, minimizing the need to demolish buildings in the urban barrier's path.

The rest of the barrier is a formidable system at least 45 meters wide. At the center is a "smart" wire fence equipped with electronic sensors and video cameras that immediately alert the security forces of any attempted infiltrations. A military patrol road runs alongside, flanked by two sand tracking paths that would reveal the likely direction taken by any infiltrator who succeeded in getting through. On the Palestinian (eastern) side lies a deep ditch to prevent vehicles from crashing through, and the whole apparatus is bordered by mounds of coiled razor wire on either side as an extra means of deterrence, and to mark the limits of the closed military zone.

Stressing the purely security aspect of the barrier, Israeli officials go so far as to call it an "anti-terror obstacle" at times, so as to leave no doubt about its purpose, while Palestinian officials routinely refer to it as the "racist separation" or "apartheid" wall, an unwelcome physical intrusion that divides Arabs from Jews in some parts and Palestinians from Palestinians in others. The semantic difference reflects a conceptual chasm. If this barrier promises Israelis a sense of security, to the Palestinians it feels like a noose closing in, cutting into the territory of their future state and creating what they fear will become a series of barely connected "Bantustans" in the West Bank.

The Qalqilya wall has become a particular symbol of perceived Israeli inhumanity in the Palestinian anti-separation-barrier campaign. Khadar is almost proud to show it off, like a national treasure. This two-kilometer stretch of concrete went up along the city's western boundary in the second half of 2002, designed both to stop suicide bombers reaching the Israeli coastal cities and to protect the Trans-Israel Highway from Palestinian sniper fire. It has not been 100 percent effective: One night in June 2003, gunmen from Qalqilya slunk through a water sluice running under the wall, shot dead a 7-year-old Israeli girl, Noam Leibowitz, who was sleeping in the back seat of her parents' car driving along the highway, and escaped back into the city the same way. The entrances to the water tunnels have since been sealed with alarmed metal grates.

Qalqilya's geographic location at Israel's narrowest point, where only 14 kilometers separate this West Bank city from the Mediterranean Sea, has defined its recent history for good and bad. In 1948, the city was used as a staging area for Iraqi forces that had joined the Jordanian, Egyptian, Syrian, and Lebanese troops, along with other Arab irregulars, in an all-out attack on the newly declared Jewish state, hoping to cut it in two. At the moment of Israel's birth on the night of May 14–15, a young Ariel Sharon was crawling along the ground here, leading a platoon to blow up a bridge on the outskirts of Qalqilya, under the cover of darkness, in order to slow the Iraqi advance.

Israel's victory in the war simultaneously sealed the Arab defeat, known in Arabic as the *nakba* (catastrophe) that turned some 700,000 Palestinians into refugees, stranded across new borders and unable to return to their former homes. After the war, representatives of Israel and the Arab states had congregated, under the auspices of the United Nations, on the Greek island of Rhodes to officially terminate the hostilities. In what would be a harbinger of the results of many future efforts to bring peace, the Arab countries rejected any possibility of a permanent treaty and accepted only an armistice, or an ending for the time being, of active fighting. By the end of the negotiations over the armistice lines, Israel was established on 78 percent of the territory of what had been Mandatory Palestine. Of the remaining 22 percent, the West Bank, including East Jerusalem, fell under Jordanian control while Egypt took over the Gaza Strip in the south.

Still the hostilities continued, with constant Palestinian infiltrations over the Green Line. Sharon was again in command in the field in 1956 when a reprisal raid against Qalqilya went badly wrong and turned into a pitched battle with Jordanian troops, leaving 18 Israelis and over 100 Jordanians dead. Moshe Dayan, one of the outstanding Israeli commanders of 1948 who personally negotiated the Green Line with Jordan in 1949, was by now the army chief of staff. He had ordered the raid against the Qalqilya police fort in retaliation for a series of attacks from the area by Palestinian *fedayeen* (literally, fighters willing to sacrifice themselves), attacks which had culminated in the murder of two Israeli workers in the orange groves of nearby Tel Mond. Dayan was criticized for what was seen as bad planning, but the Qalqilya battle also led to a serious debate in the defense establishment about the effectiveness of such deterrent operations in fighting Palestinian terror. After all, the Arabs had come to expect the reprisals, and yet the terrorist infiltrations continued unabated.

On June 7, 1967, in the heat of the Six Day War, Qalqilya was conquered by Israel, along with East Jerusalem, Nablus, Tulkarm, and Jericho, ending Jordan's war for the West Bank. Right after the war, Dayan, who was now defense minister, discovered that a third of the buildings in Qalqilya had been blown up by Israeli forces in punitive actions for sniper attacks. This was contrary to the Israeli government policy of the time that called for avoiding harming the civilian population in the war. As a result, some 12,000 of Qalqilya's residents had fled or been chased away. Dayan visited the West Bank town, famous for its citrus, and accompanied the mayor, Hajj Hussein Ali Sabri, to the surrounding groves where many of the new refugees were camping out under the trees. With Dayan's support, the government donated building materials and money for the reconstruction of the town. A year later, when Dayan was injured in an accident at an archeological site, several Arab mayors from the newly conquered West Bank towns came to visit him in the hospital. He was particularly touched by the visit of Qalqilya's mayor, Sabri, who brought him a cluster of oranges still on the branch. Dayan wrote that a personal relationship had formed between them, "two men jointly concerned with the fate of their populations—their bread, their homes, their livelihood, and their health."

Israel's sweeping victory in the Six Day War left it in control of all the territory of Mandatory Palestine and reestablished access to Judaism's holiest sites. For the vast majority of Israelis, the reconnection with the ancient Biblical heartland of Judea and Samaria in the West Bank hills was an exhilarating moment; some saw it as a messianic sign of redemption. For the Palestinians, however, it was a second *nakba* that left almost a million of them under Israeli domination and sent a second wave of refugees east across the Jordan River.

In the immediate aftermath of the 1967 war, it was unclear exactly what Israel wanted in the newly conquered territories, how long it would stay, or what kind of regime would emerge. Dayan, for one, envisioned a functional arrangement whereby the new Israeli rulers would keep open borders and encourage economic integration with the Palestinians, canceling the need for permits and allowing them free movement and access to the Israeli job market. He also established an "open bridges" policy allowing the Palestinians of the West Bank to continue selling their produce over the river in Jordan. Dayan wanted Israel to interfere as little as possible in the day-to-day life of the territories, advocating a policy whereby "an Arab can be born, live, and die in the West Bank without ever seeing an Israeli official." As he once told a journalist, "We must not become involved, issue permits, make regulations, name administrators, become rulers."

Nearly 40 years later, the same questions about Israeli intentions in the conquered territories could just as well apply, while Qalqilya and its environs have turned into the absolute antithesis of all that Dayan desired. Qalqilya's immediate neighbors today include the Israeli coastal plain suburbs of Kfar Saba and Kochav Ya'ir on one side of the Green Line, and Alfei Menashe and Tzufin on the other, two of the scores of Jewish settlements built by Israel in the West Bank since 1967. Precisely because of this proximity, Qalqilya has arguably suffered more harshly than any other West Bank city from the Israeli-imposed security closures and restrictions on movement following the outbreak of the second intifada in September 2000. At first a strict checkpoint regime regulated the flow of people and goods in and out of the city, often closing it down altogether. Three years later, the completion of the first phase of the security barrier had put Qalqilya in virtual solitary confinement.

The 6,000 laborers from the city who used to be able to walk across the Green Line every day for casual work in Israel now stayed home, and the 40 joint business ventures that had opened up over time between Qalqilya and towns in Israel shut down. The Israelis who would flock here on weekends for cheap shopping, dental work, and car repairs stopped coming, prohibited by military order from entering this city—and other cities in the West Bank—following the brutal lynching of two Israeli reservists in Ramallah a few days into the intifada.

Access to the city was also blocked to the 45,000 Palestinians in the 32 rural villages that make up the Qalqilya governorate, Palestinians who look to the city as a center of commerce and services. Moreover, the fences around Qalqilya separated villagers from their lands within the city environs, while landowners inside Qalqilya were separated from their plots outside. With no industry to speak of, Qalqilya still relies on its agricultural base. Yet according to the Palestinian Authority-appointed mayor, Ma'rouf Zahran, some 58 percent of Qalqilya's farmland has ended up beyond the barrier, with the only access to it via a number of farmers' gates that open for a few hours per day, and that on occasion remain closed altogether for security reasons. The UN Relief and Works Agency put unemployment in the city at 76 percent by mid-2004. During the four years of intifada, Mayor Zahran frequently claimed that some 10 percent of Qalqilya's population had abandoned the city in despair.

Nobody stops me as I drive into Qalqilya on the road from the east this Friday afternoon in late February 2005. It is less than three weeks after Prime Minister Ariel Sharon and the newly elected Palestinian leader Abu Mazen, the late Yasser Arafat's successor, met at another historic Middle Eastern summit, this time in the Sinai resort of Sharm el-Sheikh, and declared their commitment to end all violence. The notorious Israeli army checkpoint that used to regulate—and sometimes choke—all traffic in and out of Qalqilya was removed the previous November, around the time of Arafat's death, in an Israeli acknowledgement that the intifada had calmed down; a few armed Palestinian Authority policemen in black uniforms, relics of the Oslo peace process of the 1990s, saunter by the roadside where the checkpoint once stood. At the end of the road lies Route 55. A right turn leads to the Tzufin checkpoint, a yellow-gated border crossing in the fence on the way into Israel. A left turn sets you on the road to the Palestinian city of Nablus.

On the edge of Qalqilya, set in a park is a large black marble monument inscribed with about 500 names of the city's martyrs who have died in battle since 1948. The names of the 74 killed since September 2000 have yet to be added. A little further on, stores appear along the roadside, selling mostly junk. Men sit around in shabby armchairs and sofas on the dusty sidewalk, the used furniture presumably for sale, while secondhand fridges and washing machines looking worse for wear are unloaded off the back of a truck. Children dart by on old bicycles while the odd donkey cart weaves among the light traffic, stopping on red like everyone else. Though it is altogether a drab, cement-colored town with its buildings of two, three, and four stories conforming to no obvious urban plan, the municipality has at least made some effort at the aesthetic level, planting the sandy borders down the middle of the roads with flowers and spindly palms.

Being a Friday there is not much action in the streets, so I head for the zoo. While, during the height of the intifada, the animal park could go for weeks or even months without a single visitor, there is an almost festive atmosphere here this sunny afternoon. Groups of rowdy youths are visiting from the Askar refugee camp near Nablus, and from the Amari camp near Ramallah. Young women in Islamic headscarves are swinging skittishly along with young men and children in a colorful playground while men grill meat on portable barbecues for family picnics on the small patches of lawn, filling the air with the aroma of animal fat dripping on the coals. On the terrace of the no-frills zoo café, more men are sitting drinking black coffee and smoking narghiles to the sound of chanting and drum beating from the small municipal sports stadium next door, where a soccer game is being played.

Sami Khadar has been summoned from home by the duty manager to show me around, and drives up in a beat-up white Renault. He is a patriot at heart and, unusually, a Qalqilyan by choice, who immigrated a few years ago from the diaspora. Khadar's father, a pharmacist, left Qalqilya in 1958 when it was still in Jordanian hands, and went to live in Saudi Arabia with his Egyptian wife. Sami was born there, studied to be a vet, and worked in the oil-rich kingdom for various corporations. When it was time to find a bride, though, Qalqilya called. Sami married, took his wife back to Saudi Arabia for a while, and in 1999 they returned. "It wasn't easy. It took three years of paperwork," he says, until the Israeli authorities allowed him in under a "family reunification" clause by virtue of his marriage. "I had to come back to my country," he explains simply, adding, in another attempt at humor, "Who can live in the 60-degree heat of Dahran all year round?"

Khadar's zoo tour starts at the giraffe enclosure on the edge of the park, between two schools. There is a lone giraffe inside a treeless pebbly square of ground with a few tufts of grass and a tall shelter in the middle. The only information the bent tin sign on the fence provides is that the animal was born in 1995. Khadar introduces her as Ruti, and tells her tragic intifada tale. In response to a sharp escalation in Palestinian terror, the Israeli army reinvaded Qalqilya in the spring of 2002 as part of the massive military campaign, Operation Defensive Shield. The night of the incursion, Ruti's mate Brownie, a nervous type, took fright at the sound of shooting nearby and went running into one of the shelter's metal poles. The giraffe knocked his head and fell down, and with nobody around to raise his long neck up, the drastic change in blood pressure caused him to die. Ruti, who was 13 months in to a 15-month pregnancy, cried for a week, says Khadar, then aborted because of her broken heart. Three zebras and a lama died from tear gas inhalation the same day.

These weren't the zoo's first martyrs to the cause. Opened in 1986 by the city's then Israeli-appointed mayor, Abd al-Rahman Abu Sneineh, the animals had already lived through one intifada, the popular unarmed Palestinian uprising that lasted from late 1987 until the signing of the Oslo accords in 1993. Another male giraffe, who arrived from Israel called Eli but whose name was changed to Ali in deference to his new surroundings, died from tear gas in the early 1990s when soldiers clashed with students from one of the neighboring schools.

But Khadar always tries to make the best of a bad job. If he can't enjoy his animals alive, he puts his skills as a taxidermist to use to preserve them after death. Khadar leads me into a large hangar where hay and animal feed is stored. There stands Brownie and next to him his aborted baby, both stuffed and covered with cobwebs. Khadar would love to keep them in a glass house. "Maybe when the municipality builds me the new museum they've promised me," he says.

In the meantime, Khadar makes do with a small, smelly office where a bearskin is soaking in a bucket of secret formula. Another vat has antlers sticking out, there is a monkey skeleton on the desk, and a half-stuffed zebra, Julie, is propped up in a dark side room on a metal frame. Khadar then leads me to another room that he officiously unlocks. Serving as the beginnings of a natural history museum—Palestine's first—it contains more stuffed animals, a camel skeleton, cases of dead bugs, and fetuses of a sheep, a horse, rabbits, and chickens in various stages of development, the latter grotesquely suspended in jars of formaldehyde. A muezzin calls the faithful to prayer on a crackly loudspeaker from a ladies-only mosque on the floor above us. Khadar wants to turn the mosque into a cinema where the public could instead see educational movies about animals.

Despite the pitifully small cages of the pacing wolves, the grumpy-looking Syrian bears, the lean leopards, and the castrated male lions with nothing more than grimy tubs of water in the middle, Khadar is surprisingly optimistic and bursting with plans for the future. The three lions came as a gift from the Israeli Ramat Gan Safari near Tel Aviv in September 2004, an early sign of renewed Israeli-Palestinian cooperation after the four years of violence, and a resumption of the long-standing association between the safari and the zoo. Cooped in a 12-square-meter cage, Khadar says the lions need at least six times more space, and adds that the Qalqilya city council, which maintains the zoo, has promised to fund development of new areas and larger, more natural enclosures as soon as the PA local elections are over in a few months' time. Khadar recently visited Israel's exquisite Biblical Zoo in West Jerusalem to get some ideas and says he was impressed.

Altogether, Qalqilya appears to be coming to terms with its new, if ugly, reality. Speaking to me on his cell phone a few days after my visit, Mayor Zahran sounds upbeat and states that "Things are definitely improving." Israel recently completed the construction of a $2 million underpass that burrows under the fences to Qalqilya's south and connects the city with the equally isolated neighboring Palestinian locality of Habla, creating a second way in and out of the city. The initial problems that plagued the farmers' gates seem to be smoothing out, with opening times becoming more reliable. Some other smaller roadblocks have been removed, giving some 60 percent of the villages in the Qalqilya district free access to the city, according to Zahran. There is even talk that Israel will hand Qalqilya back to full Palestinian Authority control, returning to the status quo of before September 2000.

From ground level on Qalqilya's densely built city streets, the separation wall and fences are mostly not visible. For a moment they can almost be forgotten. But when I ask Sami Khadar about life on the city's edge, he takes me straight to the nursery of Hassan Kharuf. Because even if Qalqilya is beginning to recover, it is unlikely that Kharuf, a small-time victim of greater powers, ever will.

At the end of a bumpy dirt lane on the western edge of Qalqilya, amid the rows and rows of lush green nursery plants and miniature trees that grow on his family estate, Hassan Kharuf built his dream house and moved in with his wife and four children at the beginning of 2001. The pretty stone bungalow is surrounded by a strip of well-tended garden and bordered by bushes clipped to perfection. "I built out here to see the sunset and breathe fresh air. We used to sit on the porch and look at our lands," says Kharuf, who claims that before there ever was a Green Line, the family property extended for several kilometers toward the sea, all the way to what is now the Israeli town of Ra'anana. Today there are just 37 meters between the house and the 8-meter-high concrete separation wall that Khadar dares to go up and touch for the first time.

The first thing you notice about Kharuf, 45, are his bloodshot eyes. A pot-bellied man with a shock of black hair, a graying mustache, and thick, Shrek-like features, he says he has developed diabetes, an ulcer, and high blood pressure in the past three years. He has also taken up smoking since the wall arrived, and goes through three packs a day. It's like a slow suicide.

The first blow to the Kharuf family came after 1948, when most of their lands ended up on the Israeli side of the armistice line. Israel took another 148-dunam (37- acre) chunk when it conquered the West Bank from Jordan in 1967, he says, and seized a further 40 dunams (10 acres) in 1996 for the Trans-Israel Highway. The army bulldozers and cranes arrived in the second half of 2002 and, panel by panel, put up the solid gray wall, eating up another 40 dunams of land. And his woes are not over yet. A few weeks ago, Kharuf says, a man arrived from the army district liaison office and said Kharuf would have to remove several hothouses that are closest to the wall to clear a 17-meter strip and make way for a proper military patrol road. In all, he says, Israel has offered him a total of $9,000 in compensation. He refuses to take it "because history would judge me. In our religion, anyone who sells land to the Jews buys hell."

He could certainly use the money. Over the past few years, Kharuf has gone from being a wealthy farmer and employer to near bankruptcy. He had to sell his late parents' home in the old quarter of Qalqilya in order to cover a large debt and keep open the nursery he inherited from them. Kharuf's main market used to be in Jordan, and from there, the Gulf, but he claims that since the Israeli-Jordanian peace treaty was signed in 1994, formalizing trade agreements, the bridges are no longer open to him. The security closures and tightened regulations have dried up his market within the territories, and in Qalqilya—impoverished after four years of intifada—gardening is not exactly a priority. Kharuf is ruined. All the PA has been able to offer by way of compensation, he says, is a 100 shekel ($25) monthly food coupon.

We are sitting in an office with a sofa, TV and kitchenette in a large barn where Kharuf—which means young sheep in Arabic—keeps his livestock. Someone brings in a pot of tea that has been burnt on wood to give it a special flavor. "That's how the *fellaheen* [peasants] drink it," says Kharuf, proud of his rural stock. The windows look west toward the wall but the shutters are drawn. "In addition to all this," he relates, referring to the poverty visited upon him by both peace and war, "I have a daughter, Lana, who is three years old. In January 2004, soldiers came to the house to carry out a search at 3 a.m. and said everyone had to come outside into the street. It was very cold. I told them my daughter was ill with fever. I told them, 'You already took my land and I didn't resist you. I'll come out with my older kids, but let Lana and her mother stay inside. She's sick.' One of the soldiers said, 'I'd like to see her die.' Where's the democracy? They claim they have mercy for animals, but they had no mercy for us. Lana came out, and because of that her health deteriorated. She spent 27 days in the intensive care unit in hospital in Nablus. I myself have many Jewish friends. It doesn't mean that all the Jews are bad. The problem is with the leaders who issue the orders to be cruel and send young and ambitious soldiers here instead of 40-year-olds who would have some mercy. The Berlin Wall went. The Jews are rebuilding it. Apartheid has ended in South Africa and they're reestablishing it here! *Khalas*, it's over," he says, brushing the palm of one hand against the other, looking hunched, tired, and terribly sad. "I'm defenseless. It's the big sharks eating the small fish. Before the intifada, a farmer would support his brother, pay for him to study, and even build him a house. The farmers were rich. Now it's the other way round. The university graduate is supporting the farmer." Some would call that progress, but for Kharuf, it's another dishonor and humiliation brought on by the wall.

We walk out, cross the lane, and enter the black-and-gold painted wrought-iron gate into Kharuf's garden. To the west, toward the sea, the horizon is blocked by the line of mammoth, man-made concrete slabs. "The Jews have stolen the sunset," Kharuf declares. "In what religion is that allowed?"

⟶⟦○⟧⟵

Along this particular section of the Israeli-Palestinian seam, at the slimmest part of Israel's "narrow waist," the barrier twists in and out of West Bank territory like spaghetti, contorting itself to take in the Jewish settlements of Alfei Menashe, which lies southeast of Qalqilya, and Tzufin to its north, ensuring that both remain on the western ("Israeli") side of the fence. In these parts, the barrier route clearly adheres to the Israeli fence planners' demographic imperative of "maximum Israelis in, maximum Palestinians out." In doing so, the route has created a number of enclosures like Qalqilya, where Palestinian localities are almost completely looped in by the barrier, or even more bizarrely, the route has created enclaves in which Palestinian villages have become stuck, along with neighboring Jewish settlements, in pockets of land between the fence to the east and the Green Line to the west.

These pockets have been named the "Seam Zone," their new and special status determined by the Israeli officials responsible for the barrier project at the Kafkaesque-sounding Seam Zone Authority at the Defense Ministry in Tel Aviv. All areas between the fence and the Green Line were declared a "closed military area" by the commander of the IDF Central Command forces in October 2003. The military order prohibits entry to the Seam Zone for anyone other than Israeli citizens, West Bank Israeli settlers, and, curiously, Jews from anywhere else in the world, even if they are not citizens of the state.

By contrast, the 10,000 or so Palestinians who live in the villages inside the Seam Zone dangle in a kind of bureaucratic limbo between Israel and Palestine. To stay in their homes, they need to obtain special "green permits" from the army, named for the color of paper on which they are printed and renewable every few months or year. Those with no security record can apply for other permits from the army district liaison office to be able to work in the neighboring Jewish settlements or in Israel proper. Permits and the cooperation of the soldiers at the gates are also required to cross to the agricultural lands the villagers might own on the eastern side of the fence, further inside the West Bank, or to get to the nearest clinic, hospital, or school. Relatives and friends from the West Bank who want to visit families inside the Seam Zone need a special one-day permit to get in. It is as if the Seam Zone residents woke up one morning and found themselves in a new fictional country where permits are the equivalent of bread and air, their fate having been determined by an unseen hand drawing a line on a map.

One example of the new modus vivendi in the Seam Zone is the saga of Khirbet Jubara, an otherwise undistinguished hamlet of around 350 residents in a small enclave between Qalqilya and Tulkarm, the Palestinian city a few kilometers to the north. Khirbet Jubara shares its particular pocket of land between the fence and the Green Line with a Jewish settlement called Sal'it, which has a population of around 400. An April 2002 map drawn up by the Defense Ministry's Seam Zone Authority had also marked what are now open fields between Khirbet Jubara and Sal'it as an invisible settlement called "Ya'arit"—which does not yet exist, and possibly never will.

Colonel (res.) Dany Tirza, the army's head of operations for the fence project, told me in January 2004 that the placement of the fence west of Khirbet Jubara, cutting it off from the rest of the West Bank, had nothing to do with Sal'it but was based purely on security considerations. Many of the houses of Khirbet Jubara are built very close to Taibeh, the Israeli Arab town just across the Green Line, he explained. The army needed to create an "operational margin" between the fence and the Green Line, he continued, or otherwise anybody who managed to cross the fence would disappear inside Taibeh before the army could even give chase. Putting the fence west of Khirbet Jubara provided a two-kilometer security margin.

At first the inhabitants of Khirbet Jubara rebelled against the military authorities, refusing to take out the "green permit" required to continue residing in their homes. "What if they decide one day to take the permission away?" asked Faruq Awad, one of the local council representatives, as we walked down Khirbet Jubara's main drag one drizzly day in late December 2003, among the unimposing houses, neglected hothouses, and chicken coops that make up the village. He noted that the permit includes a clause in the small print specifically stating that it doesn't guarantee any legal right to permanent residency, leading to fears that Israel planned to formally annex the pocket of land and expel its Palestinian residents one day. However, the villagers had relented. This happened after several of them had gone to nearby Tulkarm to tend to their daily affairs but then were not allowed to cross the "Kafriat" army checkpoint, near the dusty quarries south of the city, in order to get back home. After being stuck for two days, the residents of Khirbet Jubara decided en masse to accept the permits, which are valid for one year. About 25 men in the village had initially been refused a green permit by the army, apparently on security grounds. One of those refused, Mustafa Tahina, the 34-year-old bearded imam of the local mosque, said he had spent 1988–89 in prison "for throwing stones during the first intifada." In the end, as part of the green-permit deal struck with the rest of the village, the "security cases" like Tahina all got passes, though theirs would have to be renewed after three months—presumably to allow the army to keep closer track of those it suspected of being potentially troublesome.

Even with the permits, life in Khirbet Jubara is a precarious affair. At the end of 2003 there were 98 children in the village, which has no school. Israel had recently turned down a request from the village council to build a primary school of its own. So while ten pupils were attending school in Tulkarm, most of the children, from first grade up, went to learn in the neighboring villages of Al-Ras, Kafr Zibad, and Kafr Sur, all of which now sat on the other, eastern, side of the fence. To get there, the pupils and several teachers from Khirbet Jubara had to pass through Gate 753, the heavy yellow-painted "schoolchildren's gate" in the barrier that soldiers were supposed to come and open three times a day at fixed hours. When I visited Khirbet Jubara on a school day, a midday batch of first- to third-graders who poured out of a minibus on the West Bank side of the padlocked gate waited only ten minutes for the army jeep to arrive with the key so that they could continue on foot to their homes. Perhaps the conspicuously marked UNICEF vehicle bringing observers from Jerusalem, which was parked on the Khirbet Jubara side of the gate, helped hurry things along. Even so the children were impatiently shaking the gate and tweaking the electronic sensors fixed to it in the hope of getting home sooner for lunch. "We can wait here for ages, and we've got nothing to eat," complained a husky-voiced 7-year-old boy called Hussam. Sometimes, said Nazmia Zibdeh, a school principal and a resident of Khirbet Jubara who was accompanying the children, "You can wait half an hour, an hour, an hour and a half. It depends on the mood of the soldiers."

Everyone spoke about the day in November when it had poured rain, and the drenched children stood at the gate for two hours. After that, UNICEF reached an agreement with the army to erect one tent on either side of the gate so that the children could at least be protected from the elements. Later, the Defense Ministry agreed to fund special buses to take the children door to door. Nevertheless, since the beginning of the school year in September, 15 schooldays had been lost when the gates didn't open at all because of a terror attack in Israel or an intelligence alert of an impending one.

The adults of the village complained of 90 percent unemployment. Faruq Awad said he had lost his job selling tiles in Tulkarm because the frequent security closures had made him an unreliable employee. And while many of the village families still had access to land or hothouses from which to supplement their incomes, many hesitated to invest in seeds and water,

2. It is as if the Seam Zone residents woke up one morning and found themselves in a new fictional country where permits are the equivalent of bread and air: A soldier coming to open the 'schoolchildren's gate' in the fence at Khirbet Jubara, 2003. Credit: NAD-NSU.

fearing that the closures would prevent them from getting their produce to market whether in Israel or the West Bank.

On the first day of 2004, I called Awad on his cell phone from Jerusalem. The village had woken up that morning to a full security closure. "Nobody can come in or out of Jubara today," Awad declared, asserting that even an ambulance called for a sick 40-year-old resident of the village had not been allowed in from Tulkarm. Awad was about to accompany the patient to the checkpoint and "let the soldiers see him," in the hope that something could be done. Jubara itself has no clinic, no doctor, not even a trained midwife or nurse. "Call me any time, you're welcome," Awad signed off, happy for contact with the outside world. At least the airwaves were still open.

In a surprising flip-flop, on January 8, 2004, five days after Colonel Dany Tirza had so painstakingly explained to me the security imperative of placing the fence east of Khirbet Jubara, the army announced that changes in the route were being planned that would put Khirbet Jubara back on the West Bank side of the fence. It was surely no coincidence that the announcement came just ahead of the February hearings against the barrier at the International Court of Justice in The Hague. The changes were reportedly based on the army's desire to ease the life of the Palestinian population and to save the army the added effort of dealing with the villagers' daily needs. Over a year later, in early 2005, Colonel Tirza assured me that the decision to change the barrier's route at Khirbet Jubara remained in place. In the meantime so did the old fence, leaving Khirbet Jubara stranded like a landlocked island.

If the twisting barrier route has created winners and losers, Hisdai Eliezer, the mayor of Alfei Menashe, the West Bank Jewish settlement just south of Qalqilya, is most definitely on the winning side. He receives me at 9:30 on a Monday morning in early 2005 in his functional office in the whitewashed council building overlooking the Samarian hills, animated, invigorated by the flavor of victory and of power. His political stock has definitely gone up: by being placed to the west of the barrier, Alfei Menashe has been saved, its future as a permanent part of Israel apparently assured.

Alfei Menashe is strategically perched 300 meters above sea level on the edge of the West Bank, about five kilometers east of the Green Line. The climb to the settlement is up a winding, scenic road from Route 55, which passes between Qalqilya and Habla and is flanked by the security fence on either side. At the entrance of Alfei Menashe, which is guarded by an armed Israeli in civilian clothes, placards dot the roadside advertising new housing projects that promise to "turn your dream into reality." It is a glorious day up here, bright with sharp blasts of wind. Getting out of my car in the neat parking lot at the small commercial center where the council building sits, I am immediately struck by the splendid view spread out before me of the Tel Aviv skyline and the sparkling blue waters of the Mediterranean beyond.

Alfei Menashe, a middle class, mostly secular "quality of life" settlement, was founded in 1983 as part of Ariel Sharon's Judea and Samaria population plan. Jewish settlement of the Samarian hills in the northern West Bank was initially spearheaded in the mid-1970s by Gush Emunim, the Bloc of the Faithful. This militant, messianic group arose in the aftershock of the 1973 war. It dedicated itself to settling the Arab-populated heartland of the West Bank in order to ensure that no inch of the Land of Israel would ever be relinquished, contrary to the policy of the government of the time, which was led by Yitzhak Rabin and the Labor party. When the Likud party rose to power in 1977, Gush Emunim's settlement enterprise found a willing partner in the industrious minister of agriculture, and later defense, Sharon. But despite its fervor, the Gush Emunim core of ideological settlers proved too limited for Sharon's strategic grand vision of mass Jewish settlement in Judea and Samaria, so in 1980 the Likud hit on the strategy of offering financial incentives to attract ordinary Israelis to swap their small city apartments for more spacious surroundings and fresh air over the Green Line.

Located only a few minutes' drive from the bourgeois towns of Kfar Saba and Kochav Yair in Israel proper, Alfei Menashe, a beautifully landscaped, meticulously maintained community of 6,000, offers Israelis suburban comfort at a more affordable price. The price of an ordinary four-room apartment in Kfar Saba will fetch you a semidetached house with a red-tiled roof and a garden out here. "Upgrading" is the operative word in the buzzing property market on this manicured patch of the Promised Land.

The settlement's main selling point was—and is—that it is "five minutes from Kfar Saba." It is not ideology that brings people out here, but the lure of an extra bedroom or a bigger yard. All this was endangered by four years of intifada and even more by the Sharon government's plans to build a barrier that would put Alfei Menashe on the Palestinian side of the fence. Obviously "quality of life" in the form of an extra bedroom would be no compensation for the risky present and highly uncertain future that would ensue, and property values would plummet accordingly. Subsequent changes involving extraordinary contortions in the route of the barrier have allowed Alfei Menashe to remain within, creating a special enclave in which Hisdai Eliezer is king.

A tall, athletically slim almost 50-year-old with smooth brown hair, hazel eyes, and a thin silver chain round his neck, Eliezer takes full credit for that, though not without some personal qualms. Unlike most of his constituents, who span the Israeli political spectrum but mostly crowd the middle, Eliezer is, by his own account, "very right wing." A member of the powerful Likud Central Committee, the body courted by all the party politicians seeking support in the primaries, he is also vice chairman of the board of the YESHA Council, the Council of Jewish Communities in Judea, Samaria, and the Gaza District, YESHA being an acronym of the Hebrew for Judea (Yehuda), Samaria (Shomron), and Gaza (Aza). To its right-wing supporters, the YESHA Council, founded as a pro-settlement lobby group in the late 1970s, represents the hardy spirit of Zionism, the core dedicated to settling the "greater" land of Israel by all means and against all odds. To its detractors, it is a frighteningly influential organization that has wielded disproportionate power over successive governments and set the country's agenda for decades, managing to exploit the usual Israeli fractiousness and indecision through its own unity and solid sense of purpose.

"When the fence project first came up, we on the YESHA Council were very confused about how to react," Eliezer starts, launching into a spirited monologue that makes my list of prepared questions almost irrelevant. "If we said we were against it, the people of Israel would say, 'Hey, what about our security?' Yet it was clear to us that any route chosen could be seen as the future border of Israel. What if it was to run along the 1967 border?" (which would leave all the settlements out). "We were faced with a very complicated set of dilemmas. We in the YESHA Council sat and drew ourselves a map of a proposed route, and I began a lobbying process in the Knesset to get them to draw the route with us." Eliezer sent his own map to the Defense Ministry, proposing that the barrier extend several fat "fingers" into the West Bank to take in most of the settlements.

The cooperative approach with the government and the military did not work out. The fence architects—chief among them both Colonel Tirza and Prime Minister Sharon—kept their plans under close wraps. "When the bulldozers began marking out the route in Salem in the summer of 2002 and started heading down toward us," Eliezer continues, warming up to his favorite part, "I got calls from the media asking for my reaction to the fact that Alfei Menashe was to be left out, on the east of the fence. I went to war because it was clear to me that if we were left east of the fence, this community would become extinct."

This, he explains, is because unlike the religious Gush Emunim-type settlements, "There's no ideology in Alfei Menashe. This is not a Whole Land of Israel place. People came here apolitical, from all parts of the political spectrum. They came because they assumed Alfei Menashe would always, always remain a part of Israel. They came for quality of life at a reasonable price. Not cheap, but reasonable. If we were fenced out, people would begin to leave because economically, people here can afford to lock up house and rent in the city. Plus there would be no development or growth."

Immediately recognizing the implications of the barrier, Eliezer began intensive work in the Knesset, "putting pressure on Sharon, on Uzi Landau [the hard-line Likud minister for public security who sat on the Knesset fence-route committee], and on elements in the Likud Central Committee, to get them to exert more pressure on Sharon. I chased ministers around the country, organized demonstrations and sit-in strikes opposite the prime minister's office in Jerusalem. I raised an absolute ruckus. After two weeks, on the Wednesday, I gathered the citizens in the amphitheater here to plan the next week's actions." His lobbying and political activity appeared to pay dividends when, the following day, Sharon arrived with defense minister Binyamin Ben Eliezer, IDF deputy chief of staff Gabi Ashkenazi, Tirza, and other top officials to take a first hand look at his concerns. Eliezer recalls: "We sat at the lookout point. Sharon spread the maps out on the hood of the jeep as he likes to do, and on the spot, they redrew the route."

"I didn't blow my own trumpet in the media at the time because I didn't want to kill anything before the fence was built. I wasn't looking for publicity, but for the work to get done. It works. It prevents terror. It hasn't removed my initial dilemmas," he says of his fears that the barrier will turn into a permanent border, condemning much of the settlement enterprise. "Till today, it is not clear to me how it will all end. But a great thing has happened. If property prices went down here 30 percent during the intifada, now we're flourishing! We have 1,000 new housing units planned in [the new neighborhood of] Givat Tal; 300 are already under construction. People say it's my success, but I'm not looking for headlines."

Modesty aside, the victory has also had a sobering effect and has given Eliezer pause, not only because dozens of Jewish settlements will remain outside the fence, but because of what it taught him about the inner workings of the Jewish state. "I understood in those two weeks that we live in a country where the decision-making process is fundamentally flawed. Uzi Landau said to me at the time, 'Hisdai, what are you making a fuss about? It's not such a big deal. It's not a border.' They misled him! Not a border? We don't even have such a barrier between us and Lebanon! How does a local council head manage to move a fence, with no experts committee, nothing? It was a victory for me, but it left a strange, bad taste."

The battle might be won but the war continues. On the last day of August 2004, "two years after the fence has been living and breathing," as Eliezer puts it, ACRI, the nonprofit Association for Civil Rights in Israel, had submitted a petition to the Supreme Court against the Prime Minister, the Minister of Defense, the army commander in the area, and the fence administration to demand the dismantling of the section of the barrier around Alfei Menashe. The case is still pending when Eliezer and I meet.

The petition was submitted on behalf of five tiny Palestinian villages entrapped within the Seam Zone, lassoed in the loop of the barrier that forms the Alfei Menashe enclave. The largest of the five, Ras al-Tira, has a population of 400. Its squat flat-roofed gray houses and water tower sit untidily on a hilltop opposite the settlement, clearly visible from Eliezer's office window. Alfei Menashe may be only minutes away from Kfar Saba in real estate terms, but the lay of the land here is unmistakably Palestinian. Even Hisdai Eliezer can't change that. Another cluster of houses halfway up the road to Ras al-Tira makes up the hamlet of Wadi al-Rasha, with 180 inhabitants, while 250 more live in the community of Daba, according to Bimkom, an alternative Jerusalem-based Israeli planning NGO that was asked by ACRI to survey the enclave. On the side of the road up to Alfei Menashe, on a grassy, stony slope, there is a bedouin encampment of the Arab Al-Ramadin tribe. The encampment is a scrubby looking conglomeration of tin shacks and semipermanent one-room dwellings that are home to another 176 souls. From the outside, though, the dwellings appear more fit to shelter the donkeys, sheep, and goats that graze all around. Over the hill, 77 bedouin live in a smaller encampment of the Abu Farda tribe. This encampment does not make it onto most maps.

ACRI has argued that the creation of the Alfei Menashe enclave has damned the residents of these villages to a miserable existence of economic, social, and cultural atrophy, separating them from their pasture and agricultural land, from their extended families, and from the public services required to maintain a normal life. The permit regime imposed on the Seam Zone residents by the army, according to ACRI, has created a situation of conditional residency, while the lack of sources of livelihood within the enclave has caused the Palestinians to seek "temporary work for starvation wages" in Alfei Menashe, resulting in a "terrible process" of "indentured servitude of the Palestinians by their lords, the settlers." The barrier along this route, the petition contends, will generate a process of "voluntary" transfer of Palestinians from the enclave. Moreover, it contravenes the July 2004 ruling of the International Court of Justice in The Hague which deems the construction of the barrier in the West Bank territory as a violation of international law. The petition was submitted by an Israeli attorney in the name of six residents of Ras al-Tira and Wadi al-Rasha.

⤙⟨⟩⤚

The ACRI petition is worrying Hisdai Eliezer. But glancing out of the window over his mini-empire, still ebullient, he claims that his Arab neighbors have never had it better. "I have a great relationship with the Palestinians," he declares. "They say life is good for them. They are flourishing too. They work all over Judea and Samaria as well as here, *and* they get permits to work inside Israel. They're laughing! You saw the bedouins living there by the road? I couldn't stand to see their kids waiting in the sun and rain for the gate in the fence to open to let them go to school in Habla, so I took action and together with the army, organized them transportation. When they have a family event, the army says it will give their families special permits to come in here on such occasions. And there are no problems now with the farmers' gates. On balance, they're much better off than worse. If you did an anonymous poll, they'd tell you. That's the biggest paradox of all. The bedouin have been included in the Supreme Court case, yet the whole village signed a petition saying they wanted to stay in with us." I ask to see a copy. "You can trust me," Eliezer replies. "You're not taking testimony."

Eliezer sits behind his desk cluttered with a laptop, two landlines, two cell phones, a beeper, a pack of Marlboro Lights, and a kitschy rabbit-shaped ashtray. Born in Haifa, he is the son of a Greek Holocaust survivor and a Turkish mother. "There was war in the house," he quips, "and they divorced." He stayed in the army till the age of 32, reaching the rank of lieutenant colonel, settled in Kfar Saba, and worked in several commercial companies. He married and had four girls, the oldest of which was killed in a traffic accident, and he got involved in local politics before moving to Alfei Menashe in 1990, where he has been mayor since 1998. Next he intends to run for the Knesset. During his mayorship, he says, Alfei Menashe has expanded from 900 households to 1,400. The plan is to grow to 2,500 in the next five years.

On an otherwise empty hill between Alfei Menashe and Ras al-Tira, bulldozers are noisily constructing what looks like a fortress, the sound of the mechanical diggers magnified as it bounces off the surrounding hills. This is Alfei Menashe's largest new project, the terraced garden apartment complex of Givat Tal, or Dew Hill. It will be connected to the main part of the settlement by a bridge spanning the valley. "My next meeting after this is to find solutions for education, to be ready," Eliezer tells me, anticipating an influx of young families. For now, the settlement's children learn in Alfei Menashe until middle school and then attend high school in Kfar Saba.

When I suggest that the rapid construction here appears to confirm Palestinian fears that the barrier project is in fact a "land grab," and hardly conforms to the Israeli government's recent commitments to President Bush to freeze settlement expansion, Eliezer retorts that while the prime minister had promised that the settlement blocs would get priority in building funds, he has had nothing but cuts. "They're not doing me a favor by approving building here," he says. "These were all existing plans." In Alfei Menashe, which means "the thousands of Menashe," a biblical phrase referring to one of the ten lost tribes, it is less about ancient patrimony and more about supply and demand.

A couple of blocks from the council building, a new neighborhood of luxury villas is going up. Half a dozen are under construction, and there is room for half a dozen more. Privately built to order, most belong to residents already living in Alfei Menashe who are upgrading their domestic conditions. Amos Kachlon, a tall, successful-looking contractor with short cropped hair and a satisfied expression, is overseeing the work at what will be his own new home. He came to Alfei Menashe from the coastal town of Herzliya 15 years ago "for the quality of life," and started building this villa six months ago "without connection to the fence." Kachlon sold his current, smaller house to someone else from within the community; they sold theirs to people from outside.

The builders of these new settler homes are all local Palestinians. Perversely, some of them have practically built the place from scratch. "I was born here 35 years ago," says Muhammad, a dark, smiling bedouin; "this is where we used to graze our goats." He's been working on construction sites in Alfei Menashe since 1982. Muhammad Shbeita, 43, a father of seven with thinning hair, has been plastering and painting here since 1986. He comes from Nabi Elias, a village north of here, on the other side of the fence. He has a three-month permit allowing him to cross the Tzufin checkpoint and come here to work. There is one laborer from Qalqilya, Abdallah, who says he worked here for eight years before the intifada, then had to spend the best part of the last four years sitting at home. Seven months ago, he came back to work. And in the next house, there is a group of builders from neighboring Wadi al-Rasha. One, Subhi Odeh, ginger-haired with freckles, complains that he earns 100 shekels (less than $25) a day here, whereas inside Israel he would get double. But it is still more than he could earn building in the Palestinian Authority. Asked how they feel about building for settlers, all the laborers react with a resigned shrug and a comment about having to make a living.

Now the houses are just cement skeletons but soon they will be crowned with the slanting red roofs that have become the trademark of the settlements. They will be surrounded by gardens and trees, and look like they have been here 20 years. A few minutes' walk away is the country club, which has an indoor pool, an outdoor pool with a Jacuzzi and waterslide, and a health club advertising free exercise classes for women and martial arts for kids. It is a suburban Eden where ideology—even the mayor's—is kept mostly at bay.

In a quiet playground in a far corner of Alfei Menashe, Livnat Rafaeli, an average-looking 24-year-old with maroon-rimmed glasses, is spending the afternoon with her one-year-old, Niv, an olive-skinned cherub with a mop of black curls. Like one of the billboards at the entrance of the settlement, she immediately pronounces Alfei Menashe a "fabulous place, a small community that has everything. Soon we'll be able to sign Niv up for toddler activities." Rafaeli moved here with her parents from Herzliya three years ago, married, and became a mother. She and her husband, who also came from Herzliya, have bought an apartment in Givat Tal that will be ready in a year. In the meantime, Rafaeli's main ethical dilemma is whether to leave her current job at an office supplies firm near Netanya for a rival company that is offering her better terms. When I ask her if it is of any significance to her that her new home lies over the Green Line, she looks at me blankly and asks, "In what sense?" Politically, I say. "No, not really," she replies. "You mean will they [the Israeli government] give up the land? I don't believe they will." She asserts that the fence route was also not a factor in the decision to buy in Givat Tal. She says the only reason she would not move to a community deeper inside the West Bank, such as Karnei Shomron further up Route 55, on the other side of the barrier, is because the drive there between two Arab villages is "scary." Pressing on, I ask Rafaeli if she has any political opinion about the West Bank at all. "Look, I think there could be coexistence," she says. "Maybe, but it's hard to believe. Two states? Only if they put them [the Arabs] far away in a remote place." That does not mean Rafaeli is devoid of conscience. When I ask her what she thinks of the wall around Qalqilya that she drives past every day on her way to work, she does not hesitate to respond: "In my opinion, we've made them a prison. It's like a ghetto there. I wish they'd take it down."

Once, when he lived in Kfar Saba, Eliezer traveled to Qalqilya with a toothache to see a dentist. His wife would drive into the Palestinian city with a sleeping baby to buy diapers on the Sabbath when the Jewish stores were closed. Now, the mayor says, he would like to renew links between Alfei Menashe and its neighbors in Qalqilya and Habla in order to find joint solutions to utilitarian problems such as the air pollution resulting from burning garbage. He has not gone soft. He believes that the end of the second intifada merely means the Palestinians are gearing up for a third one. As such, Eliezer's political mantra is not the redemption of the Promised Land, but security. "There's a big difference between the other YESHA people and me," he says, producing a miniature Bible. "It's this. In here you'll find Ofra, Beit El, Hebron"—the ancient landmarks of the Jewish people in Judea and Samaria—"not Tel Aviv. My ideology comes not from the right to territory, but the right to life. I'm for 100 percent security. No less. If we lived in Switzerland or Lichtenstein, I'd have no problem, but I don't see that on the horizon. And to get close to 100 percent security, I believe we have to be in every place in Judea, Samaria, and Gaza. I'm for the right to life, not turf. I'd send my family to Australia if I saw a holocaust coming. It's a big and significant difference, but it doesn't make me any less right wing than them. So meantime I'm here, and I will fight for all the land of Israel with all my might."

Eliezer has no explanation for how his former settlement guru, Ariel Sharon, the ultimate Likud security hawk, could have thought of leaving Alfei Menashe out in the first place, not to mention much of the rest of the West Bank. "Who would have thought?" Eliezer declares. "Then again, who would have thought that Arik would remove settlements unilaterally?" he goes on, referring to the prime minister's decision to remove all the settlements from the Gaza Strip and another four isolated ones in the northern West Bank in the summer of 2005. "Nobody can work out what has happened to the man. There are speculations. And his own explanations that as prime minister, what you can see from up there, you can't necessarily see from down here," suggesting that having reached the pinnacle of political power, Sharon has become more attuned to the regional realities. "Nobody has a clue. I don't think it's because of U.S. pressure. Arik is not an easily pressured man. No one can believe it."

In Alfei Menashe, security seems to be something of an obsession. Settlement security vehicles patrol the streets at all times. One, a blue Nissan pickup truck, is parked in the lot outside the council building, in the square with the post office, library, and health center. Painted on one of its doors are the words, "Dedicated by the Young Israel of Monsey and Wesley Hills, Monsey, NY," and in smaller Hebrew letters below, "With the help of YESHA council." Now and then a khaki jeep or a more serious-looking armored military vehicle sweeps through. Alfei Menashe is surrounded by its own state-of-the-art electronic perimeter fence, just beyond the last houses on the edge of the settlement. And in the distance, the security barrier itself can be seen from almost every direction weaving through the hills. "I never compromised on security," Eliezer boasts. "I even put it before education, because if people get killed, they won't be educated either."

In 2001, one Alfei Menashe resident, Ruth Shoai, a 46-year-old mother of two, was killed by a sniper on the road near Habla. But there have been no terrorist attempts to infiltrate the settlement during the Al-Asqa intifada. "They feared failure. They went for easier targets," Eliezer asserts. "One Arab thief got shot through the head by a resident here. They knew not to mess with us."

At the same time, Eliezer's creed of Israeli hegemony requires the cooperation of the neighbors, which he believes is best guaranteed by beneficence. "I'm looking for the kind of cooperation that can solve problems together. For example water. I can give water to Habla. I'm not speaking in terms of politics, the conflict. In the meantime we're all here, so we might as well make our lives easier. The bedouin of the Ramadin tribe are like family here. When we have fairs for the kids with bouncy castles and the like, my heart breaks when the bedouin come to sweep up afterwards, knowing that their kids are playing in the mud. So one day last year I took the bouncy castles, music, and everything to them. We have soccer games together—it's a bit awkward because they lose like crazy. But we're trying to create a decent relationship with our neighbors, until whatever is to be decided gets decided. Our firemen once risked their lives to save kids from a burning building in Qalqilya. Not all Qalqilya's residents are terrorists. And not all of Alfei Menashe wants to kill Arabs. In fact nobody here does. You see Ras al-Tira out the window here? After the security fence blocked their only access road, from Habla, the army made them an alternative route, a dirt track up to the village. I said what's wrong with asphalt? You've paved hundreds of kilometers along the security fence with asphalt. Is asphalt not good enough for them? It took two years, but finally the army just paved the road with asphalt. That makes me feel good. I'm very right wing. I think all of Israel is ours etc., etc., but they deserve to live like us. Envy only leads to hatred and frustration, and in the end they blow themselves up."

That afternoon, when I try to drive up the mountain to Ras al-Tira, the asphalt ends halfway up the narrow, winding road. Soldiers leaning on a jeep by the roadside, who assume I've lost my way, say they have no idea when the new road surface will be completed. When I return a week later, the smooth black asphalt reaches all the way to the entrance of the village, and the edges of the road are marked with freshly painted yellow lines.

⊷⊜⊜⊶

The first house in Ras al-Tira belongs to Sami Hamdallah Marabi, a pleasant-looking 40-year-old in a faded denim shirt and jeans. I meet him hanging around outside late on a Friday afternoon with his brother, Azzam, 33, and a couple of the village youths. Like alter egos, Sami is handsome and cheerful while Azzam is sour-faced and glum. It does not take long to find out why. For this is a realm where opposites can be true, where apparently both Eliezer and ACRI can be right, and where one brother can prosper while another despairs.

Azzam used to work in Kfar Saba in construction but two years ago he was caught there without a permit. He cannot risk going back to work over the Green Line, even though from Ras al-Tira, as from Alfei Menashe, there is no fence or checkpoint blocking the way. "If they catch me again, I'll get three or four months in prison and a 3,000 shekel ($700) fine." He has applied to the army district office a few times since for a precious magnetic card that would allow him to work legally inside Israel, but has always been turned down. "That's because I have a police record from when I was caught," he explains. Azzam could easily pass through to the east at the new Tzufin checkpoint in the barrier for a job inside the West Bank, but he says he will not work for 20 or 50 shekels ($5 or $12) a day, a fraction of what he could earn in Israel. So the father of three is *qa'ed*, or "sitting," meaning unemployed. "We're inside Israel, but we aren't allowed in, not officially at least," he says, trying to articulate the surreal nature of life in the Seam Zone, where luck, not logic, holds sway.

Sami, on the other hand, has a magnetic card and works in construction in Tel Aviv where he earns 250 shekels (approximately $55) a day. Maybe a third of the men in the village have one, he says, allowing them to work either in Israel or inside the Jewish settlements such as Alfei Menashe. Not only that, but Sami, a father of seven young children, was also chosen by the village council to receive a recent donation of two hothouses in which to grow cucumbers. The donation came from a French humanitarian aid agency called Premiere Urgence. He can hardly believe his good fortune. "France gave them to me," he says, pointing to the new acquisitions that went up a few months ago on the empty ground by his house. "I didn't pay a cent. They even gave me the cucumber plants, the string to tie them up with, everything! They gave some other people five sheep, and food for them besides. They have supported this village a lot, because we are inside the fence and surrounded."

Sami is now selling boxes of cucumbers at a good price down the road at a vegetable market in Alfei Menashe's small, clean industrial zone. Inside one of the hothouses, in the clammy, almost tropical atmosphere, Sami's pretty wife Amal is spraying the plants. Dressed in pants and a smock top, with a pink scarf loosely covering her hair, she looks young to be the mother of seven children. "I married at 16," she laughs, bright faced. Amal, which means "hope," came from Ras Attiya, a village neighboring Habla, on the other side of the fence that winds down through the valley below us.

The family indeed seems to be prospering. Perhaps, as Eliezer says, they have never had it better. When I am invited into Sami's front yard for tea, however, it becomes abundantly clear that the family is still dirt poor. Sami started building this home ten years ago. It still has no glass in the windows, and other than a decorative archway over the front door, which Sami created out of pebbles gathered in the valley, the walls are all raw cement.

The whole village is basic, to say the least. Its internal un-made-up roads lead nowhere in any direction. The center is nothing more than a bare, dusty clearing between the newer houses of recent decades and the old neighborhood where the parents of Sami and Azzam live. Other than a few French sheep wandering around, the streets are deserted.

The two clans that make up the village population of 400, the Marabi and Shawahneh, originated from the village of Tult, to the north. About 150 years ago, the families started moving here to live on their agricultural lands, at first living in nearby caves. It was only in the 1940s that they started to build permanent homes.

Even today, the village is not hooked up to electricity, and the well Sami built in his yard provides his family's water. As we sit in the yard, a huge generator provided by the Palestinian Authority roars constantly outside. Directly over our heads, the power lines pass from the Israeli community of Matan, near Habla, on their way to Alfei Menashe. All the major Palestinian cities in the northern West Bank get their electricity from Israel, Sami explains, as his wife serves glasses of thick and sticky artificially flavored strawberry juice and several small children mill around. Now, Sami notes, "Israel has promised to supply us with electricity too," adding with a wink: "They're trying to appease us, also with the new road, so that we'll stay quiet about the fence."

Azzam sits by me in silence most of the time, looking lost in thought. At this point he pipes up, "They should at least give us permits to work in Israel." Then Sami pulls out the green permit authorizing his presence as a "permanent resident of the Seam Zone," a legal alien at home. It is valid from June 2004 till June 2005. After that, the mayor is supposed to organize its renewal. "The old people sometimes forget their permits, and the soldiers send them back from the checkpoints," says Amal. "Once we didn't even have ID cards. Now we have IDs, permits to live, magnetic cards to work—you need a big bag to hold them all."

The villagers of Ras al-Tira can still joke. Because, compared with the neighbors in Wadi al-Rasha down the road, their situation is relatively good.

Three days ago, Sami says, "they," meaning the army, came to register the names of everyone in the nearby hamlet. Rumors are rife that homes are about to be demolished there. Wadi al-Rasha, like Daba and the bedouin encampments, sits on land that is defined as agricultural according to the regional zoning plan dating back to the British Mandate that ended in 1948. Building there is considered illegal, and the military authorities have handed out dozens of demolition orders over the years that may not have been carried out, but that can become effective at any time. In the warped world of the Seam Zone, the residents of Wadi al-Rasha have permits allowing them to build other people's villas in Alfei Menashe, but they cannot legally put up a hut of their own.

"They want to put all the Arabs together, not to have them scattered around," Sami surmises. And there is general agreement in the family that Israel's true aim is to expand the settlements. "We'll be surrounded by settlements. They'll build down here too," says Azzam, gesturing toward the valley below us. "In the end all we'll have left is our houses."

Neither Sami nor Azzam nor Amal nor the youths who have tagged along are aware of any Supreme Court petition to dismantle this section of the barrier on their behalf. "No, no, that's in Qalqilya," Sami offers helpfully. Meanwhile, Sami is certain which side he would rather be on. "I want a blue [Israeli] ID," he says. "Nobody has told us we'll get one, but that's what I'd like."

Dusk begins to fall and the air suddenly turns chill. The sun turns into a huge red ball and starts slowly sinking into the Mediterranean. From up here, in the Alfei Menashe enclave, the sunset is magnificent. I cannot help thinking of Hassan Kharuf, against the wall in Qalqilya down below. Tel Aviv shimmers along the coast in the distance, its glass skyscrapers silhouetted against an orange sky. Down there, in that other world, security officials have been charged with studying the options for Sami, Amal, Azzam, and all the other Palestinian residents of the Seam Zone, and the officials will determine their future status, whether as citizens of Israel, or of Palestine, or of somewhere in between.

2

Paradise Lost

Yoav Ben Naftali is bumping through the fields of Kibbutz Metzer, a communal farm in central Israel, in a dirty white pickup truck, hurtling past lush banana plantations and orchards of avocado and persimmon, beeping his horn at the blond cows lazing in his path. It is raining on and off, heavily at times, and the rich brown earth has churned itself up to the surface, turning the barely discernible gravel track into mud. Soon he reaches his destination and gets out of the truck, slamming the door shut with a thud. We are standing on the high ground, practically on the Green Line, the old 1949 armistice line between Israel and the West Bank that is marked out here by nothing more than a few knee-high stone pyramids dotted at regular intervals across the countryside over half a century ago.

As a lifelong Zionist and socialist, Ben Naftali, 59, a wiry, bespectacled man with ruddy cheeks and a ginger-gray beard, is anxious to prove that he does not lay claim to anything that is not rightfully his. He picks up a handful of the wet, brown soil and rubs it through his fingers, as if feeling the history and texture of the conflict in every grain. "This is ours," he declares, raising his voice against the gathering storm. "It was given to us at Rhodes in 1949."

At this point, Israel's "narrow waist" is less than 20 kilometers wide. To the west, despite the looming November rain clouds, the apartment blocks of Netanya are visible on the Mediterranean coast, as are the ghostly outlines of the chimneys of the Hadera power station and the Carmel ridge leading to the strategic port city of Haifa about 20 kilometers to the north. On a clear day, Ben Naftali says, you can see the Haifa University tower on top of Mount Carmel. Even to a leftist and peacenik like him Israel seems tiny, but this is not his point. The reason we have come up here lies a short distance to the east, where the coastal plain rises into the rolling hills of the West Bank. Straight ahead of us, Israel's new separation fence slices surgically across the stony grassy slope, a band of steel cutting a path through the silver-green olive trees whose leaves have turned iridescent in the rain, before snaking round a bend and disappearing into the valley out of sight. Just beyond the fence, on the opposite hill, is a cluster of old stone houses belonging to the West Bank Palestinian village of Qaffin. The houses are perhaps only a kilometer away as the crow flies, but the distance between the village and the kibbutz cannot be measured in ordinary dimensions of space and time. For Metzer and Qaffin, by virtue of their shared history and location, lie at the crux of this century-old struggle of two people over one land, neighbors who are doomed to live together and yet destined to part. The point that becomes clear here, on the seam of the conflict, is that even with the best intentions in the world, the line between accommodation and enmity is very thin indeed.

Kibbutz Metzer lies at the end of a twisting road lined with fields of cotton and wheat, staples of the Zionist socialist dream. A faux-rustic wooden sign at the entrance, just inside the electronic gate, states that the commune was founded on September 8, 1953 by immigrants from South America, members of Hashomer Ha'tza'ir, a pioneering left-wing Zionist youth movement. An Israeli flag hangs on a pole alongside, and further in, pedestrian pathways and green lawns are bordered by low whitewashed houses where the 220 kibbutz members live. An unimposing building in the center contains a simple communal dining room and in a far-off corner of the farm ostriches stalk along a fence in a children's zoo. It is a quiet life. Even the kibbutz factory, Metzerplas, which produces piping for irrigation and construction, barely disturbs the pastoral tranquility of the place.

Among Metzer's founders are people like Yitzhak Nisselbaum, a lean and gray 75-year-old who arrived in Israel as a young immigrant from Argentina five years after the state was born. He and the three friends he came with, all graduates of Hashomer Ha'tza'ir, were committed to a communal farming life guided by Marxist principles of social justice, equality, and peace. They had dreamed of setting up a coastal commune and in preparation had learned to fish. But "someone decided to set up a kibbutz here," says Yitzhak, so he and his friends were sent inland instead. "We climbed the hill and looked around. There was nothing to see," he recalls. Yitzhak's wife-to-be, Fanny, arrived soon after with another group of pioneers from Argentina and got to work manually clearing the rocks from the land. Today a round, spectacled grandmother with her short hair dyed red, she speaks nostalgically about how their early living quarters consisted of a tin shack divided down the middle with a sheet, with cartons from Tnuva, the cooperative dairy company, as furniture. Gradually, native Israelis from the local branches of Hashomer Ha'tza'ir came to join the enterprise as well, among them Yoav Ben Naftali, born in 1945 to parents he describes sarcastically as "Polish capitalists" who had settled in Yehud, a Jewish town east of Tel Aviv. Ben Naftali was 18 when he came to Metzer in 1963, in the days, he quips, when "you still heard more Spanish than Hebrew around here."

For these young idealists, peace was not an abstract notion but a practical way of life. The kibbutz is located in an area of the country known as "the Triangle," the fertile, soft underbelly of Israel where Arabs far outnumber Jews even today. In these parts, Arab villages and towns zigzag from one side of the Green Line to the other, refusing to conform to the maps and defying any simple definition of Israel and Palestine. Metzer, which means "boundary" in Hebrew, and a few other rural cooperatives were set up here in the early years of the state as wedges of Jewish settlement intended to secure the Green Line, to assert ownership over as much newly acquired state land as possible, and to prevent the chain of older Arab communities from melding into one formidable bloc.

Metzer was, and still is, surrounded by Arab villages on all sides. Nestled in a shallow dip outside the kibbutz gates is the village of Meisar. In the 1950s this was a sleepy hamlet with 140 inhabitants who didn't want to receive electricity at first for fear, according to Ben Naftali, that modernization would "spoil" the children. Today its rural simplicity is embellished with a number of contemporary pastel-colored homes. Another Arab village, Um Qutuf, is perched on a hill to the north of the kibbutz, and across the fields to the south sprawls the bustling Israeli Arab town of Baqa al-Gharbiya. Over the valley to the east lies Qaffin.

While Meisar, Um Qutuf, and Baqa al-Gharbiya all fell on the Israeli side of the 1949 line, making their residents full citizens of the new Jewish state, the village of Qaffin remained out of bounds in the Jordanian-held West Bank. Though there was no physical barrier between Metzer and

Qaffin—other than some concertina wire here and there to deter thieves—
a veil of hostility punctuated by occasional Jordanian and Israeli army patrols was enough to keep the populations apart. Yet the two were
symbiotically linked, for when the armistice lines were drawn up by the Israeli and Jordanian negotiators, about half of Qaffin's farmlands fell on the
Israeli side of the divide. Four years later, when Kibbutz Metzer was established, the Israel Lands Authority allocated some 2,000 dunams, or 500
acres, of the Qaffin lands, half cultivated, to the new communal farm. Ben
Naftali relates the fact unapologetically, for that is just the way things are.

Still, in an attempt to reconcile the Marxist and humanistic principles of
Hashomer Ha'tza'ir with the practical demands of Zionism and building the
Jewish homeland, Metzer's founding generation made political activism its
hallmark. The members would attend Israeli peace rallies by the busload and
organize joint Jewish-Arab May Day parades. Ben Naftali, Nisselbaum, and
others devoted themselves to weaving friendships and partnerships between
the Arabs and Jews sharing this soil, creating a loose patchwork of coexistence along the way.

Special relations were forged with Meisar. In the old days, Fanny recalls,
sitting in the simply furnished living room of the Nisselbaums' small bungalow in the old people's quarter of the kibbutz, the villagers and the kibbutzniks attended each others' weddings and paid condolence calls whenever
anybody died. A joint Metzer-Meisar soccer team functioned for a while.
And when the Metzerplas factory was built on a plot that had been expropriated from a member of the Abu Obeid family of Meisar, Ben Naftali organized a land swap. (As it turned out, the alternative plot the kibbutzniks gave
Meisar as compensation had itself once been expropriated from another of
the Abu Obeids.)

In June 1967, following Israel's victory in the Six Day War, the invisible
curtain between Metzer and Qaffin suddenly came down. Two weeks after
the war's end, in the euphoric aftermath, a curious Ben Naftali, who had returned from battle as a reservist with the paratroopers in Sinai and Jerusalem,
gathered a few friends from Metzer and Meisar and hiked across the valley to
Qaffin. There had been no serious fighting in the area and the Jordanian legions had fled. The Palestinian villagers hung white flags from their
rooftops, waiting to be conquered by the Zionist army. But nobody came except for the kibbutzniks and their friends, so the farmers of Qaffin surren-
dered to these amicable strangers instead.

The kibbutzniks, uncomfortable with their new role as occupiers, were eager to show a benign face. They promised to supply the Palestinian villagers with anything they needed and offered one group work picking oranges and cotton in the kibbutz fields. A few weeks later, in August, Yitzhak Nisselbaum joined another Jewish-Arab delegation to Qaffin, and was honored with a lunch of chicken and rice. Soon after, Qaffin's notables paid a return visit to Metzer where they were hosted in the clubhouse in an atmosphere of great excitement. Over the years the two communities developed a relationship of sorts based on good neighborliness, mutual respect, harmony with the exquisite rural surroundings, and a lulling sense of security that allowed the kibbutzniks to sleep soundly at night for 35 years.

The idyll came to an abrupt end on November 10, 2002, as Kibbutz Metzer prepared to celebrate its jubilee year. Just after 11 p.m. a 19-year-old Palestinian called Sirhan Sirhan crept unhindered across the Green Line and, under the cover of darkness, crawled beneath Metzer's flimsy perimeter fence. On a pathway in the heart of the kibbutz he shot dead Tirza Damari, 42, a visitor to the kibbutz who was out strolling with her boyfriend, a Metzer member. Yitzhak Dori, 44, a holy land guide, the kibbutz secretary, and a member of the emergency response team, rushed to the scene. Sirhan killed him before he could even get out of his patrol car, sending it crashing into a water pipe which burst into a rushing fountain. The intruder then made for the nearest home, a white stucco corner bungalow that used to be a kindergarten. Failing to kick down the door, he climbed through a small side window into a bedroom. There he found Revital Ohion, 34, and her two sons, Noam, 5, and Matan, 4, huddled on one of the children's beds. He shot each of them at close range as the mother tried to shield the terrified children with her own body. The security forces arrived soon after and ordered the kibbutzniks to lock themselves inside their homes with the lights off, fearing that the gunman was still on the prowl or holed up somewhere in the kibbutz. Ohion, recently divorced, had moved to Metzer only two months earlier to rent a home in what she had assumed would be a calm and nurturing environment. The next morning's papers printed harrowing pictures of the bloodied floor and a pair of little muddy boots in the hallway waiting by the door. The nation cried on its way to work.

The day I find Ben Naftali careering through the wet fields of Metzer happens to be the first anniversary of the attack. Back at the kibbutz, on the sloping lawn leading up from where the murders took place, a modest memorial has been fashioned out of a rough local rock, bearing the names of the victims and set amid artificial streams of running water. Extinguished *yartzheit* candles and a black plastic bucket of wilting red roses are left over from the service of the night before. At the entrance to the communal dining room, a collage of black and white photos pinned to a screen celebrates the early years of kibbutz life as the jubilee draws to a close. Back from the fields, sitting at a Formica table with a tray of canteen food before him, Ben Naftali mutters once, and then again, "The killer didn't come from Qaffin," as if to vindicate the decades dedicated to coexistence, to convince himself that they were not entirely in vain. Nor, Ben Naftali stresses, did the gunman seek refuge there after his escape.

By all accounts, Sirhan Sirhan first ran north to Um Qutuf but was chased away with gunshots. He then made it to the nearby Israeli Arab town of Baqa al-Gharbiya bordering the kibbutz to the south, where he dropped off his gun. From there he slipped back into Tulkarm, a Palestinian market town hugging the other side of the Green Line in the West Bank, and became a fugitive. It took the army 11 months to catch up with Sirhan but finally, in October 2003, undercover soldiers shot him down in an alleyway near his home in the Tulkarm refugee camp abutting the town. Forty days after Sirhan's death, a ceremony was held in Tulkarm in his honor; local militants and Palestinian Authority dignitaries alike eulogized the murderer of children as a "martyr" and a "struggler."

Even before the terror struck at Metzer the ground between the kibbutz and Qaffin was being prepared for Phase One of the barrier, a roughly 130-kilometer stretch of fence from Salem in the north to the Jewish settlement of Elkana, about a third of the way down the West Bank. By the fall of 2002, army bulldozers were already cutting a swathe through the countryside, uprooting thousands of Palestinian-owned olive trees in their path.

One would have imagined that Ben Naftali, having spent all his adult life in the relentless pursuit of peace, dialogue, and coexistence with his Arab neighbors, would hate everything about this new band of steel that runs like a scar across the landscape he so loves. It ought to be the antithesis of all he stands for. But his is a world of shattered illusions. Ben Naftali, like many on Metzer, has always tended toward a practical, grass roots approach to peacemaking. He once helped a father from Qaffin recover the body of his teenage son from a morgue in Tel Aviv after the youth was killed during clashes with Israeli troops in first intifada, the popular uprising of the late 1980s. Also

around the time of the first intifada, Ben Naftali helped establish a network
on the ground for B'Tselem, the Israeli Information Center for Human
Rights in the Occupied Territories, now a well-respected organization. He
became a member of the secretariat of the left-wing Meretz party, and entered into political dialogue with some of the local Palestinian leaders over
the Green Line—not the corrupt cronies that Yasser Arafat imported from
Tunis under the aegis of the Oslo peace accords in the mid-1990s, he stresses,
but men he describes as the "authentic" West Bank leadership, home-grown
Palestinian nationalists who grew up nearby breathing the same air, pragmatic partners who seemed ready for a compromise.

The second intifada has forced Ben Naftali to radically reevaluate his positions. Ben Naftali fervently opposed the Israeli occupation of the 1967 territories from the outset, an occupation, he says, that has had "terrible things"
done in its name. Nevertheless, he muses later, sitting in his small office in
the Metzerplas factory where he is a foreman, "I thought we should take our
time and get to know these people and their leaders on the other side a little
before leaving. Now I think I was wrong."

The Oslo process, launched in 1993, was supposed to bring about a
final peace treaty based on a negotiated partition of the land between the
Jordan River and the Mediterranean Sea into two states, one Israeli and
one Palestinian. The idea of dividing the land was first raised as far back as
1937 when the Peel Commission, appointed by the British who then controlled Mandatory Palestine, concluded that partition was the best solution.
The opinion has informed countless proposals for peace since, including
the United Nations partition resolution of 1947, UN Resolution 242 following Israel's conquest of the West Bank and Gaza in 1967, and most recently, the U.S.-sponsored attempt to reach a final accord at Camp David
in July 2000.

However, Yasser Arafat rejected the "most generous offer" for a Palestinian state on most, though not all, of the land conquered in 1967, the offer
that Israeli Prime Minister Ehud Barak made behind the closed doors at
Camp David, and the peace process exploded into violence that fall. The
armed uprising and cycle of Palestinian terrorism and Israeli retaliation
would rage for the next four years. In the course of the intifada, the two "authentic" Palestinian figures that Ben Naftali repeatedly names as his peace-
time dialogue-partners, Thabet Thabet and Raed Karmi of Tulkarm,
grassroots leaders of Arafat's mainstream Fatah faction, were both killed by

Israel for their alleged involvement in the very terror network that would later send Sirhan Sirhan on his murderous mission to Metzer.

Considered an incurable leftist—even by Metzer standards—by some of his comrades, Ben Naftali claims that the two were killed precisely because they were pragmatists ready to strike a territorial deal, and as such they presented a threat to the Israeli leadership's real goal of maintaining the occupation and the settlement enterprise. In the meantime, with all avenues of dialogue and reconciliation closed in the political desert of the post-Oslo era, Ben Naftali has come to believe that the best option for Israel vis-à-vis the territories is just to get out: to put up an impenetrable fence and withdraw behind it, to shrink the Jewish state back to its original proportions, and to bring about a Palestinian state by unilateral separation if it cannot be brought about by negotiation. "We need a fence," he asserts, "to put limits on the occupation in the Jewish mind."

Other kibbutz members had been opposed to the notion of a fence, but the terror that struck that night in November 2002 drew new boundaries in blood. On Metzer, not another word would be uttered against the barrier. The only issue was where exactly it should run. The kibbutzniks had been horrified to find that the Metzer part of the security fence was slated to detour up to a kilometer from the Green Line into the West Bank, skirting the last houses of Qaffin and, disastrously for the local farmers, cutting them off from 70 percent of what remained of their olive groves and fields. For two months prior to the attack, Metzer activists including Ben Naftali and Yitzhak Dori, the kibbutz secretary who would later be slain by Sirhan, had been campaigning on Qaffin's behalf, writing the Defense Ministry and calling on the media in an attempt to get the route adjusted to run closer to the kibbutz, on the armistice line itself.

In what would prove to be one of their final acts of neighborliness, two weeks before the Metzer murders, about 40 kibbutzniks and a similar number of villagers from Qaffin met on the Green Line where their fields touch, and held a joint demonstration against the approaching bulldozers. The Israelis were careful to limit their protest to the planned route, and not to object to the fence itself, sensitive to the feelings of the rest of the terrorized Israeli society. A bad fence, they argued, would threaten their own security, which was based on decades of mutual trust. As Doron Lieber, who would become the next kibbutz secretary, told the Ha'aretz newspaper during the quiet demonstration: "We're living in a fool's paradise compared to the situa-

3. Two weeks before the Metzer murders, about 40 kibbutzniks and a similar number of villagers from Qaffin met on the Green Line and held a joint demonstration against the approaching bulldozers: Laying the razor wire during construction of Phase One of the barrier in the north, March 2003. Credit: Amos Ben Gershom, Israel Government Press Office.

tion in other parts of the country. I fear that once there is a fence here, we'll find that we've moved to hell."

The campaign was partially successful. Some time after the Metzer attack, the Defense Ministry agreed to create a special bulge in the barrier around Qaffin to accommodate more of the village olive groves. At its closest point, however, the barrier would still fall three or four hundred meters east of the 1949 line, on Qaffin's land. Army planners argued that they needed an "operational margin" on the Israeli side of the fence to allow security forces to catch up with any infiltrators who managed to cross it, before they could reach the kibbutz or other built up areas nearby.

At the demonstration on the Green Line where the fields touch, though, the disconnect between Metzer and Qaffin became abundantly clear. The two neighbors stood together but divided, a wall of misunderstanding between them. The Palestinian villagers were not protesting the route, but the essence of the fence itself. While the kibbutzniks were trying to help, the villagers brooded as the wounds of half a century ago resurfaced, cast in concrete and steel.

⟡

Abu Rushdie's house is the one in Qaffin's sleepy old center with the rusty blue tractor parked outside and taking up most of the narrow alleyway. The aroma of home-baked bread wafts out of traditional *taboun* ovens on the spring breeze as it has probably done for centuries. The village is 200 years old, or 600, or 4,000, depending on who you ask. The residents, traditionally harvesters of the bounty of gnarled olive trees on the surrounding slopes, have seen controlling powers come and go, whether Roman, Ottoman, British, Jordanian, or, as now, Israeli, embodying the Palestinian ideal of *sumud* (steadfastness on the land).

Muhammad Toameh, known to all as Abu Rushdie (the father of Rushdie), was born here in 1934, a scion of Al-Toameh, the largest of the four clans that make up Qaffin's population of 8,000. Spry and balding, his permanently tanned face deeply creased around his sparkling eyes, he is delighted when I turn up unannounced with one of his distant relatives, a well-known Palestinian journalist now living in Jerusalem. The journalist remembers last visiting Qaffin over 30 years ago as a boy, arriving on donkey-back with his grandfather.

Abu Rushdie's grin is as broad as his jaw will stretch though he has little in the way of teeth, just two sharp black stumps jutting out of his upper and lower gums at odd angles. Um Rushdie (the mother of Rushdie), Muhammad's wife, a tubby woman with a bright white headscarf and a synthetic long dress, joins the gathering, a bouncing baby grandson in her arms. She and Abu Rushdie have produced 16 children, six boys and ten girls. The oldest, Rushdie, is now 41 and the youngest is 17. The family living quarters are built traditionally around an inner courtyard, surrounded by high stone walls. The compound has expanded across the alley over the years, where a new reception area has been built above a donkey stable and is reached by stairs running up beside a haystack.

It is now the spring of 2004 and the intifada has been waged for three and a half years, not here so much as elsewhere, in the more populous cities and refugee camps of the West Bank and Gaza Strip. One Qaffin resident, a taxi driver, was sent to prison and had his house demolished by the army for allegedly transporting a suicide bomber, the villagers say. His son then ran with a knife at an Israeli soldier at a checkpoint and got nine years. Otherwise the only outward signs of the uprising are the graffiti on the walls, in support of one militant faction or another, and the odd poster here and there of a *shahid* (martyr to the cause) that has found its way here.

The days of being able to walk from Metzer to Qaffin are over. Instead, visitors from Israel now require a special permit from the army enabling them to cross a military checkpoint in the fence. The closest crossing point is at Baqa al-Gharbiya, where an 8-meter-high gray concrete wall, part of the security barrier, has gone up between the houses in a residential area straddling the Green Line. The opening in the wall is heavily guarded by soldiers and is overshadowed by a gray cylindrical watchtower with narrow bullet-proof peepholes. Though this is now by far the quickest way to get to Qaffin we are refused permission to cross here, told by a young soldier that we are "not on the list." We are directed on to the next crossing point in the barrier, which is beyond Barta'a, another Arab village that straddles the Green Line, a 20-minute drive to the north.

The Barta'a checkpoint, a gap in the fence where the road from the village into the West Bank dissects it, is manned by more khaki-clad soldiers, flak-jacketed, helmeted, and armed. A straggling line of cars, taxis, and trucks wait on either side of the gap, some Israeli and some from the Palestinian Authority, all laden with produce and people. Progress is slow this morning, with one car passing through every ten minutes or so. Drivers wave permits and papers at the soldiers; tempers flare.

The soldiers won't be rushed, though, afraid of another security lapse. Only six months earlier, in October 2003, a 29-year-old female suicide bomber, Hanadi Taysir Jaradat, had passed through this very gate in a taxi with the aid of a Jordanian passport. The trainee lawyer rode on to the crowded, Arab-owned Maxim restaurant on the Haifa beachfront, where she ate lunch, paid the bill, and then blew herself up, killing 21 Israelis—Jews and Arabs, grandparents, parents, and children alike. It was one of the rare instances in which the barrier system had failed. When we reach the crossing, the soldiers check our papers and wave us through. We follow the winding road a few kilometers south until the houses of Qaffin come into view. The hills all around are a riot of wild flowers, the same species as on the other side.

Once everybody is settled in the Toamehs' reception room above the stable, Um Rushdie bustles back to the main house, a few daughters in tow, to produce an impromptu lunch. The room is decorated in unconsciously kitschy Palestinian style with flowery-upholstered couches, artificial flowers in vases, and more false flowers framed on the wall. Soon a procession of Toameh women are carrying trays up the stairs and a white plastic garden table is filled with dishes. The country feast consists of huge poached eggs floating in olive oil, triangles of fried white salty cheese, fried cauliflower florets, sharp-flavored *labaneh*, crushed *za'atar* (wild thyme), home-produced spicy green olives, vivid wedges of tomatoes and cucumbers, and hot flat breads from the *taboun*. Fat plastic bottles of soda are passed around in accordance with the more modern rules of Palestinian hospitality.

At first the atmosphere is festive as the long-lost relative, from the more sophisticated "city" branch of the family, is grilled for gossip and news. Beneath the peals of laughter, though, are undertones of uncertainty, anxiety, and pain. The generations-old rhythm of life here is on the cusp of dramatic change. Abu Rushdie has always lived a simple life on the land, working the 45 dunams, or 11 acres, of land he inherited from his father, tending his 150 or so olive trees, and caring for his animals. The family's fields abut Metzer's. One plot is even shared, he says, and is now planted with the kibbutz bananas. Now, though, all of Abu Rushdie's birthright, and that of his own considerable progeny, lies on the other side of the fence. With the roads to Israel closed and the villagers' previous jobs there having been taken by guest workers from as far away as Thailand and China, agriculture has, for many villagers, become the main or only source of livelihood. In Qaffin, the fence has brought with it an existential fear for the village's future.

At olive-picking time the previous fall, Abu Rushdie and a few hundred other villagers from Qaffin got special permission from the army to cross the fence via a small "farmer's gate" in the fields near Baqa al-Gharbiya, in order to pick their fruit. It was the first harvest since the fence went up, around the time of the first anniversary of the Metzer attack. Abu Rushdie got a permit valid for 15 days. None of his sons got permission, but Abu Rushdie pleaded with the soldiers at the gate that at 68 he could not do it alone, so they "unofficially" let Um Rushdie and one daughter in with him to help. Though the three picked as quickly as they could, two-thirds of the fruit remained on the trees, left to rot, to be eaten by goats or to be stolen by thieves. The following year the army would invest tremendous efforts to facilitate the olive picking season, issuing over 2,000 temporary permits to residents of Qaffin and other villages in the area whose orchards fall across the fence. The situation improved somewhat but the villagers complained that the system still fell short. In some cases only the women of the family got permits, while in others the papers were only valid for a few days. The harvest, traditionally a festive occasion in the Palestinian countryside when whole families would picnic under the trees, has turned into a bureaucratic nightmare. The rest of the year, the orchards are completely out of bounds.

"The wall has destroyed us," Abu Rushdie declares, sitting after lunch with a coffee and cigarette. Um Rushdie chimes in with local rumors that when "the Jews," as the Israelis are routinely referred to in the local dialect, were digging for the fence, they found cases of gold and a golden statue in caves nearby, but they loaded the gold onto trucks and drove away.

The implication is that the land is being raped and plundered yet again. Once, according to the villagers, Qaffin's agricultural land used to stretch all the way to Hadera. Most of it was lost to Israel after 1948, much of it going to Metzer. Later, another 500 dunams (125 acres) were confiscated for the nearby West Bank Jewish settlement of Hermesh, established in 1982. Now, the security barrier has eaten up another 600 dunams (150 acres) in its path, and has cut off a further 6,000 dunams (1,500 acres), over half of the remaining lands, from the village.

Ironically the old weather-beaten farmer Abu Rushdie seems more forgiving of the Israeli neighbors than his sons. Having lived a lifetime under foreign

4. One of the most expensive and ambitious national infrastructure projects Israel has ever undertaken: The fence going up between the Jerusalem suburb of Gilo and Beit Jalla in the West Bank. Credit: Esteban Alterman

authorities, Abu Rushdie deferred to fate and accepted them almost like a force of nature. So even though the Arab defeat of 1967 was considered by the Palestinians to be a second *nakba* (catastrophe), when the soldier-farmers of Metzer showed up in the village, the Palestinians, both humble and proud, received them in the time-honored tradition of hospitality and good neighborliness. The Israeli conquest in a way reconnected Qaffin with its former lands; a number of villagers took up the kibbutzniks' offer and went to work as hired laborers on Metzer, while Abu Rushdie mentions that he used to gather fodder for his cows from the kibbutz. He says he personally misses the contact with Metzer, "a relationship of years," and acknowledges that the kibbutzniks "helped us a lot here with the wall, with drawing the border."

The better educated sons are more cynical. Growing up alongside Israel, a vibrant democratic society with little respect for hierarchy, has influenced them. At the same time, the smarting sense of dispossession and injustice stemming from 1948 has not gone away. It has been passed on from generation to generation, seemingly becoming more intense the younger the population gets.

Rushdie, thin, dark, and sullen, has a leg injury from a recent accident and is unemployed. A member of Qaffin's "Anti-Wall Committee," he harbors little nostalgia about the past. While his father fondly reminisces about working side by side with the Israelis in the fields, Rushdie is quick to point out that "the kibbutz was built on land confiscated from the village" in the first place, then complains that since the 1950s, Metzer has done nothing really to help Qaffin "other than employ a couple of people. That's it. They only wanted to make a show of liking us for their own security," he continues bitterly, adding that it was "important for us to keep up the tradition of good neighbors. Nobody can say we hurt them."

"We even acted as guards for them in their fields," his father interjects. "Last year," Rushdie goes on, becoming more and more animated by his own cynicism, "the kibbutz threw a party for its jubilee. So as not to offend us, they told us it was a party for 'peace and coexistence.' Some people from the village even went to celebrate with them," he smirks, "despite the fact that we've lost 6,000 dunams belonging to 400 families who indirectly support another 200."

If in the past the whole village would turn out for the olive picking, this last time Israelis from leftist organizations like B'Tselem, Rabbis for Human Rights, the Peace Bloc, and Ta'ayush came on buses from Tel Aviv and

Jerusalem as substitutes for those Palestinians who could not get permits, to lend a hand with the harvest, however symbolic. Foreign activists from the pro-Palestinian International Solidarity Movement came from as far as the Americas to help. But nobody came from Metzer, Rushdie remarks.

"Ah," sighs Abu Rushdie, at his son's side sipping the thick black coffee, "now you see the gap in the generations. When I used to go down to the kibbutz and the *mukhtar* (local chief) would greet me with a hello that was enough for me!"

Echoing the fears that some on Metzer had, Rushdie describes the fence project as a "barrel of explosives. The wall will create a reaction," he warns. "It creates hatred in the people that will only lead to more attacks."

The two generations do agree on one thing, though: the pain they felt when they heard about the killing spree of Sirhan. "It was as if it happened here," says Abu Rushdie. "That's true," says his son, "we were affected by this. We consider the kibbutz members to be moderate people. We had a different attitude when there was an attack at the settlement of Hermesh." (Just days before the Metzer attack, another Palestinian gunman from Tulkarm had infiltrated Hermesh, just south of Qaffin in the West Bank, killing a woman and two 14-year-old girls.)

In truth, Qaffin's younger generation has in any case aspired to more than the frugal living that can be made off the land. Casual work in Israel has proved more lucrative, and some four to five thousand individuals from the village are currently living and working abroad.

As we are talking, an overweight young man, Muhammad Khasib, drops by and plops into an armchair. He is just back from 15 years in Brooklyn, where he studied chemistry, worked in wholesale, and brought out a bride from his native Qaffin, one of Abu Rushdie's daughters. Khasib says he became homesick and nostalgic for village life. Having returned eight months earlier, he found Qaffin closed off by the fence and by army checkpoints from every side. Now he is "sitting," too. "Maybe coming back wasn't such a smart idea," he murmurs in a thick, Brooklyn-accented English drawl.

Meanwhile, with unemployment in Qaffin standing at 90 percent, according to the mayor Taysir Harasheh, everybody seems to be going back to school. Abu Rushdie's third son, Jamil, who used to work in construction in Israel, is now studying English at the Open University in Tulkarm. His blushing 22-year-old sister is studying social services at the same place. In all, 200 students from Qaffin are said to be enrolled at local colleges.

And yet, for all the modernization and progress underway in the village, the rift between Qaffin and Metzer only seems to yawn wider. A few weeks before our lunch above the stable, Rushdie saw Avi Ohion, the bereaved father of the two murdered little boys, on TV. Ohion had traveled to The Hague as part of a delegation of Israeli terror victims to demonstrate outside the International Court of Justice while hearings on the legality of Israel's new security barrier went on inside. At a televised press conference in the Dutch capital, Ohion had tearfully described how Sirhan Sirhan had cold bloodedly looked one of his children in the eye before shooting him through it. Had the section of the security fence by Metzer been completed a year and a half earlier, he said, he would be the happiest man on earth because Revital, Noam, and Matan would still be alive. Rushdie expressed his dismay at Ohion's words in favor of the fence, mistakenly assuming that he was a resident of the kibbutz as well, as if the distraught and broken man should have been more sensitive to Palestinian feelings.

When I return to Metzer at around the same time in the spring of 2004, the fields all around are magnificent carpets ablaze with wild mustard and poppies. The velvety wheat is thigh-high and pink and lilac blossoms adorn the trees. It has been 16 months since the murders. Oblivious, the birds are singing so loudly in the trees outside the Metzerplas factory that Ben Naftali, just back from a trade fair in Milan, can hardly hear himself speak. Further inside the kibbutz, on the grassy slope outside the white corner bungalow where Revital Ohion and her children died, the artificial streams around the memorial have dried up.

Taking to his car and driving through his beloved fields again, Ben Naftali declares he is "absolutely in love" with this place—with the tranquility, the nature, and the "fabric of life" that has been woven here between the Jews and Arabs. Metzer's location still gives him purpose. But his reflective mood betrays disappointment and gloom, for like Qaffin, the future of Metzer, as a radical experiment in social equality, is no longer secure. Today, agriculture is Metzer's least profitable branch, making up only 15 percent of the income. In the fields and in the factory, the kibbutzniks are mostly managers now. The workers from Qaffin cannot get here anymore, but Metzerplas's staff of a hundred is made up of new immigrants from the former Soviet Union and

Ethiopia living in nearby towns like Hadera, as well as Arabs from Baqa al-Gharbiya and Meisar.

Most of the kibbutz children—the "best and brightest," according to Ben Naftali—have flown the coop in search of new opportunities, the kibbutz having failed in providing them with suitable challenges. Meanwhile, like most kibbutzim, Metzer is undergoing a slow process of privatization. A differential salary scale has been introduced and the communal dining room, traditionally the hub of kibbutz life where members used to congregate three times a day, only operates at lunchtime and on Friday nights for the Sabbath meal.

The Nisselbaums, whose three children have all left the kibbutz, should be enjoying the fruits of a lifetime's labor; Yitzhak worked in plumbing and irrigation, and Fanny labored in agriculture, in the now-defunct communal children's houses and in Metzerplas. The idea had been to work according to one's ability, and in return, to be looked after until the end, in the tree-shaded kibbutz cemetery overlooking a vale of blossom trees. The Nisselbaums are anxious about the changes, though, and say they are paying for the kibbutz movement's mistakes of the past. "At our age we have nothing," frets Fanny. "No pension, no rights, no property, nothing to leave our children."

Ben Naftali lives in a modern two-story house, expanded to accommodate his family once the communal children's houses closed down. In the back garden he shares with his neighbors, there is a majestic palm that grew out of date pip he once discarded. "We're in crisis," he pronounces. "The old structure is disintegrating and we don't know where we're going."

Here at Metzer, one of the last bastions of the *yefei nefesh* (do-gooders or "sensitive souls," as the peace camp is sometimes patronizingly called in Hebrew), even political enthusiasm has been replaced by apathy and self-doubt. Matti Bardosh, a skinny 18-year-old with tussled hair, came to Metzer with his immigrant parents from Hungary at the age of six. The only contact he remembers having with Meisar was a couple of exchange visits when he was in kindergarten. His father Ephraim, who watches the Hungarian news on cable TV, says he brought the family to Metzer because relatives already living in Israel had advised him that a kibbutz was his best bet in terms of guaranteeing food and a roof over his head. He says he would leave if he could afford to, but he does not have even 100 shekels ($25) in his pocket.

Essentially, however, the story of Metzer falls into two eras—the period before the attack, and the period after. Before, people felt they were immune—that because of their relations with the Arab neighbors on both sides of the Green Line, nothing could possibly happen to them. "Our defense against attack was that we were peace activists," says Ofer Wagshall, a strapping man with a moustache and curly hair who was born on Metzer in 1958 to immigrants from Argentina. Wagshall, a deputy managing director of the Metzerplas factory, is married to Rosie, also from South America. They have two little boys of their own. Since the attack, this once-open, once-peaceful utopia has been invaded by the psychology of self-preservation and fear. Two days after the murders, an electric fence went up around the kibbutz perimeter, skirting the Wagshalls' garden. Yitzhak Nisselbaum fixed bars on the windows of his home while Fanny started locking the front door from the inside for the first time in fifty years. For nobody accepted the suave explanations of Palestinian Authority spokespeople who claimed that the novice Sirhan Sirhan had lost his way and blundered into the kibbutz by mistake, believing it to be a Jewish settlement in the West Bank. On the contrary, the kibbutzniks are convinced that Sirhan was dispatched to Metzer deliberately, to sabotage the model it had built of peaceful coexistence. States Wagshall: "Somebody dropped Sirhan off and pointed him our way."

As a result, a pall of uncomprehending confusion has descended on the place. The Nisselbaums are almost at a loss for words. "We didn't think we'd come to this," says Fanny. "There are no more free rides, it's over," sighs Yitzhak, as a muezzin's call to evening prayers drifts on the air from a mosque in Baqa al-Gharbiya. Asked if he sees any solution to the conflict, he just shrugs and suggests asking the politicians, apparently having no use for ideology any more.

Ben Naftali has not entirely given up, but like many on the disillusioned Israeli left, his support for the Palestinian national cause has become more conditional. "I'm not Mother Theresa," he says. "There'll be a Jewish state here. I tell the Palestinians, if they help me stand up for my rights, I'll help them stand up for theirs."

As we sit on his back porch in the spring evening, under the majestic palm, Ben Naftali asks me what people are saying in Qaffin. He listens and nods knowingly at all that I relate. Tellingly, he cannot remember the name of a single villager when I ask, though when I mention Abu Rushdie, he says he remembers him from the fields. In Qaffin, nobody I spoke to could remember any of the kibbutzniks by name either.

At the center of Qaffin is a small clearing, a kind of town square with cars parked unevenly outside an unimposing building where the mayor and the village council sit. A man hawks squeaky toys from a cart but there are no customers in sight. Up a dingy stairway Riad Khasib, 35, the village council treasurer, is at his desk equipped with a telephone and a large calculator. His brother Atef, a council member, comes by to while away some time. Two of eight siblings, both the brothers are now married with young children of their own. Riad is a graduate of business management from Bir Zeit University in the West Bank. Atef used to work as a trader of food supplies with Israel before the checkpoints and closures made it impossible. Now he is thinking of going back to school. "If you're educated, you work. If not, you don't," he says, not wanting to spend his days like the rest of Qaffin's unemployed, "sleeping or wandering the streets."

The Khasibs' parents used to work the land with their bare hands. Their father would get up every morning for dawn prayers and then go straight to his orchards, which now lie across the barrier. There is a Palestinian proverb that says, "you'll never get rich from olives, but you'll never starve." According to Atef, Qaffin's revenues from olive oil used to reach $4 million a year, but since the barrier, the villages' three olive presses have closed down. Many of Qaffin's families are now living on charity, relying on remittances from relatives abroad in Jordan and the Gulf. When the bulldozers came, the brothers say, each family in the village gathered soil in jars to keep in their homes so they would "never forget." They also claim that twenty mostly elderly villagers suffered heart attacks, one of them fatal.

Both Atef and Riad attended the joint demonstration on the Green Line with the members of Metzer in October 2002. Riad, the treasurer, says he went as "an official"; Atef says he went as "a person who loves peace. We are two people forced to live together, like before." In the Palestinian collective memory, things were always better before: before "the wall," or before the Al-Aqsa intifada; before Oslo or before the intifada before that. Things were better before the occupation, and certainly before 1948, when the state of Israel came into being and eclipsed Palestine. Qaffin dwells on its past perhaps to take some of the sting out of the present, while the kibbutznik neighbors like Ben Naftali, who sports the tinted spectacles favored by Israeli men of his age, plow ahead with the altruistic arrogance particular to socialist Zionism, the same determination that got the Jewish state on its feet in the first place.

After the Metzer attack, Qaffin's residents and notables raised their voices in condemnation of the bloodshed. Mayor Harasheh, who was visiting Yasser Arafat a few days afterwards, got approval to organize a condolence visit to the kibbutz. About thirty villagers and officials wanted to go. The separation fence was not up yet between Metzer and Qaffin, but the village was surrounded by army checkpoints and the Israeli authorities refused the delegation permission to cross. "An official delegation can't go hiking through the fields and orchards," says Atef, so the mayor had to make do with a phone call to Metzer instead.

It is only when I leave the village council building that I notice a couple of faded posters of intifada "martyrs" pasted on the wall to the street, certificates of past deeds of "resistance" that nobody has bothered or dared to take down. One is of a female suicide bomber who blew herself up in the northern Israeli town of Afula. Another is tinged blue by the elements, a portrait of a young man posing with a gun. The words are barely legible anymore, but I suddenly feel a chill when I make them out. The poster is inscribed with the legend, "The Martyr Commander, Sirhan Sirhan."

3

The Bulldozer

It is 9 o'clock on a dark night in the quiet Israeli border town of Kochav Ya'ir, a genteel suburb of single-family homes, clipped lawns, and cul-de-sacs smack up against the Green Line, about a half-hour commute east of Tel Aviv. Though the last houses abut the old pre-1967 patrol road, not one strays over into disputed territory. The West Bank city of Qalqilya is only a few hundred meters away, but Kochav Ya'ir was always intended to remain strictly inside Israel proper.

Unlike Qalqilya, Kochav Ya'ir is perfectly planned, its streets conforming to a neat grid befitting the fact that by a quirk of real estate history, it is home to an unusual concentration of the country's military top brass and heads of the intelligence community. Kochav (the Star) of Ya'ir was founded in 1981 and named by the Likud government for Avraham (Ya'ir) Stern of the pre-state Stern Gang, a radical anti-British terror underground. That would hardly bother the generals, though, given that one of the leaders of the Stern Gang, Yitzhak Ysernitsky, later Shamir, went on to serve as the country's prime minister. Actually, Kochav Ya'ir was originally conceived as a community for South African immigrants wanting to put apartheid behind them in the wake of the Soweto riots. Many of the plots were left unsold, however, and by the early 1980s, land was being sold off at special rates to other English-speaking immigrants, to the various branches of the security establishment, and to graduates of the pioneering youth movements willing to move out of the city for a house and garden. Nonconformism was not encouraged; only married couples were allowed in this oasis of orderliness and respectability. In the end, South Africans made up only about 10 percent of the population, while over the years the junior officers and colonels rose up the ranks.

Today Kochav Ya'ir's residents include such military and political luminaries as Shaul Mofaz, the former IDF chief of staff who became Ariel Sharon's defense minister, former Mossad head and Labor Knesset member Danny Yatom, and ex-Shin Bet (internal security service) deputy head Gideon Ezra, Sharon's minister of internal security. Yossi Ginossar, a Shin Bet officer who went on to become a close confidante of several prime ministers, including Yitzhak Rabin and Ehud Barak, and their trusted go-between with Yasser Arafat, lived here until his death in early 2004. Ehud Barak himself, another former chief of staff turned politician, lived in the town's Rehov Ha-Vered (Rose Street) until he separated from his wife Nava in 2003.

Uzi Dayan is a fish in water at Kochav Ya'ir. A compact, dark-haired major general in the reserves, he served as the army deputy chief of staff in the late 1990s under Mofaz, then as Ehud Barak's military advisor, and until 2002 as head of the National Security Council. A quintessential *sabra* (the term used in Hebrew to denote a native Israeli), he was born along with the state in 1948 on a *moshav* (cooperative farm) in the Jezreel Valley. He is also the nephew of the late war hero and statesman Moshe Dayan, who helped negotiate the armistice line along which Kochav Ya'ir sits. Uzi Dayan moved here around 1990, he says, because a buddy nagged him to, and because you could build a dream house on a quarter acre for $100,000. Like the *sabra* (literally, prickly pear) that the Israelis have adopted as a symbol of their national character, Dayan is tough on the outside, often brusque and haughty in public. Tonight, though, he is charm personified, waiting outside his home to greet me and revealing the warm family man that he is on the inside. It strikes me that like Barak and Mofaz, he is probably headed for politics too. First I am introduced to the cats that come in three grades: the official house pets; windowsill cats that regularly hang around the garden and get fed; and occasional guests from the street who manage to penetrate the formidable security system around the house, installed by the Shin Bet when Dayan became senior in the military.

The spacious villa leads out onto a large garden with an orchard and a tree house, and backs up to open country. We sit at the dining table, and after making arrangements with his wife Tamar, a zoology professor at Tel Aviv University, about who will wake up 10-year-old Zohar and take her to school, Dayan chats amicably as he brings out a box of purchased brownies, a bowl of succulent peaches and grapes, and a bottle of the national beverage, Diet Coke.

Five days before our meeting, a double suicide bombing had killed 16 Israelis in the southern city of Beersheba. Two buses blew up almost simultaneously on the last day of the school summer vacation in August 2004. To Dayan, the attack was just another tragic proof, if any were needed, of the ongoing fiasco that Israel's security fence project has become. "It wasn't fate," he asserts about the Beersheba attack. "It could have been avoided. The terrorists are guilty of the act, but the responsibility for it lies with the Israeli government."

Dayan is the original architect of the barrier, having drawn up the first plans for it during his term at the NSC. He is also one of its most passionate advocates: Since retiring from the military in the fall of 2002, he has headed a slick public lobbying group called Security Fence for Israel dedicated to pushing the project through. So far, it has been an agonizingly slow and painful business.

He notes that the Beersheba bombers came from Hebron, in the southern West Bank, and infiltrated Israel without hindrance since the security barrier had not got that far. A fence has to be continuous, Dayan says, or it is like a dam with holes. But more than three years after he presented the government with his blueprint for the whole barrier, it is far from complete. And the main reason for that, Dayan insists, is that Prime Minister Ariel Sharon, who did not want a fence in the first place, still does not want one now.

Dayan was appointed to head the NSC by Sharon's predecessor, Labor Prime Minister Ehud Barak, in September 2000, exactly as the intifada was breaking out. The violence soon swept Barak out of office: In February 2001, the right-wing Likud candidate Ariel Sharon won a convincing victory at the polls. By June 2001, Dayan had presented him with the security barrier plan as a means of stopping the suicide bombers and other terror operatives who needed little more than a destructive will and a cheaply produced explosive belt or a gun to wreak havoc in Israel's cities. As the Al-Aqsa intifada progressed, Palestinian terror had taken on an increasingly freelance nature as more established groups splintered into neighborhood cells that sent youthful volunteers on missions with little training, sometimes at a day's notice. "It was clear we couldn't fight terror only on the offensive," Dayan explains. "We lacked the intelligence and other means. We needed a defense as well." Moreover, Dayan says, the military wanted definition, a fence that would delineate responsibility for who controls what, and where. The army's southern commander may be responsible for Hebron in the West Bank, Dayan argues, but he is not responsible for Beersheba in Israel proper.

The prime minister himself was actively opposed to the idea. Sharon, Dayan says, "prefers offense to defense." He was also not keen on the political complications such a project would bring. Indeed, there was no great enthusiasm for the fence plan from any quarter of the unity government that Sharon had formed. His coalition partners included the right-wing National Religious Party and the National Union, whose ideological settler constituencies rejected the idea of any physical division of Eretz Yisrael, the Greater Land of Israel. Sharon, nicknamed "the Bulldozer," had forged a formidable constituency of his own among the settlers over the past 30 years as the master builder of the settlements. And while some Labor Party politicos, notably Haim Ramon and Dalia Itzik, were vocal fence supporters, the head of the party, Shimon Peres, the foreign minister at the time, was not keen on the notion of a barrier for reasons of his own: Dayan remarks that the champion of open borders and regional cooperation "didn't want a fence running through the salon of his 'New Middle East,'" a sarcastic reference to Peres's grand plan, laid out in a book by the same name, for economic development—with Israel playing a central role—leading to regional peace.

Dayan's plan gathered dust in the prime minister's office for almost a year until Palestinian terrorism reached intolerable levels in March 2002, the month when 17 suicide bombings killed almost a hundred Israelis. Under tremendous popular pressure to find an answer to the bombers, Sharon launched Operation Defensive Shield, retaking all the Palestinian cities of the West Bank, and finally, by public demand, he brought the fence plan to the cabinet table in May 2002. In June, the cabinet approved the first third of the route, from Salem in the north down to the settlement of Elkana, where Israel is at its narrowest, as well as another two sections of around 10 kilometers each on Jerusalem's northern and southern flanks to hamper access to the capital from the nearby terror-launching pads of Ramallah and Bethlehem. Phase One of the fence was completed by the following summer, and in October 2003 the government gave the go-ahead for the rest of the barrier to be built. Yet a year on, in September 2004, I am sitting with Dayan and practically nothing more than that initial third has physically gone up.

Ostensibly, the delay was caused by international pressure on Israel and legal problems with the barrier's route, which Dayan says had changed

5. The military wanted definition, a fence that would delineate responsibility for who controls what, and where: Prime Minister Ariel Sharon (center) and Defense Minister Shaul Mofaz (at right) touring the northern seam line, January 2003. Credit: Avi Ohayon, Israel Government Press Office

somewhat from the one he had originally proposed. Cases had been brought against the route both in the International Court of Justice at The Hague and in Israel's own Supreme Court, sending the army back to the drawing board. But Dayan calls this a poor excuse for foot-dragging that is costing lives. While he and Security Fence for Israel, the pressure group Dayan heads, avoid taking a position on the crucial and controversial issue of the route, he says that "there's a government in Jerusalem; let it decide." It is the government's responsibility to choose where to build the fence as quickly as possible, he insists. And if the route is not rational, the government will pay. While clearly, building the barrier on the Green Line itself would present the least problems on the ground, Dayan goes along with the general Israeli consensus that doing so would make an undesirable political statement: Israel fears that any apparent recognition on its part of the temporary 1949 armistice line as a legal border would prejudice its position in future negotiations with the Palestinians over the West Bank, parts of which it intends to keep. "But if you ask me today do I prefer a fence on the Green Line or no fence at all," Dayan says, "I'd say put it on the Green Line." Conversely, if the government insists on extending the fence all the way out to Ariel, a large Jewish urban settlement that lies 22 kilometers east of the Green Line, in the heart of the West Bank—a highly controversial possibility that has generated considerable international opposition—Dayan is just as clear. "If it's between that or no fence at all," he says, "then I'd say include Ariel. I can agree to a route I don't like as long as the thing gets built."

In fact Dayan's original plan had neither stuck religiously to the Green Line nor included Ariel, a point that Sharon had not objected to at first despite a long-standing national assumption that Ariel would remain under Israeli control under any final status agreement with the Palestinians. Perhaps that was because Sharon insisted on belittling the significance of the barrier he had been forced into building, seeing it as neither a political nor a security border, but just as another operational means of fighting terror. Soon, however, the question of Ariel and the fence would come to plague him, encapsulating all the problems any Israeli leader faces in trying to set the boundaries of the state.

The settlement of Ariel, built on a long, narrow strip of land in Samaria, or the northern West Bank, has a mostly secular population of 17,000, half made up of new immigrants from the former Soviet Union attracted by the cheap housing and relatively good standard of living. Many came as a result of the recruiting efforts of Ariel's mayor, Ron Nahman, a rough-talking, blunt-featured Likud politician who pays little attention to social graces. In the early 1990s, as waves of immigrants were arriving on planes from Russia, Nahman would go to Ben-Gurion Airport to pick new arrivals off the tarmac himself. Some of them may have had no idea they were going to live over the Green Line, if they even knew what it was.

Though Ariel was officially founded in 1978 by the Likud government of Menachem Begin, the Samarian location also accorded with the vision that many in the Labor party held of building an Israel with a wider waist. Indeed, it was Moshe Dayan, Golda Meir's defense minister, who first approached Nahman and his "Tel Aviv group" of urban, secular pro-settlement colleagues, all employees of the military industries, in the early 1970s and asked them to "raise the flag of security and Zionist settlement." The signature of Labor's Shimon Peres is on the government document, dated March 29, 1977, permitting the purchase of the first 1,000 dunams (250 acres) of land for Ariel from the nearby Palestinian village of Hares. Nahman produces a copy from his files to prove his point that Ariel has always been part of the Israeli consensus. With Ariel recently having been connected to central Israel by the fast, new Trans-Samaria Highway, Uzi Dayan, the nephew, confirms that Ehud Barak never intended giving it up.

When I visited the settlement-city one weekday in the fall of 2002, I found the streets quiet, almost deserted with all the children in school and the adults at work, some in the factories of the nearby Barkan industrial zone. The neat apartment blocks and rows of houses stretched for miles. At one of the small commercial centers, the Milky Way restaurant was serving light Italian lunches while Thai workers swept leaves outside. No Palestinians had worked here since the outbreak of the intifada in 2000. Nahman proudly showed me around the 6,000-student Judea and Samaria College—later upgraded as the West Bank's first Jewish university, where 85 percent of the students come from inside Israel proper—as well as the settlement's cultural center and Internet café. Then there was the state-of-the-art radio and TV studio donated, according to the plaque, "as a blessing to Ariel" by Nahman's Christian friends at the Maranatha Chapel in San Diego. Nahman, like some other settler leaders, had found a ready source of funding among some evangelical and fundamentalist Christian communities of America whose End of Days vision apparently includes the Jewish settlement of all the holy land.

Nahman's ambitions for Ariel knew no bounds. Next, he told me, he was planning to build a zoo.

When I asked the mayor about the recently approved fence project, he responded with a dismissive "eh" and a flick of his hand, suggesting that he doubted it would ever get built. Instead, he asked me to write that he was looking for up to $2 million in donations to complete a state-of-the-art laser security system around the town's own perimeter fence. However, once the bulldozers got to work and it became clear that the government security barrier plans did not include Ariel, Nahman changed his tune. He railed on the radio that Sharon and Peres, the fathers of Ariel, the capital of Samaria, were "abandoning" the settlers, using the same word in Hebrew for abandoning wounded soldiers in the field. It was an emotionally laden charge, given the enormous value Israelis place on recovering their soldiers under almost any circumstances, often at a high price, and particularly since Sharon himself had been left for dead during the battle for Latrun in 1948. On one occasion, Nahman verbally attacked Sharon at a Likud faction meeting. When the prime minister blustered that he was intending to make Ariel and its satellite settlements into an undefined "special security zone" outside the fence, Nahman retorted that Israel's last special security zone was in South Lebanon, and "we all know what happened to that." Eighteen years after Ariel Sharon, as defense minister, had masterminded the Israeli invasion of Lebanon, Ehud Barak had withdrawn the troops in May 2000. After several months more of intense pressure from the settler lobby, the government eventually pledged that Ariel would be included inside the fence, a decision no less political in its future implications than one to build the barrier on the Green Line, leaving Ariel out, would have been.

Once Sharon gave into the domestic pressure to include Ariel and other settlements deep inside the West Bank within the barrier, foreign pressure came to the fore. The Americans put their foot down when it came to Ariel on grounds that extending the barrier in a "finger" more than 20 kilometers long inside the West Bank would severely hamper the Palestinians' territorial contiguity and the viability of their future state. In the summer of 2003, Washington officials even threatened that the United States may, for every kilometer the barrier strays from the Green Line, start docking dollar sums from the loan guarantees Israel receives.

Caught between the conflicting pressures, Sharon couldn't make a decision one way or another about the course of the fence, his dithering rather uncharacteristic for a man more famed for his decisiveness and initiative.

Construction had started on a nine-kilometer curved section of the fence, referred to by the army as one of the "fingernails" that would go up around the back of Ariel and some of its smaller satellite settlements that make up the Ariel bloc. But for the time being the nail would not be joined up with the main barrier to create the finger. Instead, as an interim solution, a gap would be left in the main barrier several kilometers long, meaning that Ariel would be neither in nor out.

The illogic of this halfway measure was neatly, if unintentionally, caught by the Defense Ministry's Seam Zone website in Hebrew, which noted that the prime minister had, contrary to previous fence plans, adopted the principle that a "non continuous obstacle would not fulfill the objective" and that to avoid infiltrations, a route for a continuous barrier had to be found.

In Dayan's view, the barrier saga goes from the illogical to the almost absurd. His next example of the defective implementation of the project is the case of the towns of Baqa al-Gharbiya and Baqa al-Sharqiya (Baqa West and Baqa East), the first Arab-Israeli and the second West Bank Palestinian, just south of Kibbutz Metzer and Qaffin. The two towns are located on either side of the Green Line about a kilometer apart, and have grown toward each other over the years to the point where they now meet up in the middle. Originally, Dayan had proposed building the barrier more or less on the Green Line between the two Baqas, which he saw as the only logical route at this point. The alternative was to include Baqa al-Sharqiya and a few adjacent tiny villages within the barrier. The problem with that was that it meant stranding some six thousand West Bank Palestinians in an enclave between the fence and the Green Line, with free access to neither Israel nor the rest of the Palestinian Authority.

In the cabinet discussions of May 2002, Sharon insisted that the fence should run east of Baqa al-Sharqiya, several kilometers inside the West Bank, for no apparent reason, according to Dayan, other than not to build it on the pre-1967 border. "I think he just wanted to please his right-wing coalition partners from the National Religious Party and show them he was not sticking to the Green Line," he says. Only one minister, the Likud's pragmatic Dan Meridor, backed Dayan. The fence went up, effectively cutting Baqa al-Sharqiya off from the rest of the West Bank, and became a showcase of Israeli irrationality at home and abroad. Sure enough, in February 2004, one day before the start of The Hague hearings on the legality of Israel's construction of the barrier inside the West Bank territory, the army bulldozers arrived to pull the

8-kilometer section of the fence around Baqa al-Sharqiya down. Israeli officials claimed unconvincingly that the timing was purely coincidental.

The cost of the whole exercise ran to millions. Aside from the original construction of the barrier, built on a budget of 10 million shekels (over $2 million) per kilometer, there was the cost of its removal, then of rebuilding the barrier between the houses more or less on the Green Line, where Dayan had originally planned. Security officials claimed that the fence around Baqa al-Sharqiya had always been planned as a temporary stopgap measure to provide security while a path could be cleared along the Green Line, between the two Baqas, wide enough for a wall. That required demolishing a number of houses that had been built without permits, and the legal proceedings were bound to take some time. Army fence-planner Dany Tirza, on the other hand, told me that Baqa al-Sharqiya had first been included on the western, Israeli side of the fence because the residents of the two Baqas, some of whom have intermarried over the years, wanted to stay together. Only afterwards, he said, Israel found itself accused of having designs on the chunk of West Bank land.

Either way, about 20 bulldozers roared up at 6 a.m. on August 21, 2003, according to Moin Asad, 25, a resident of the seam between the two Baqas, and razed seven houses mostly belonging to the Asad clan. Moin's own apartment was turned to rubble. Due to be married the next day, he summoned the wedding photographer to take pictures of the demolition instead. About 60 members of the Asad clan, including Moin, his new wife and baby daughter, have since moved into the four family properties that survived, all on the Israeli side of the wall. They have special permission to live in the houses even though they are West Bank Palestinians, and can pass through the checkpoint to the eastern, Palestinian side whenever they want. But they are forbidden from moving any further beyond their houses into the Israeli Baqa al-Gharbiya. A cousin was recently detained when he was caught buying vegetables in the town.

—◦═◦═◦—

Dayan says the government's handling of the fence project reminds him of a tale from Chelm, the fictional village in Jewish folklore inhabited by *schlemiels*, Yiddish for fools. "One day the people of Chelm decided their mayor should wear gold shoes in keeping with his status," he says. "But in

6. About 20 bulldozers roared up at 6 a.m. on August 21, 2003 and razed seven houses mostly belonging to the Asad clan: Moin Asad (left) with family members by the wall between the two Baqas. Credit: Esteban Alterman/The Jerusalem Report

Chelm it was muddy, so they sewed him boots from felt to put over the gold shoes. They made holes in the felt to let the gold show through, but of course the mud got in. Then a man was given the job of filling the holes with straw."

Major General Dayan does not suffer fools. In his opinion, this is no way to build a fence. The route, he goes on, has been dictated by petty political calculations, and its progress has been determined by attacks. In December 2002, for example, an additional 60-kilometer section was approved by the government and hastily constructed along the northern edge of the West Bank from Salem east to the mountains of Gilboa. That came after a November 28 terror attack at the Likud party headquarters in the northern Israeli town of Bet She'an, in which six Israelis were killed. The local regional council head, Laborite Danny Attar, had threatened to start privately building a northern barrier himself. And five days after the Beersheba attack, Defense Minister Mofaz announced on Army Radio that the bulldozers had started laying the ground for the first six-kilometer stretch of barrier in the south. He added—again unconvincingly—that there was "no connection" between the timing and the Beersheba attack.

The security barrier is undoubtedly one of the biggest infrastructure projects Israel has undertaken, its total estimated cost running to "many billions" of shekels according to a Defense Ministry source. Other than the settlements, it is the most politically significant and decisive "fact on the ground" since 1967. Yet with all the dust and broo-ha-ha stirred up by the bulldozers, Dayan says, he has found it hard to convince people that not much has actually been built. "The story of the fence is a typical Israeli story," he goes on. "We say we're doing it, but we aren't exactly doing it, and in the process we just create trouble for ourselves." Israel, he points out, had already faced international censure for a barrier that mostly did not exist.

Uzi Dayan's call for defensive measures could be taken as a personal barb against Sharon, for the prime minister had long built a reputation for taking the offensive, for initiative and deeds, and for actions that sometimes went badly wrong. As a commander during the 1956 Sinai campaign, for example, Sharon sent a group of paratroopers on a daring and controversial attack on the heavily defended Egyptian position at the Mitla Pass deep in the desert.

The pass was captured, but it cost 38 Israelis and over 200 Egyptian soldiers their lives.

After the 1967 war, Sharon played a central role in destroying Palestinian terrorist organizations in the Gaza Strip. Finding that the militants often hid their bunkers among the cactus thickets that lined Gaza's roads and fields, he gave a standing order that battalion commanders charged with checking suspect areas should always bring a bulldozer along with them. "Behind every commander's jeep I wanted to see a bulldozer," he wrote, explaining how he first got his nickname.

Later, after Israel was surprised with the outbreak of the 1973 October War, Sharon, by then a general, planned the stunning crossing of the Suez Canal to encircle the attacking Egyptian forces and clinch Israel's victory. And in 1982, as defense minister, he was the architect of the invasion of Lebanon and the siege of Beirut. The campaign, which Israel called Operation Peace for Galilee, went far beyond the original stated aim of flushing out the PLO that had long engaged in terror over Israel's northern border, and ended badly for Sharon. The massacre of Palestinians at the Sabra and Shatilla refugee camps in Beirut at the hands of Christian Lebanese militias but under Israeli eyes resulted in a state commission of inquiry which concluded that Sharon bore indirect responsibility and judged him unfit to serve as defense minister.

It was not the first time that Sharon's actions had been called into question in his 50-year war on terror. As a promising young commander, he was tasked in 1953 with creating an elite counter-terror squad, Unit 101, in response to the escalation of infiltrations from the then Jordanian-controlled West Bank. Israel's political leadership had concluded that if the Jordanians would not take active measures to prevent these attacks, Israel would have to take its security into its own hands. The unit's first major mission, on the night of October 14–15, 1953, gained Sharon notoriety and left a stain on the young Jewish state.

Two nights earlier, Arab *fedayeen* had entered the Israeli town of Yehud, east of Tel Aviv, and murdered a mother and her two infants in their sleep. There were indications that the killers may have come from the direction of Qibya, a rural hamlet not far away on the other side of the Green Line in Jordanian-held territory. It was decided Sharon would lead a retaliatory raid. The orders were clear. According to Sharon's own account given in his autobiography *Warrior,* Qibya was "to be a lesson. I was to inflict as many casualties as I could on the Arab home guard and on whatever Jordanian army reinforcements showed up. I was also to blow up every major building in the town. A political decision had been made at the highest level. The Jordanians were to understand that Jewish blood could no longer be shed with impunity. From this point on there would be a heavy price to pay."

Sharon set out with a hundred paratroopers, 25 of his specially trained 101 commandoes and 600 kg of explosives. After the raid, he reported that his men had inflicted 10–12 casualties—two of them Jordanian soldiers, the rest home guards killed on the approach to the village. He also reported the demolition of 42 buildings which soldiers had checked first, to ensure they were empty.

It was only the next morning, he recounts, that he heard on Jordanian radio that 69 people had been killed, mostly civilians, including women and children. Several of the destroyed homes had apparently not been empty at all: The terrified inhabitants hiding inside had merely kept quiet when the soldiers came banging on the doors. The United Nations Security Council passed a resolution, also numbered 101, condemning the Qibya raid as a violation of the cease-fire provisions and censuring Israel for the act.

Sharon describes Qibya as both a tragedy and a turning point in Israel's war for survival. He recalls that prime minister David Ben-Gurion called him in afterwards and told him that despite how it was seen around the world, "this is going to give us the possibility of living here." In his own account, Moshe Dayan, who was appointed army chief of staff a few weeks after the incident, said the incident also taught Israel that the world would not tolerate its army retaliating against anything but military targets, and moved to merge Unit 101 into the paratroopers.

The botched operation came at the "time of the olives," or picking season, in Qibya. Fifty-one years later, one October morning in 2004, it is olive time again. The approach to the village is lined with olive trees and sabra bushes, the latter resplendent with rosy fruit. The hardy cactuses were planted, locals say, after the young Jordanian king Hussein visited here following the disaster and urged the villagers to have patience, for which the word in Arabic is *sabr.*

Abu Antar, 70, a retired shepherd, is whiling away the hours on a plastic chair outside a clothing store in the ramshackle center of the village, in the company of a young man. Some of the old men are sick of telling outsiders the story, but Abu Antar readily launches into his rendition of the events of that terrible night. Approaching Qibya from the terraces below, he recounts, the Israeli commandos first came across two villagers who were out guarding the olive groves, the trees heavy with ripe fruit, from thieves.

"The old one was wearing a kaffiyeh. They wound it round his neck and stuffed the black cord in his mouth. The man was killed," Abu Antar relates. A younger boy with him was tied up, but managed to escape. Though he was shot at and wounded in the leg, he raised the alarm, shouting into the night, "The Jews are coming!" Hundreds of villagers, including Abu Antar's family, heeded the warning and headed for the mountains, seeking refuge in the nearby Shukba caves. Others stayed behind, barricading themselves in their houses, caught unawares or perhaps assuming that, as in previous raids against villages in the Jordanian-held territory, the Israeli forces would blow up a few outer buildings before retreating. "When a hunter comes to hunt deer," Abu Antar explains, "they don't all run away."

Sa'id, 38, Abu Antar's half-brother and the owner of the clothing store, comes out onto the sidewalk to join the conversation. He tells the story of the Abd al-Majid household, where two young men were hiding with their wives, mothers, and children in the family's old stone house. The mothers urged the young men to jump from the windows and escape "so that at least they could keep the family name alive." When they returned, they found the rest of the family under the rubble.

Sharon was telling the truth, according to Sa'id. The soldiers did check the houses before blowing them up. "Old Abd al-Majid told me they banged on the doors shouting '*jaish, jaish* [army], is anyone in there?'" he says, banging on the metal shutter of his store by way of demonstration, "but the people were too scared to come out."

When Abu Antar came back down from the mountains, he says he found an 80-year-old woman lying dead in the street. He remembers seeing Musa the schoolteacher's house blown up and Musa's wife brought out dead, her hair uncovered and flowing loose. He saw a mother and her four children under the ruins of one house, and a dozen more people in another. "For two weeks there was a very bad smell here," he recalls. "There was nobody to bury the bodies."

The victims, whom the villagers counted as 75, were eventually buried in the old cemetery in what is now the heart of the village, by a new mosque. With a distinct lack of sentimentality for the dead, their graves have long since vanished, having been replaced by new ones or covered by buildings. A modest memorial in the village marks the number of deceased but not their names.

If, as the villagers believe, Israel's intention in razing the village had been to drive the inhabitants away from the border—Qibya sits a few hundred meters beyond the Green Line, about 10 kilometers east of Ben Gurion Airport—it did not work. Qibya has been rebuilt and now has a population of around 4,000. Thousands more are living abroad. Many left with the Israeli occupation in 1967, and settled in the town of Salt, in Jordan.

Qibya claims no martyrs in the Al-Aqsa intifada, having remained out of the sphere of violence for the past four years. The last two villagers who set out from here seeking revenge died carrying out attacks against Israelis in 1988 and 1993, both times in the month of October. Nevertheless, situated between the villages of Shubka and Budrus, Qibya's lands lie directly on the route of the security barrier going up along the Israel-West Bank seam. A beige scar is clearly visible on the high ground across the wadi where the bulldozers have prepared the ground for the fence. Stormy protests have been taking place in Budrus, where whole olive orchards have been uprooted. Residents from Qibya have joined the popular resistance there, Budrus being a small village of 1,200 souls.

About half of Qibya's village lands—some 16,000 dunams, or 4,000 acres—were lost after 1948, having fallen over the armistice line. More lands will now be lost to the security barrier, planned to run along the ridge east of the Green Line and built by the villagers' old nemesis Sharon, who does not want it any more than they do. It is an ironic fate. Despite all the trauma of the past, in Qibya, the idea of separation from Israel is considered not a comfort, but a curse.

According to Jihad Ajrab, a 32-year-old English teacher and a member of Qibya's small educated class, some 80 percent of the village men currently work illegally in Israel, mostly in construction. The fence will spell economic ruin. Sharon will "kill us with this wall," says Ajrab, sitting in his village home located behind a chicken coop, with an old IBM computer in the corner of the sparsely furnished lounge. A father of three, Ajrab supplements his own meager teacher's salary of $350 a month by working during school vacations on a building site in the airport town of Lod.

For over three decades since Israel conquered the West Bank in 1967, the villagers of Qibya have enjoyed free access to relatively lucrative jobs over the Green Line. Even now that it is illegal to cross without a permit—a precious commodity that few Qibya residents possess—the traffic has not ceased. Ajrab says Palestinians come here by the bus load from more northerly towns like Qalqilya and Tulkarm, which are already sealed off from Israel by high concrete walls and fences. From the village, they take taxis up to the top of the ridge and continue into Israel to work. Once the barrier is up, the flow of illegal laborers will come to a stop.

A few of Qibya's young men bear the wounds and scars of this new border regime; infiltrating Israel without a work permit apparently comes with a certain degree of risk. Outside Sa'id's clothing store, the youth who has been sitting in respectful silence next to old Abu Antar suddenly pipes up. Ahmed Qadah, 20, lifts his T-shirt to reveal a metal body brace. He was caught working illegally in Lod two months earlier and, he alleges, was severely beaten by the border police. He says that they broke four of his ribs with their rifle butts.

Another young man with an Elvis hairdo is passing by and comes to join the group on the sidewalk outside Sa'id's store. Esam Jamil, 19, says he too was caught without a permit on a construction site in Tel Aviv just over a week ago, and claims to have been beaten by regular police. He has bruises over his left eye, a cut on his left shoulder, and complains of continual headaches. Asked whether they have filed complaints, Qadah and Jamil shrug off the suggestion with amusement, dismissing it as a waste of time.

Obviously, notes a police spokesman in Jerusalem, there is no way of telling whether these injuries resulted from police beatings or not. In general, the only cases that come to the attention of the authorities are ones where Palestinians land up in an Israeli hospital. In 2003 alone, according to the police files, 258,481 illegal Palestinian workers were stopped and checked in Israel. Most were simply sent home. "We don't have the means to deal with a quarter of a million people," the spokesman says, noting that for that matter there are not a quarter of a million Palestinians walking around in body braces either.

Villagers say that on a clear day, you can see ships sailing on the Mediterranean from the top of the ridge. For months after 1948, they relate, Palestinian refugees from the coastal plain camped out there in tents, determined to keep their former homes within sight. Eventually they were moved further in to the West Bank, to organized camps such as Jalazoun, near Ramallah. After the barrier, Qibya's permanent population will have to turn its face to Ramallah too. But unskilled laborers working in the West Bank city will earn a fraction of what they could in Israel.

In Qibya, the fence is seen as just another proof of Israel's ill intentions and its desire to drive the Palestinians off their land. Ajrab the English teacher says he told his daughter the other day that he loves her like the sea. "She asked me 'What's the sea?' I told her the Jews stole it from us." Here, 1948, 1953 and 2004 are all part of the same timeline, with the Palestinian tragedy as a constant theme.

From the military Sharon went into politics, joining Menachem Begin and his Herut party in a rightist coalition called the "Likud," or union. Once the Likud came into power in 1977, Sharon went on to use his appointment as minister of agriculture to shape the country according to his strategic vision. Unlike the gentlemanly, more theoretical, and legalistic minded Begin, Sharon describes himself in *Warrior* as having come from "pragmatic Zionist" stock. In those circles, the goal was to create facts on the ground, "reclaim another acre, drain another swamp, acquire another cow," all according to the motto "Don't talk about it, just get it done."

Since 1967, Sharon had been afraid that the Arab towns on either side of the Green Line would join up and create a densely populated area that would constrict the narrow corridor between Israel's center and north to almost nothing. New communities like Kochav Ya'ir were built on the Israeli side of the Green Line to fill up the spaces. But Sharon was convinced that in order to strengthen the corridor and protect the coastal plain, Israel also had to control access from the east. This meant settling the high mountain ridge that runs like a spine down the center of the West Bank, and in parallel, the Jordan Valley on the eastern border with Jordan. In addition, Sharon envisaged an east-west artery linking the two that would be guarded by Jewish settlements as well. Sharon linked up with the messianic Gush Emunim (Bloc of the Faithful) settlement movement and set about the task with gusto, barging through the state bureaucracy in true bulldozer style. In his four years as agricultural minister he managed to establish no fewer than 64 Jewish settlements in Judea and Samaria. In a sense, the almost 240,000 Jewish settlers now living in communities scattered throughout the West Bank are the children of Sharon.

Sharon's antipathy to the very notion of the barrier is not surprising, especially since it had its genesis in the opposing political camp in Israel and was born not only out of a desire for security but for physical separation and disengagement from the Palestinians as well. Sharon had vehemently opposed the Oslo peace accords from the start, protesting the partial Israeli withdrawals from the West Bank and Gaza Strip and rejecting any attempts to partition the land.

The fence plan first started percolating among the staff of Sharon's Labor predecessor, Ehud Barak, as a kind of Plan B should the peace process ultimately collapse. Specifically, Uzi Dayan, then a close advisor of Barak, says the idea came to him as he searched for a possible exit strategy should Camp David fail. "I advised Barak not to go for an all-or-nothing negotiation with the Palestinians because I thought he wouldn't be able to bridge the gap," Dayan says, "but he insisted. I asked him 'What if there is no agreement? We need to prepare a safety net because you're taking us to the edge.' That's when we started to build what we called a policy of 'initiated disengagement' in the case of finding we have no partner on the other side— despite Barak's offer which was generous by all means."

Initiated disengagement is unilateral separation from the Palestinians by another name, but Dayan says he avoided the term "separation" because it "sounds like something between apartheid and divorce." Dayan's idea was to put up a fence between Israel and the West Bank and to withdraw gradually from some areas on the other side, while at the same time leaving the door "wide open for negotiations." Israel's pragmatic center-left felt increasingly that in the absence of a true partner on the Palestinian side, unilateral separation was the only way left of realizing the vision of the late Yitzhak Rabin and the Oslo Accords: to partition the Land of Israel, or historic Palestine, into two states. If a barrier went up, it was assumed, the remote Jewish settlements falling beyond it would be perceived as having no future. They would naturally start to dry up "like grapes left out on the vine," as Rabin used to say, facilitating their eventual removal.

Parallel to the political vision, the Israeli desire for separation from the Palestinians has always been rooted in terror. Back in 1990, after a Palestinian stabbed three Israeli civilians to death on the street one morning in the quiet Jerusalem neighborhood of Baka, Israelis started calling for the 160,000 or more Palestinian laborers who came to work in Israel each day to be kept out. Security closures were imposed on the territories for a few days at a time at first, banning the workers from entering Israel proper. An extended closure of a few weeks was imposed at the time of the 1991 Gulf War, and after that, Israel began instituting more control along the Green Line. Main entry points slowly turned into ad hoc checkpoint crossings, usually consisting of a few concrete blocks manned by soldiers. By the time the PA arrived in 1994, a permit system was put in place.

While security was always the prime motive, Barak's staff saw other good reasons for wanting a fence. With Israel's GDP being 17 times that of the Palestinians in the territories, Israel has long suffered from the scourge of car and property theft, particularly in areas along the seam. And despite the permit system, tens of thousands of unauthorized Palestinian workers have continued to enter Israel to work, walking through fields or using side roads to avoid the checkpoints. Thousands have failed to return home, taking up illegal residence in the Arab villages of the Galilee and the Triangle instead.

There was no sense of urgency to start construction of the barrier during Barak's last months in office, however, perhaps because the prime minister did not see the failure of the Camp David summit in July 2000 as the end of the peace process. Rather, there was talk of another summit and hope that a final status agreement could still be reached. Over the next three months, no fewer than 38 Israeli-Palestinian secret meetings took place. The talks focused on finding a breakthrough on the unresolved and seemingly intractable issue of sovereignty over Jerusalem's Temple Mount, known to Muslims as the Haram al-Sharif (Noble Sanctuary). The ancient site of the First and Second Temples, the plateau is the most sacred place in Judaism. And as the location of Al-Aqsa Mosque and the Dome of the Rock, it is also revered as the third-holiest site in Islam. On the domestic front the Barak government was facing meltdown, while the outgoing President Clinton was running out of time. By early fall, the feeling was that there was a two- to three-week window left in order to reach agreement.

After refusing to have any direct contact with Yasser Arafat since the beginning of the Camp David summit, Barak's advisers persuaded him that he had to meet face to face with the Palestinian leader in order to gauge the true intentions of the other side. On September 25, 2000, Arafat came to Barak's home in Kochav Ya'ir accompanied by his closest aides. According to Gilead Sher, Barak's senior advisor and negotiations coordinator who was present at the meeting, the atmosphere was "festive and all smiles." Barak and Arafat left their colleagues and went to talk in the garden, alone, for an hour. The negotiators, who were about to leave for a round of talks in Washington, felt they were embarking on a historic mission.

Then three days later, on Thursday, September 28, Ariel Sharon, as head of the Likud opposition, paid his fateful visit to Temple Mount. The ensuing Al-Aqsa intifada swallowed the Barak government and the peace efforts in its storm. Many Israelis believe this was Arafat's intention all along. The Palestinians believe it was Sharon's.

⟶≡⟸

Among the first families to build a home in Kochav Ya'ir was that of Mark Heller, a Canadian immigrant who came to Israel with his wife Barbara and their young children in 1979. They moved there in the mid-1980s before the town was hooked up to electricity. Heller, an articulate, urbane man with snow white hair, radiates calm and intensity at the same time. Now the principal research associate at the Jaffee Center for Strategic Studies, a highly respected think tank at Tel Aviv University, he describes himself as a member of the Israeli peace camp, but not of the "sentimental left," whose politics, he says, are primarily derived from personal encounters with "nice" Palestinians. In 1991, he co-authored a groundbreaking book with prominent Palestinian academic Sari Nusseibeh, the scion of an aristocratic and politically active Jerusalem family and a salt-and-pepper-haired scholar of Islamic philosophy.

Nusseibeh, who was born in 1949 in the old East Jerusalem neighborhood of Sheikh Jarrah, is now president of Al-Quds University, whose campus buildings are spread around East Jerusalem and its environs. The book, called *No Trumpets, No Drums—A Two-State Settlement of the Israeli-Palestinian Conflict*, laid out the pair's principles and pragmatics for implementing peace between the two peoples. The close Israeli-Palestinian collaboration entailed in the project was unusual, even daring at the time. Nusseibeh was well known for his moderate approach toward Israelis and his often controversial positions that occasionally got him in trouble on the Palestinian side. In 1987, he was beaten up by masked Fatah activists on the campus of Bir Zeit University in the West Bank for his contacts with young members of the Likud—after delivering a lecture on tolerance.

In the book, Heller made no bones about the fact that to him, a two-state settlement of the Israeli-Palestinian conflict is the most desirable choice "from a short and not very appealing list of options." Nusseibeh, who was jailed without trial for three months by Israel during the 1991 Gulf War on what turned out to be the ludicrous accusation that he had been guiding in

Saddam's Scud missiles, had his own reservations. "Bluntly put," he wrote, "Palestinians essentially believe that any bargaining with Israel over Palestinian territory is like bargaining over stolen property with the very thief who stole it by force." Heller retorted that the West Bank and Gaza, "which were ruled by Arab governments before 1967, came under Israeli control as a result of a legitimate war of self-defense against unprovoked aggression."

But Heller comes to the same conclusion now that he did then. "Peaceful coexistence of Jews and Palestinians within the same structural framework is impossible," he states, sitting at his kitchen table in Kochav Ya'ir. "The only solution is separation, whether done unilaterally or by negotiation. It has taken the Israeli public 37 years, and four years since Camp David, to conclude that what was, couldn't be sustained forever."

Heller has never had any illusions about a shared existence with the Palestinians. In the 1980s, he says, life in Kochav Ya'ir was "OK. It was fine. I wouldn't say it was idyllic. We went cycling to [the nearby West Bank Palestinian village of] Falamiya and did shopping in Qalqilya. That's where we bought the kitchen tiles. And the bathroom mirror. On occasion we took the kids to Qalqilya zoo." In those days, maids and technicians would come from Qalqilya to render services in Kochav Ya'ir, but there had long been undercurrents of resentment on the Palestinians' part. "Most people's pipes were clogged with concrete when they moved in," Heller notes dryly, pointing to the petty sabotage that Palestinian construction workers engaged in at the time.

The barrier now seals Kochav Ya'ir off from Qalqilya and the rest of the West Bank. Heller considers it a necessary evil, the intifada and absence of a serious Palestinian partner having turned him into an advocate of unilateral separation. To the south, between Kochav Ya'ir and Qalqilya, the security fence runs a few hundred meters away. To the east, it digresses more than four kilometers into the West Bank to take in the expanding Jewish settlement of Tzufin, in the process enveloping significant tracts of agricultural land that belong to the nearby Palestinian villages of Falamiya and Kafr Jamal. The landowners from the villages have permits to cross through a farmers' gate in the fence to reach their fields, but the hyper security sensitivity of Kochav Ya'ir only adds to the usual bureaucracy. In the summer of 2004, a military order was given to chop down an orange, tangerine, and guava orchard belonging to a 72-year-old widow from Kafr Jamal on grounds that it presented a security threat to the Kochav Ya'ir home of Defense Minister Shaul Mofaz, which sits a few meters away inside the Green Line. A petition to Israel's Supreme Court resulted in a stay of execution: The court ruled that the trees could be pruned but not destroyed.

Indeed, it may strike outsiders as somewhat odd that the cream of Israel's military and security establishment has chosen to live here on the Green Line, a boundary that has not always been hostile, but was never born of peace. From the end of Ehud Barak's former street, the hothouses, mosques, and apartment blocks of the West Bank are clearly visible, spilling down the next hill. "There's almost no place in Israel that's not in short rocket range from some Arab location or other," Heller, the strategic analyst, says. "It's so small that being on the border doesn't make any difference."

Nusseibeh, like Heller, still supports a two state solution, but quite literally from the opposite side of the wall. The main campus of Al-Quds University now sits behind an 8-meter-high barrier of concrete in Abu Dis on the edge of Jerusalem. And contrary to Heller, Nusseibeh, an advocate of nonviolence, never gave on political dialogue. In July 2003, together with Israeli former Shin Bet chief Ami Ayalon, he came up with the "Destination Map," a joint document of principles for a negotiated settlement of the conflict based on two states split more or less along the Green Line.

One Friday afternoon in July 2004, on the first anniversary of the signing of the Destination Map, Nusseibeh headed up a national-scale Palestinian peace demonstration, the first of its kind, in the city of Qalqilya. In the style of the Israeli pressure group Peace Now, many of whose rallies Nusseibeh has attended as a speaker, activists were bused in from various West Bank cities. Not all made it through the checkpoints; six coaches, from Ramallah, Salfit and Jerusalem, were turned back. Nevertheless, people had arrived in the hundreds and Nusseibeh, out of the ivory tower and connecting with the grassroots, was buoyant. "It's a good beginning," he said, beaming from underneath a white baseball cap and surrounded by knots of supporters who all wanted to be introduced, "the Israelis do it all the time."

Organized by Nusseibeh's People's Campaign for Peace and Democracy, known by its Arabic acronym HASHD, the event was supposed to revolve around the slogan of "Smarter without Violence" which Nusseibeh wore on his T-shirt. The location of the demonstration, though, on the roof of the Al-Shariqa Girls School overlooking the mammoth concrete wall and foreboding watchtowers that separate Qalqilya from the Trans-Israel Highway and the Israeli middle class suburbs beyond it, gave it more the flavor of a rally against the wall. Indeed, many of the activists who showed up came from nearby villages like Jayyus and Zawiya, where the bulldozers were working to construct the fence and separate them from their lands. Across the wall, on top of a converted garbage dump, Ayalon and a group of Israeli supporters from his People's Voice Campaign, HASHD's Israeli counterpart, came to show their solidarity.

At this particular part, the wall sits on the Green Line, making it less controversial even to HASHD. Nusseibeh agreed that in this regard, the wall here "is OK. We just chose this bit because it offers high points on both sides." Still, he stressed, such a barrier is "not a solution, and is not a substitute for a negotiated border that would guarantee both sides what they seek: for Israel, security, and for us freedom and dignity."

After half an hour of standing around as demonstrators flew kites and raised a few chants, Nusseibeh, in his usual self-deprecating way, said he wasn't quite sure what was supposed to happen next. A couple of rough-looking activists from the villages barked spontaneous speeches through megaphones, and Nusseibeh tried to hold a public dialogue with Ayalon on the other side. The two connected by cell phone but the plan didn't quite work out. "It's a bit disorganized," Nusseibeh remarked. "I spoke to the other side but there are no facilities here for them to speak to us." However, he had made his point: There are partners for peace on both sides.

Nusseibeh and Heller are an eminently reasonable pair. Yet in their book, they too were unable to agree on a precise demarcation line between the future Israeli and Palestinian states, confining themselves instead to "overall guidelines" for negotiators. They agreed that in the absence of a river or a clear demographic divide, the 1949 armistice line provided the most salient political and historical marker. But the realities on the ground, in part the result of Sharon's strategic settlement-building policies of the past 30 years, have seriously complicated the possibility of implementing any such solution even if the political leaders were ever to agree on one.

Meanwhile, as prime minister, Sharon had undergone a kind of epiphany of his own. In May 2003, he stunned his party and the whole nation when he announced at a Likud faction meeting in the Knesset that "It is not possible to continue holding 3.5 million people under occupation" and suggested that the Palestinians should have a state of their own. "You may not like the word," he went on, underlining the political taboo he had just broken, "but what's happening is occupation. This is a terrible thing for Israel, for the Palestinians and for the Israeli economy."

Sharon was again sailing with the wind, this time blowing from the United States. For just one day earlier, Sharon, under international pressure, had persuaded his government to endorse the Road Map, a U.S.-backed peace plan calling for, among other things, an end to Palestinian terror and an Israeli settlement freeze to be followed by the establishment of a temporary Palestinian state in provisional borders and swift negotiations for a permanent settlement by 2005.

More drama was to come. In late 2003, Israeli and Palestinian unofficial negotiators unveiled a draft permanent status agreement for a Palestinian state based on the 1949 lines to international applause. The heads of the freelance process, known as the Geneva Initiative, were former Israeli justice minister and leftist politician Yossi Beilin and on the Palestinian side, Yasser Abed Rabbo, a former PA minister and close confidant of Arafat. Apparently in response, and to head off pressure to enter into formal negotiations, Sharon came out with an initiative of his own calling for unilateral disengagement from the Gaza Strip and the removal of all 21 Jewish settlements there by the summer of 2005, as well as the evacuation of four isolated Jewish settlements in the northern West Bank. Despite strong internal opposition, also from within his own party, Sharon resolutely carried out the withdrawal in the second half of August that year, bulldozing the former settler homes in his wake—this time, with the agreement of the Palestinians.

The reasons for Sharon's change of mind and his true intentions regarding the West Bank could only be guessed at since he stuck to his pragmatic Zionist habit of keeping mum. Some aides hinted that further withdrawals from the West Bank might be in the offing. At the same time Sharon's senior adviser Dov Weisglass told the *Ha'aretz* daily that the disengagement from Gaza and the northern West Bank was the political equivalent of "formaldehyde" designed to take off the international heat and put any Road Map-style peace process into deep freeze.

In some ways, Sharon has been nothing if not consistent. From the beginning of his term as prime minister, he had made it clear that he did not aspire to reach a permanent peace agreement with the Palestinians, but only what he called long-term interim solutions. Moreover, it seems he has long considered the Gaza Strip dispensable. Bassam Abu Sharif, a one-time close Arafat aide and senior PLO official, asserts that Sharon suggested as much back in 1989, when the two men engaged in secret contacts. Sharon was industry and trade minister in Yitzhak Shamir's government at the time. According to Abu Sharif, he and Sharon sat in separate rooms in Paris's Hotel Plaza Athenee— Israeli law barred officials and citizens from meeting directly with the PLO— while an Israeli businessman and a French Jewish lawyer relayed messages between them. At first, according to Abu Sharif, the discussion focused on Sharon's request for help in locating missing air force navigator Ron Arad, shot down over Lebanon in 1986. But after several hours, he claims, they turned to political issues and Sharon proposed that the Palestinians establish an independent state in Gaza. "My response was what about the West Bank?" Abu Sharif recounted. Sharon, he went on, "kept the door open on that."

Even now, Sharon's intentions vis-à-vis the future of the West Bank remain ambiguous. On the one hand, his vision of an east-west axis of settlement seems finally to be coming to fruition. North of Ariel, a string of unauthorized new outposts founded with Sharon's encouragement in the late 1990s are taking root, forming a contiguous chain of Jewish settlement almost to the Jordan Valley. Despite repeated American demands, little has been done to take them down. On the other hand, the future of the isolated settlements of the West Bank is no longer guaranteed. For Sharon himself has endorsed the idea of a Palestinian state there, even if he personally will not sign on to anything more than a minimalist one in provisional borders.

Having been forced into building the barrier by public pressure, Sharon later attempted to make it fit his map, insisting on overseeing every detail of its route. That meant at the very least ensuring that the large settlement blocs of Ariel, Gush Etzion south of Jerusalem, Ma'aleh Adumim to the capital's east, and Givat Ze'ev to its north, containing a majority of the settler population, would remain on the Israeli side of the fence. There were plans to build an eastern fence as well, on the far side of the West Bank, to protect the settlements of the Jordan Valley, and to ensure future Israeli control over the strip of land along the Jordanian border. But that, together with the western barrier, would have placed about half the territory of the West Bank out of bounds for the Palestinians. In the face of an American veto, the idea was quietly dropped, as were plans for a complicated system of "secondary barriers" delving deep into the West Bank.

Originally, the barrier route approved by the government in 2003 left some 20 percent of the West Bank land on the Israeli side of the fence, according to Shaul Arieli, a colonel in the reserves and mapping expert who headed Ehud Barak's "peace administration," the team of advisers and technocrats who handled the implementation of the Oslo accords and prepared the Israeli proposals for Camp David. Ironically, Arieli had worked in the peace administration with another colonel, Dany Tirza. While Tirza became the army's main point-man on the security barrier, Arieli, a consultant and leading participant on the Israeli side in the Geneva Initiative, went on to become the planner of an alternative, more Palestinian-friendly fence route.

I meet Arieli, a nondescript looking man with sandy cropped hair, in an office in Tel Aviv. He is poring over topographical maps, aerial photography, and data of the West Bank all available at the press of a button on his laptop. With the original barrier route, he explains, "The thinking was that the Palestinian residents would leave those areas of the West Bank that landed on the Israeli side, and the West Bank would go 80:20 between Israel and the Palestinians. Sharon offered Gaza to the Americans in return for a fifth of the West Bank."

The combination of international pressure and rulings from The Hague and the Supreme Court in Jerusalem shuffled the deck. Sharon remained obliged to carry out the Gaza disengagement, but could no longer deliver 20 percent of the West Bank. According to the army's own calculations, the revised route for the remainder of the barrier approved in early 2005 leaves only 7 percent of West Bank land on the Israeli side—roughly the amount of territory Barak had reportedly hoped to annex by the end of Camp David. And given that at certain points on the map, like the Ariel settlement bloc, the conflicting demands of the settlers and the international community cannot be reconciled, it is entirely possible the fence will never get finished at all.

Accordingly, the barrier project has become subject to the ambiguity of Sharon's policies and intentions, the imperfect product of no clear strategy. Israeli officials and military personnel have altogether stopped referring to it as a "separation" fence, downplaying the political implications, calling it a security or anti-terror fence instead. The officials also stress its "temporary" nature, pointing to the Baqa al-Gharbiya / Baqa al-Sharqiya episode as proof that sections can easily, if expensively, be taken down and changed.

Sharon, for his part, stalled bringing the revised fence route to the cabinet for approval for months on end, despite the best efforts of Uzi Dayan and his lobbyists. He was in no hurry to press ahead. After all, having invested decades in blurring the 1949 borders fixed by Dayan's uncle Moshe, Sharon was now charged with physically dividing the land and coming to terms with placing some 93 percent of the West Bank on the other side of a barrier, with all the future military, social, and political implications that could entail. The barrier had ended up more Shaul Arieli than Ariel Sharon. No wonder that this time, the Bulldozer was idling.

4

Arafat's Intifada

It has taken a while to find the house deep in the warren-like heart of the Tulkarm refugee camp, but a small blue metal sign hanging above the alleyway, now named "Sirhan Sirhan Street," has an arrow pointing to the local landmark.

The intifada posters and leaflets produced here call this the "Martyrs' Camp," offering a kind of twisted consolation to the families of the hundred or so Palestinians who have met a violent end over the past four years in this miserable, decrepit slum. Compared to the bare concrete and cinderblock dwellings typical of the camp, a militant hotbed of 17,000 inhabitants abutting Tulkarm town, the Sirhan house stands out as a new and relatively luxurious abode. The outer walls are painted light terracotta pink and there is an intercom by the wrought-iron gate leading in from the street.

Once inside, sitting in the lounge, Su'ad passes around a soft-covered pocket-sized Quran. It belonged to her son, Sirhan Sirhan, the perpetrator of the killings at Kibbutz Metzer in late 2002. Scrawled in Arabic on the inside cover, in faint blue ballpoint pen, is his will and testament, written during his year as a fugitive after the Metzer attack: "Oh brothers in arms, I ask you to pray, to read the Quran, and to love the people. Make every effort to die as martyrs. Love each other. Take care of my family. I call on you to continue the jihad."

Hearing the words read out loud Burhan, Sirhan's father, can't contain his tears. More than a year has passed since Israeli elite forces lured Sirhan out of hiding with a phone call and gunned him down in a street not far from here, outside a mosque on the edge of the camp, also killing a 10-year-old boy standing by. Burhan gets up to leave the room. By the time he reaches the door he is audibly sobbing.

◈

The family only recently moved back here, having built on the ruins of their old home that the army demolished on December 18, 2002, a typical response to an attack meant to deter other terrorists from carrying out similar deeds. The new house was built "with my own money," Burhan stresses, distancing himself from others who had received cash for their martyred children whether from the PA, Saddam Hussein, or some Islamic charitable organization or other in the Gulf.

The reception room has glistening floor tiles that are shell-pink and white, thick carpets, pearl-colored drapes, new sofas, occasional tables, and a pine dining suite. Burhan and Su'ad are articulate, dignified, and smartly dressed, she in a traditional long black robe with understated decorative stitching, he in a pressed shirt and pants. The Sirhans are disarmingly polite and gracious hosts, even though I have turned up unexpectedly with a small entourage of men from Tulkarm who have helped me locate the house. Hot, milky coffee is served in tall, decorative glasses, followed by sweet tea. On the walls there is a portrait of Yasser Arafat, the recently departed leader of the Palestinians, and a studio photo of Sirhan standing with his father against a backdrop of Jerusalem's Dome of the Rock. Over the dining table hangs a framed poster, a photo-montage of Sirhan in multiple poses with a gun.

"When we heard, we couldn't believe it. I still can't. There wasn't even a hint," says Burhan of the night in November 2002 when their 19-year-old first born, Sirhan, infiltrated Kibbutz Metzer and gunned down five people, including Revital Ohion and her two small boys. Sirhan Sirhan had left the house at four that afternoon and came back at nine the next morning. "He seemed completely normal," says Su'ad, a pleasant-faced woman with smooth skin. "He went to play on the computer in his room."

The first the family heard of the attack was that morning on Al-Jazeera, the popular Arabic satellite TV channel, when it was announced that the Fatah-affiliated Al-Aqsa Martyrs Brigades in Tulkarm had claimed responsibility for the Metzer killings in the name of the "martyr" Sirhan Sirhan. They were surprised to hear this, especially since Sirhan was here, in the flesh, sitting with them in their Tulkarm refugee camp home when the news came in. Obviously Sirhan's handler, Muhammad Naifeh, known also as Abu Rabi'a, a key member of the local Al-Aqsa Brigades militia, had never imagined that the amateur terrorist would return from his mission alive. The gunman he had sent to the settlement of Hermesh just days earlier had not come back. In April 2003, Naifeh was convicted in an Israeli military court and sentenced to 13 life sentences plus 50 years for dispatching the terrorists to Metzer and Hermesh.

The following day Sirhan Sirhan fled into hiding. It is not clear where he spent all the eleven months it took for Israel to hunt him down, but Burhan says his son spent three months in the Jenin refugee camp, another militant stronghold in the northern West Bank, and returned to Tulkarm two months before he died.

Burhan also reveals that Sirhan had had three brushes with the army before the Metzer attack, and a particularly close one after, from which he had escaped. During routine army raids on the camp beforehand, he had been taken from school once and detained for three days at an army base, like thousands of other Palestinian youths, and twice the army came to search the house. On one occasion after the attack, soldiers caught him wandering near a Jewish settlement and he was routinely detained. Sirhan was not carrying any ID at the time, and the soldiers failed to recognize him. He supplied them with a false identity, giving details of an acquaintance in Jenin that checked out, and two hours later they let him go.

When he had set out for Metzer, Sirhan was in his first year at the Open University of Tulkarm, studying economics. Having scored a high 92 in his school matriculation exams, he was considered to have a promising future. Burhan insists that Sirhan didn't belong to any militia and had never trained with a gun. The parents can only guess, with hindsight, at what led him to kill. Su'ad starts with the fact that Sirhan kept a picture on his bedroom door of Iman Hijjo, a four-month-old baby killed in a Gaza refugee camp by shrapnel from IDF shells in May 2001. The army was retaliating for Palestinian mortar fire that landed on a nearby Jewish settlement earlier in the day. Hijjo became the youngest victim of the intifada and Prime Minister Ariel Sharon issued a rare apology for what he called her "tragic" death. Gruesome pictures of Hijjo's tiny, shattered corpse had flooded the Palestinian Authority's media, a new emblem of Palestinian suffering at Israel's hands. To the Israelis, this was a campaign of incitement designed to provoke more violence. In Sirhan's case, it obviously worked. "He wouldn't allow anyone to remove her picture. He swore he'd avenge her death," Su'ad recalls.

Burhan adds that two of Sirhan's friends had been killed in the camp. "Together with the Iman Hijjo story it all affected him," he says. "He was a very emotional boy, very sensitive and easily moved. One guy from the Al-Aqsa Brigades, Jarrad, was killed right outside our house. It all built up."

While it's not unusual for the parents of Palestinian terrorists to protest the innocence of their sons who "couldn't harm a fly," Su'ad and Burhan do not for one second deny Sirhan's murderous act. Su'ad, ever the protective mother, exudes understanding and even a flash of defiant pride.

"He didn't act out of a void," she continues. "It was a reaction. The Jews kill our children, and force our young men to go out and respond. I sat with him afterwards and asked him if he regretted what he'd done. He said 'No.' After the baby in Gaza, how can they blame us for killing theirs? He was happy with what he'd done."

Burhan, a distinguished-looking man with gray-speckled hair, is clearly less at ease with the glib justifications and the image of his son as such a callous killing machine. "He wasn't trained. I don't think it was his intention. He probably just opened fire," he surmises. Asked about his feelings when he heard that the victims included young children at Kibbutz Metzer, a reputed bastion of the Israeli peace camp, Burhan responds after a pause. "In my personal opinion, this war has to end," he says softly. "There might have been a mistake. But how many children have they killed in Nablus and Jenin?"

It turns out that in the intense, crowded world of the Tulkarm refugee camp, Sirhan Sirhan was something of an outsider, not one of the regular *shebab*, or youth, who had grown up in the camp, having only come to live here in 1996. Burhan's parents had fled from their native Haifa in 1948 and made a home here, where Burhan was born. In 1974, however, Burhan left for Beirut, joined Fatah—Arafat's faction and the central component of the Palestinian Liberation Organization—and became an officer in the PLO army. He met Su'ad, the daughter of a Palestinian refugee family living in Beirut. Following the Israeli invasion of Lebanon in 1982 and the PLO's expulsion from the country, the couple moved to Aden, in South Yemen, where Sirhan was born. The Sirhans then moved around the Arab capitals, living in Jordan, Libya, and Algeria. Sirhan Sirhan's younger brother Abed, now 16, and his four younger sisters were born along the way.

Burhan brought his family home—that is, to the Tulkarm refugee camp—in the heady days of the Oslo peace process, as Israel withdrew from the Palestinian cities of the West Bank. He joined Fatah's Force 17, the PA's elite presidential guard. After being watched and hounded by secret police all over the Arab world, he says, "I thought here we'd find stability and peace."

The Al-Aqsa intifada came instead. Burhan is not opposed to the armed struggle, having built a career on the ethos of fighting for the Palestinian cause. But he has his criticism about this latest war, and by implication, about his own son's part in it. This intifada would have been better, Burhan says, had it been restricted to the occupied territories, the 1967 lands the Palestinians claim for their state, and had there been more control over the violence and use of weapons. By bringing the intifada across the Green Line into Israel proper, he acknowledges, the Palestinians have blurred their own goals. He nods in agreement when I suggest they have also brought upon themselves the wall.

As for Sirhan, his parents say, he wouldn't even have realized that he had crossed the Green Line. "He didn't even know where it was," says Burhan. "He didn't grow up here and didn't know the area. He had never been inside Israel before."

For now, the Sirhans have only one request. They want their son's body back. It lies in an anonymous, numbered grave in a secure cemetery reserved for Palestinian terrorists' remains, somewhere in southern Israel.

I visit the Sirhans in the last days of December 2004, only six weeks after the sudden and somewhat mysterious death of Yasser Arafat. The death of the Palestinian leader, the symbol of the national struggle for the past 40 years, marks the end of an era, laying to rest an intifada that had long since lost its way. By the time Arafat, the heart and soul of the armed resistance, passed away, the intifada was in the throes of death itself, only waiting, like the Sirhans, for a decent funeral.

The last few militants in the Tulkarm camp are hard pressed to explain what it was all about in the first place, let alone what, if anything, has been achieved. Outside in the alleyways, practically the only vestiges of the rebellion are the dozens of martyrs' posters staring down from every wall. The intifada has already all but fizzled out here, as in the rest of the West Bank, the

ranks of the militias decimated over the past two years by the doggedly thor-
ough intelligence work of the Israeli Shin Bet internal security service and
the army's operational brawn. By late 2004, according to the Shin Bet statistics, 959 terrorists had been killed and over 6,000 arrested.

Major attacks inside the Green Line, and even against the West Bank
settlements, have become rare. The separation barrier, although only a third
constructed, has proved extremely effective in sealing the militant hotbeds of
the northern West Bank from Israel. Meanwhile the majority of ordinary
Palestinians, worn down by years of security closures and financial stress, are
suffering from intifada fatigue, translated into a waning of support for continuing the violence.

Practically the only "action" in Tulkarm occurs when Israeli army units
raid the town or the camps in pursuit of the last remnants of the armed
gangs. For these next martyrs in line, dying has become a habit, devoid of any
discernible sense or point. In a way, the same spontaneity, randomness, lack
of discipline or clarity of purpose that led Sirhan to Metzer has marked the
intifada from its very outset to its inevitable, ignoble end.

The intifada broke out in the first place not as the result of a singular strategy
on the Palestinians' part, but more from the lack of one. While it revolved
around Arafat, it was imbued with the classic ambiguity of his intentions. It
could have broken out at any time. Then again, it need not necessarily have
broken out at all.

In the summer of 2000, Israeli Prime Minister Ehud Barak had embarked on an ambitious mission to reach a final status agreement with the
Palestinians, persuading U.S. President Clinton to convene a summit at
Camp David for that purpose. It took place from July 11 to July 25. The
Palestinians had been reluctant to come, arguing that the gaps between the
two sides on all the fundamental issues were still too wide. Barak, for his part,
refused to consider a partial agreement. Though there were no prior understandings on cardinal issues such as Jerusalem and the Palestinian refugee
question, a closely involved American official told me in the days before the
summit that Barak was convinced it could be done.

Abandoning the previous step-by-step strategy of the peace process,
Barak laid down a principle that nothing was agreed until everything was

agreed, and that the agreement would constitute the end of conflict and the end of all claims. It was a high-risk gambit, and it failed. Arafat turned Barak's "generous offer" down. The reasons were myriad. At the core of the disagreement at Camp David, though, stood the future of the Temple Mount / Haram al-Sharif. Although the Temple Mount lies beyond the old Green Line in Jerusalem's Old City, Barak insisted on Israeli sovereignty there and offered the Palestinians custodianship. The Palestinians, who refused to recognize the legitimacy and symbolism of the Jewish attachment to the Mount, replied that they did not know what custodianship was. Nor did they dare speak on behalf of all Muslims. According to several of the key participants at the Camp David summit, this emerged as the most sensitive and intractable issue of all.

It was against this background that Ariel Sharon, then the head of the right-wing Likud opposition, decided to visit the Temple Mount a few weeks later, on September 28, 2000, accompanied by scores of security men and police. The clearly provocative maneuver, mostly likely planned for internal political reasons, did not elicit a murmur of public condemnation from Labor leader Barak. He was wary of taking on an opponent who, though secular, was bent on asserting his right as a Jew to visit the holy site. Barak's silence, meant to mollify his domestic audience, further undermined his credibility with many Palestinians who saw it as proof that the visit was an Israeli plot designed to show who is really sovereign on the Mount.

The next day, predictably, as Muslims filed out of the main Friday noon prayers at the Al-Aqsa Mosque, stones were thrown onto Jewish worshippers at the Western Wall below and rioting broke out. By the end of the afternoon, five Palestinians had been killed in Jerusalem by Israeli security forces, four of them in the mosque compound itself. The Al-Aqsa intifada was born.

Every day after that for several months, Palestinians went to the barricades, marching on Israeli army checkpoints on the outskirts of the Palestinian towns, hailing them with stones and Molotov cocktails, and soon with bullets as well. While the Israeli establishment blamed Arafat for orchestrating the violence and said they had intelligence that he had handed down specific orders for the intifada to begin, most Palestinians insisted it was not planned, but came as an almost spontaneous reaction to Israeli actions on the ground. In the first six days of confrontations, some 60 Palestinians were killed and more than 2,600 were injured by Israeli fire; during the same period, four Israelis died, three of whom were members of the security forces.

The Palestinians maintain that their militants' weapons came out only as a result of the dramatically lopsided loss of life. By the end of December 2000, over 270 Palestinians were dead compared with 37 Israelis. Then the suicide bombers of the fundamentalist Islamic Resistance Movement, Hamas, began hitting Israeli cities, later followed by exploding "martyrs" sent by the secular Fatah faction, for fear of being outdone.

Despite the apparent spontaneity, however, the intifada hardly came out of the blue. There had been many predictions of a violent confrontation, and some precursors too. As early as 1995, Arafat had sanctioned the formation of an armed Fatah militia, called the Tanzim (the Organization) and led by West Bank grassroots Fatah leader Marwan Barghouti, to operate parallel to the official PA security apparatuses and to check and balance the growing armed opposition group, Hamas.

Then in 1996, when the peace process was faltering under Likud Prime Minister Benjamin Netanyahu's premiership, a spate of rioting broke out in the territories sparked by Israel's opening of a new exit to an archeological tunnel running along Temple Mount. For the first time, Palestinian police and Fatah gunmen opened fire on Israeli positions. Fifteen soldiers and over 60 Palestinians were killed. It was after that, Israeli officials believe, that the Palestinians started "institutionalizing" preparations for an armed confrontation.

The IDF learned lessons from the 1996 riots and subsequent "Days of Rage" organized annually by the Tanzim. For months in the run-up to the Al-Aqsa intifada, the army had been training snipers to station at the checkpoints and had fortified its positions, perhaps explaining the high Palestinian death toll in the first days of the uprising. Instead of quelling the violence, the army's harsh reaction merely fanned the flames. Speaking years later at a private salon gathering in Ramallah, a top PA security chief recalled the army's preparations and described the intifada as an Israeli self-fulfilling prophecy.

For months before the Camp David summit, the Israeli security establishment had been warning of the possibility of violence should the peace process end on bad terms. Even though Arafat returned to the territories not as the "failed leader" the Israeli and American leaderships saw, but as a popular hero who had not capitulated to the superpowers, the Palestinian leadership was riddled with bitterness, resentment, and internal rivalry. Ariel Sharon may have provided the spark that ignited the intifada, but in reality, the conditions for it had been brewing for years.

At first the Oslo process had been greeted with the same euphoria on the Palestinian side as the Israeli. The stone-throwers of the first, mostly un-armed, uprising of the late 1980s and early 1990s came out onto the streets of the West Bank and Gaza with olive branches, to bid farewell to the departing Israeli soldiers and to welcome the PLO returnees from exile. From the out-set, however, some were skeptical of Israeli motives and intentions. Dr. Haidar Abd al-Shafi, the elder statesman of Gaza who had headed the Pales-tinian delegation to the Madrid Peace Conference and the Washington talks that preceded Oslo, maintained soon after the agreement was signed that the lack of a clear Israeli commitment to stop settlement-building in the 1967 territories was a recipe for disaster. He sounded like a malcontent and quib-bler at the time, but the Palestinians were impatient for the Israeli occupa-tion to end.

As the Oslo process progressed, some of the worst premonitions came true on both sides. The Palestinians watched helplessly as Israeli settlement-building continued apace. The scheduled Israeli withdrawals from West Bank territory were constantly delayed. Yitzhak Rabin, Arafat's trusted part-ner in what he called "the peace of the brave," was assassinated by a right-wing Israeli fanatic and was followed in quick succession by prime ministers Shimon Peres of Labor, the Likud's Benjamin Netanyahu, and Labor's Barak. Israel had no shortage of grievances too. In the Palestinian Authority, illegal weapons were multiplying and media incitement against Israel never ceased. In many Israelis' minds, the basic premise of Oslo, land in return for security and peace, had already collapsed with a horrific Hamas bombing campaign in 1996 that killed over 60 Israelis within two weeks.

Once rightist Netanyahu was in power and started putting the brakes on the Oslo process, there were growing signs that Arafat's Fatah organization was radicalizing again. Masked and armed demonstrators started protesting against the stalemate in the Palestinian cities. Tulkarm Fatah secretary gen-eral Thabet Thabet, a large man who resembled French actor Gerard Depar-dieu and was the erstwhile dialogue-partner of Metzer's Yoav Ben Naftali and others in the Israeli peace camp, said in a January 1998 interview that he and many Fatah loyalists had come to realize that the Oslo agreements were a "mistake. Anyone who thinks Fatah has abandoned the intifada and the rifle is mistaken," he told Khaled Abu Toameh in an interview for the *Jerusalem Report*. "The intifada will return, and the guns will start shooting again, if Netanyahu continues with his extremist, uncompromising line."

By the summer of 1998, scores of young males in Gaza were attending military camps organized by the Shabiba, or Fatah youth wing, where they would spend up to 14 hours a day training and learning to fire light weapons at a base of one of the PA security branches outside Gaza City, in coordination with the PA's Military Intelligence apparatus. The PA's minister of supplies, Abu Ali Shaheen, a Fatah veteran who restructured the Shabiba in the early 1980s, told me at the time that "anything we are preparing against this Netanyahu is good." Sitting in his private office in Gaza sporting a white shirt, khaki pants and jacket, the minister, a jovial, trim man in his early 60s, epitomized the still-ambivalent political-military nature of Arafat's Fatah movement. In a prominent place above his desk hung the banner of Al-Asifa (the Storm), the military wing of Fatah established in the 1960s to undertake cross-border *fedayeen* raids against Israel. The insignia, a rifle and bayonet crossed over a grenade inscribed with the slogan "Revolution until Victory" seemed to leave little room for dialogue. When I asked Minister Shaheen whether the banner meant he was keeping all his options open, including that of a resumption of the armed struggle, he chuckled and replied, "Yes! All the options. Did Netanyahu close any of his? We don't have atom bombs. He does."

Even once Ehud Barak became prime minister and intensively re-engaged in the peace process, the militant stream within Fatah continued to gain ground. It got a particular boost in May 2000, when Barak pulled Israel's troops out of Lebanon and withdrew to the internationally recognized border practically overnight. For nearly 20 years Israel had been occupying a "security zone" in South Lebanon in order to defend its northern border, first against the PLO, and then the "Islamic resistance" of the Iranian-backed Hizballah who mounted a guerrilla campaign against the Israeli forces and their proxies on Lebanese soil. Perceived as having chased the great Israeli army out with its tail between its legs, the Shi'ite fundamentalists were hailed as heroes all over the Arab world. The Palestinian grassroots in the Fatah Tanzim started agitating in favor of getting rid of their own Israeli occupiers the "Hizballah way."

Israeli intransigence aside, the Al-Aqsa intifada was also fuelled at least as much by internal disaffection with the Arafat regime, specifically with the cronies who had returned with the leader from exile in Tunis. A young, resentful generation of "insider" Palestinians had graduated from the first intifada and served long terms in Israeli prisons, only to find themselves largely cut out of the PA decision-making apparatus and the halls of power. They were still known as the *shebab* (youth), in lasting recognition of the role they played as teens during the first intifada, though they were by now well into their 30s. Some were on the pay rolls of the various PA security agencies, but had little prospect of rising up the ranks. And though some of them weren't above crime themselves and had made lucrative careers out of weapon smuggling and car thievery, their rallying call became the corruption of the PA officials around Arafat, many of whom had come from "outside" and amassed vast wealth as a result of Oslo-generated business deals.

"Fighters trigger the revolution, brave men lead it, and the cowards reap its fruits," Jamal Tirawi, a member of one such armed Fatah gang in the Balata refugee camp near Nablus told me in late 1999. "We are now in that third stage." The words were spoken without irony despite the fact that Tirawi and his friends had reaped at least some benefits from Oslo. Tirawi had worked in the PA General Intelligence security apparatus headed by a cousin, Tawfiq Tirawi, until a recent showdown between the PA police and the armed men in the camp, a militant stronghold, had led to a termination of his employment. Fellow gang-member Mahmud Jabara still claimed to be on the General Intelligence payroll, and was driving around the muddy camp in his "company car," a flashy new gold Peugeot.

Since arriving back from Tunis, Arafat had surrounded himself with a circle of VIPs who were well rewarded for their loyalty and led an opulent life. Arafat's confidantes and moneymen managed a complex network of investments and shady deals and set themselves up with lucrative monopolies and concessions. While most Palestinians were still scratching a living, the PA was raking in a rumored million dollars a day from a casino in Jericho set up in partnership with an Austrian gambling giant who had ties to a string of Israeli prime ministers on both the left and right.

Running the PA as a one-man show, Arafat was careful to ensure himself a steady cash flow for "extras" including an extensive patronage system, assistance to ordinary Palestinians who turned to him for help, and later, funding for the militias. The population at large did not feel the benefits of peace, however, which created a ripe environment for a young-guard rebellion.

The target would not be the PA itself, however. Referring to the PA elite as "corrupt capitalists," but carefully avoiding any disrespect to Arafat himself, Balata militant Tirawi stressed that the "nationalist" weapons in his gang's possession would in "no way" be turned against the Authority. Rather, he suggested, the preferred target of the young-guard's anger would always be Israel. As the Ramallah-based Palestinian political analyst Khalil Shikaki put it, the new intifada was 50 percent directed against Israel, and 50 percent against the Palestinian Authority itself.

Once the violence had gained momentum, there was nobody to stop it. The only man who could have was Yasser Arafat, the unchallenged leader of the Palestinian cause for the past 40 years. He chose not to.

Arafat had built a political career based on a confounding combination of divide and rule, and cooptation and consensus, emerging from among his rivals as the sole figure that represented everybody. Seen as the "father" of all Palestinians and affectionately nicknamed the "old man" by many, even when he was middle-aged, he was considered the glue that united the old guard and the young, the "insider" graduates of the first intifada and the Israeli prisons and the "outsiders" who had come from Tunis, the West Bank and the Gaza Strip, the refugees in camps, the village and city dwellers, as well as the millions of Palestinians still living in the diaspora from Saudi Arabia to Santiago de Chile.

The Palestinian leader was also notorious for his autocratic style and jealous obsession with every detail of the Authority, which reportedly extended down to signing vacation forms for junior policemen. Shortly before he triumphantly arrived back in Gaza from exile in the summer of 1994, local Fatah activists, leaders of the first intifada, were warning that here, Arafat's solo, omnipotent style would not wash. "Even God had angels to help him," one commented wryly. There was already grumbling in Gaza that officials who had arrived from PLO headquarters in Tunis ahead of Arafat could not get a building painted without a decision from the boss.

Yet when it came to the Al-Aqsa intifada, Arafat essentially abdicated responsibility, abandoning his people to their fate while at the same time forbidding anybody else from acting in his place. As a matter of pride the Palestinians continued to support and defend their leader against Israeli threats to remove him. Internally, though, they became increasingly frustrated with his ways.

For six months from the fall of 2001, Arafat remained under army siege in his Ramallah compound, the Muqata'a, an old British police fort set in a large courtyard, where he gave refuge to six men wanted by Israel for the murder of a minister. When a solution for the wanted men was found (they were sent to jail in Jericho under British supervision) and Arafat finally came out in May 2002, he embarked on a "victory" tour of several West Bank cities. His appearance in Jenin had to be aborted, though, after his staff sensed the anger of the crowd there and feared a scene. Arafat beat a hasty retreat, returning to the Muqata'a by helicopter, and would not leave the compound again until, rapidly ailing, he was evacuated to his deathbed in Paris in late 2004.

With the Israeli leadership openly debating sending him back into exile and some politicians calling for his assassination, Arafat had refused to leave the compound in the absence of guarantees for his safe return. His aides vigorously protested his effective "house arrest" and humiliation. At least in the early stages of the siege, though, Arafat, who had never taken off his fatigues, seemed positively to revel in the chance to return to his revolutionary roots, holing up inside even as the army blew up and demolished the buildings around him.

The security heads and pundits in Israel continued to squabble over whether Arafat was personally spearheading the violence or was merely riding the tiger. Either way, it was clear that he was certainly enabling its continuation, oiling it with funds and infusing it with his spirit. After any particularly deadly suicide bombing, under international pressure and scared for his skin, he would come out onto the steps of the Muqata'a, ashen faced, and condemn terror in the presence of TV crews. The next day he would delightedly chant along with the "popular masses" bused in to visit him, raising his fingers in the famous V sign and calling for millions of martyrs to march on Jerusalem.

Arafat was not about to leave the pitch open to his internal enemies, the suicide bombers of Hamas. Instead, his own loyalists from the more secular-minded, Fatah-affiliated Tanzim, which morphed into smaller cells of the Al-Aqsa Brigades, entered into a deadly competition of who could kill the most Israelis. And soon, bound by the common cause of inflicting as much pain as possible on the other side, these former rivals forged an ad hoc alliance and turned terror into a joint project.

When chaos started to prevail, European diplomats who were still visiting Arafat pleaded with him to do something—anything—in order to rein it in. That way, they suggested, he would regain some of the respect he so coveted, and perhaps eventually, his freedom. But cramped inside the Muqata'a, constantly surrounded by a coterie of thirty loyal cronies described by one diplomat as "dinosaurs" and increasingly isolated from the real world, he failed to respond. He presumably knew that he was already dead in Israeli eyes as far as ever being a partner in peace again was concerned, and that nothing he could do would resurrect his credibility. The almost super-human symbol, who even managed to survive a plane crash in the Libyan desert, had met his match in Sharon.

"Sirhan who?" exclaims the PA governor of Tulkarm, Izz al-Din Sharif, his pencil-thin eyebrows dancing around on his forehead. Though Sharif himself, according to media reports, had not long ago eulogized the Metzer murderer at the memorial service held after his death, now, in the spring of 2004, sitting at his desk in a nondescript office downtown, he is feigning ignorance of who Sirhan was. When I ask him again what he thinks about Sirhan's act, Sharif, together with the Tulkarm mayor who has dropped in, parrots the now familiar refrain that it was simply a "reaction," an almost natural response to Israeli "crimes."

"There are 248 martyrs from the Tulkarm area, 25,000 wounded, a third in wheelchairs," Sharif rattles off. "These are the latest figures that have stuck in my mind."

Until the intifada broke out, Tulkarm was a pleasant, traditionally conservative, and reasonably prosperous West Bank market town lying along the Green Line with a population of 90,000, or over 130,000 if the two adjacent refugee camps are included. The district as a whole, with all the surrounding villages, numbers some 245,000 souls. During the "good years" of Oslo, Israelis would come here in droves during the weekends to shop. Now a neglected no-go zone, Tulkarm figures prominently in the annals of the intifada, having produced some of its most famous "martyrs" and most notorious acts of terror.

Thabet Thabet, the general secretary of the local Fatah branch and a dentist, gained the dubious distinction of becoming the first high-profile victim of Israel's "targeted killing" or assassination policy when he was shot by snipers outside his Tulkarm home on December 31, 2000. Thabet's former dialogue-partners in the Israeli peace camp reacted with shock to the killing, insisting that Thabet was a political figure who would never have involved himself in terror. Governor Sharif, for his part, describes Thabet as "a man of peace" who was merely "trying to organize the armed men and the illegal weapons." One member of the Tulkarm Al-Aqsa Brigades told me admiringly that Thabet "was involved in everything," backing up the Israeli security establishment's claims that Thabet had become a lynchpin in the town's terror network.

Revenge came a few days after, in January 2001, when two Tel Aviv sushi bar owners who had ventured into Tulkarm to buy supplies with an Israeli Arab colleague were abducted from a restaurant where they were eating lunch, taken to a deserted field out of town, and summarily shot dead. The executioners were Raed Karmi, the charismatic head of the Tulkarm Al-Aqsa Martyrs Brigades, and two other militiamen. A nephew of the dentist, Masalma Thabet, was one of those arrested by PA security in connection with the murders though, typical for the PA's "revolving door" justice system, he was soon released.

Payback time came in January 2002 when Karmi himself was killed by an Israeli-engineered bomb in a Tulkarm street. He'd narrowly escaped a previous assassination attempt when missiles were fired at his car. Karmi's death ended a three-week hiatus in the violence, the result of a Palestinian attempt to institute a cease-fire that Karmi was reportedly supporting, leading some Israeli officials to question the wisdom and timing of the assassination. Days later, a Palestinian gunman shot dead six Israelis at a bat mitzvah party in a hall called David's Palace in the nearby Israeli city of Hadera. Though the gunman himself was from a village near Nablus, he had been sent by the Tulkarm Al-Aqsa Brigades to avenge Karmi's death. In retaliation, Israel sent F–16s to flatten a wing in Tulkarm's government compound, which had housed Governor Sharif's old offices.

From that point on the intifada continued to escalate, culminating in the Passover-eve bombing of the Park Hotel in Netanya in which 30 Israelis and tourists were killed. Abd al-Bassat Odeh, the 25-year-old Hamas suicide bomber who carried out that attack, also came from Tulkarm. The following November, it was the turn of Sirhan Sirhan.

Blood has been spilt on the streets of this once-charming city as the result of inter-Palestinian violence too. In August 2002, Akhlas Khouli, a mother of seven, was shot dead by local militants along with her niece. They had been accused of collaborating with the Israeli authorities, of planting the bomb that killed Raed Karmi, and of passing on information about the whereabouts of another senior Al-Aqsa Brigades member who was later assassinated. Locals say people here are so poor they will agree to collaborate for little more than a pack of cigarettes. Khouli's niece is said to have helped the Israelis in return for the promise of a cell phone card, which she never actually received. On another occasion, three alleged collaborators from one of the refugee camps were executed outside the city morgue, saving their relatives the trouble of having to transport the bodies.

Like Burhan, Governor Sharif first arrived here as a PLO returnee from exile in 1996. Formerly a military man, he had helped form Fatah's Al-Yarmuk force in Syria in the 1970s and then moved on to PLO headquarters in Tunis. He entered Tulkarm just as the Israelis had withdrawn under the terms of the Oslo Accords and says he found the place a dilapidated mess. "There were no water wells, there were 90 children to a classroom, there was one hospital from Ottoman times and no clinics in the villages, and the market was flooded with rotten canned food past its legal expiry date."

Under his watch, boasts the small, lean governor with a trim moustache, PA police and security forces were trained and deployed on the streets, committees were formed to deal with education, health, and the spoiled food, the Japanese started building a new hospital, and other foreign donors worked on the water system and the roads. "Commerce prospered and the city was flourishing," Sharif enthuses. "And we were also fighting terrorism. We started meeting with the Israeli army and solving all the problems at the table. At the weekends, Tulkarm was full of Israeli families who used to come and shop. Here everything is cheaper and better. The Jews would return with wide smiles on their faces. The years from 1996 to 2000 were a golden era for us."

After years of intifada, though, Tulkarm has become what Sharif calls a "social case." Some eighteen to twenty-two thousand Palestinian laborers from the Tulkarm district used to go and work in Israel every day. Now they are prevented by the security barrier that went up during 2003. Like Qalqilya, the city's boundary with Israel is sealed by an eight-meter-high concrete wall complete with round gray watchtowers, built to prevent Palestinian snipers from shooting at passing cars on the Trans-Israel Highway that skirts Tulkarm to the west. Additional stretches of fence hermetically seal the surrounding villages off from Israel, as well as from some of their agricultural land. Thousands of families, according to Sharif, now live on charity. He himself, like many high-living officials who returned from exile with Arafat, has earned the public's disgust rather than respect. Meanwhile all the city's hard-core militants are either dead or locked up in Israeli jails, and their uninspiring replacements have been finding it increasingly difficult to act.

I met the latest, and probably the last, self-proclaimed "commander" of Tulkarm's Al-Aqsa Brigades, Hani Aweideh, in late May 2004. His predecessor, nicknamed "Jarira," had been captured by Israel four months earlier. Aweideh, 26, a slightly phlegmatic-looking young man who used to work in a picture framing shop, came to an afternoon rendezvous in a grocery store in the center of Tulkarm along with fellow gang member Mahdi Tanbuz, a tall, skinny 21-year-old with huge almond eyes and a shy smile. Aweideh was clean-cut with neatly coiffed hair. He was dressed in pressed beige denims and a matching polo shirt with fancy embroidery around the collar. Tanbuz wore a fashionably tight black T-shirt and a neck chain. Neither looked much like militia leaders. Even the highly polished AK–47 Aweideh brought with him was handled awkwardly, with obvious reverence, more like a prized heirloom than a ready-for-use weapon. Mindful of spies everywhere and Israel's undercover units that kill armed men on sight, Aweideh had requested a plastic bag in which to hide the rifle for the short hop from the car into the store. The days of swaggering with a gun through the streets of Tulkarm were clearly over.

With the store shutters drawn, Aweideh, drumming nervously on the back of his chair and with an eye fixed on the door, acknowledged that for the local Al-Aqsa Brigades, the game was up. "All we want now is to defend ourselves. That's it," he said. "Nobody is giving us any hope or security."

Apparently, residents of Tulkarm were no longer willing to provide refuge for armed men in their houses for fear of ending up on the army's demolition list. Furthermore, Aweideh revealed, the money that used to come in regularly from Arafat had dried up. "The PA used to support us, but we've had no funding from them for the past two months," he grumbled. "They make promises, but nothing ever materializes."

The grocery store owner, Abu K., told me that middlemen had occasionally left cash in envelopes in his store for the militants to pick up. He said they used to get stipends of around $200 to $300 a month, a small fortune in a city where a lawyer's secretary earns $2 a day.

Arafat always denied any direct involvement in funding the intifada, but in June 2002, he was reportedly caught red-handed. The Israeli security services reported to the Americans that they had proof that the PA head had personally handed several thousand dollars to Muhammad Naifeh, the Tanzim leader who succeeded Ra'ed Karmi and went on to become Sirhan Sirhan's handler. These reports got Arafat into even deeper trouble with the Bush administration than he already was following Israel's seizure of the "Karine A" weapon-smuggling ship earlier that year, but for a while nothing changed on the ground. Then sometime early in 2004, Aweideh said, the money had stopped coming. The people he dealt with in Ramallah were "scared for Arafat," following Prime Minister Sharon's veiled threats on the Palestinian leader's life.

In the absence of PA funding, the militants in the refugee camps, who Abu K. described as "thieves," had taken to other means of making a living. An armed gang in the Tulkarm camp had recently abducted one alleged collaborator, taped his confession then let him go in return for a ransom of 80,000 shekels ($18,000).

Elsewhere in the West Bank, particularly in the northern cities of Jenin and Nablus, Al-Aqsa Brigades cells were reportedly replacing the lost PA support with funding from Iran and its Lebanese proxy Hizballah. But Aweideh and his gang, who Abu K. dismissed as inexperienced lightweights, obviously didn't have the connections. Moreover, they were grounded. With the wall and the checkpoints surrounding Tulkarm, Aweideh attested to "100 percent difficulty" in carrying out attacks. Hiding had become their main preoccupation. Nevertheless, they remained marked men.

Eight weeks after our meeting, Aweideh, Tanbuz, and four of their colleagues were dead, shot by an undercover army unit that had entered Tulkarm on a tip-off. The *shebab* had apparently come out to meet an arms dealer and were gunned down outside a restaurant. The IDF announced that all the dead were senior operatives of a terrorist cell. One of them, Sa'id Nasser, was 16 years old. Given Aweideh's wet-behind-the-ears image in Tulkarm, he would probably have been quite pleased with his "obituary" on the army's website. He was counted as one of the masterminds of the bat mitzvah party shooting attack in Hadera in January 2002. The IDF also attributed "dozens" of shooting and explosives attacks to a cell it said Aweideh and Tanbuz had recruited at the beginning of 2003. The truth has gone with them to the grave.

⊷⊸◉⊂⊷

Arafat's physical absence and moral abandonment became the norm to the point that when he died in November 2004, following a rapid deterioration in his health, his people hardly missed him. The Palestinians, sunk in their own deep ennui, treated the historic, potentially ground-shaking event of

Arafat's sudden departure, first from the Muqata'a and then from this world, as one of astonishingly little consequence.

As Arafat lay in a final, deep coma in the Paris hospital to which he had been evacuated, I visited the Jalazoun refugee camp a few minutes away from the Muqata'a on the outskirts of Ramallah, a bleak place where the air was turning putrid from the garbage piling up and rotting in the streets because of a strike. "Everyone dies," shrugged one camp resident after another. "Even the prophet Muhammad died," said an old sheikh, Hassan Yassin, sitting out on the sidewalk, "and he was a much better man than Arafat."

Given the political and literal wasteland that Arafat left behind him, the fatalism and cynicism seemed an almost charitable response. By the time Arafat expired, a thousand Israelis and over three thousand Palestinians had been killed in the intifada and many more thousands had been injured. Whereas there were fewer than 2,000 Palestinians in prison before the intifada, some 8,000 were now crowding the security wings of Israeli jails. Israeli troops were back inside the Palestinian cities, the villages and refugee camps of the West Bank and Gaza Strip, which had been entirely cut off from each other since the outbreak of the violence. Military checkpoints throughout the territories prevented free travel between one Palestinian town and another, stifling the local economy that was already suffering from being closed off from Israel. Unemployment stood at around 30 percent, and according to UN statistics, over 60 percent of the Palestinians of the territories were living below the poverty line set at $2 per day. More than 4,000 homes had been demolished as a punitive measure by the army or as part of "clearing" operations for security purposes, mostly in the Gaza Strip. Large tracts of Gaza's agricultural land and orchards had also been turned to scorched earth, "shaved" by IDF bulldozers as a measure against the snipers, roadside-bomb layers, and mortar-shell and Qassam rocket launchers that plagued Gaza's Jewish settlements and army positions, and also plagued the Israeli kibbutzim and the town of Sderot just across Gaza's border.

Meanwhile, as long as Arafat was alive, the independent Palestinian state that he was supposed to have founded looked as far away as ever. A system of new Israeli bypass roads crisscrossed the West Bank, carving up the territory in order to serve the ever-expanding Jewish settlements and illegal outposts cropping up on the hilltops. More land was being eaten by the separation barrier or stranded on the Israeli side of it. Tens of thousands of Palestinians had reportedly left the country in search of work or a better life elsewhere.

"There's no work, no future here. Ask any ambitious young man in Jala-zoun—his dream is to go abroad," said Samer Ayyub, a 28-year-old in the camp near Ramallah. Ayyub's 31-year-old brother lay at home half paralyzed, having been shot by the army during the rioting in 1996. "Nobody cares about him," Ayyub said. "We have 5,000 martyrs, but who in the world cares? Many in the camp were involved in the resistance, but they're tired. They see it hasn't worked."

Even Arafat's ruling party, Fatah, seemed on the verge of disintegration, the battles between the old guard and the young having degenerated into fratricidal violence at times. The territories were on the brink of anarchy. Some Palestinians were calling it another *nakba*.

As the sun rose on the Muqata'a on Friday November 12, 2004, Israeli radio was playing upbeat songs from the musical "Hair" about the dawning of the age of Aquarius. Arafat was dead in Paris, and would be returning in a coffin. Oddly for the twenty-first century, the doctors at the military hospital in Paris were apparently unable to ascertain the exact cause of death, exacerbating rumors among Palestinians that he had been poisoned.

The streets of Ramallah were deserted, but in the eerie gray first light, in the courtyard of the former British fort that had been half demolished during the intifada, feverish preparations were underway for the funeral that would take place some time in the afternoon. The rubble and wrecked cars that had been demonstratively left littering the compound for the past three years had been urgently swept away. Fire engines sprayed the ground with water, to clear and pack the dust. Half a dozen men worked stolidly laying the marble slabs around the hastily dug grave, which was placed under a few spindly Cyprus trees, the only greenery in the compound. Armed and uniformed PA policemen, who Israel had not allowed on the streets during the intifada, blocked vehicles from entering the side roads leading to the Muqata'a, manning rudimentary barriers made up of an assortment of rocks, barrels, and garbage cans.

As the morning wore on, khaki- and blue-uniformed honor guards and a military band started going through their paces inside the walls of the compound while the streets outside were beginning to fill with people. Some came out of curiosity, others as an expression of Palestinian pride. Most laid aside their disillusionment and came to pay their last respects to a leader who, for good and bad, had devoted a lifetime to the cause. The atmosphere was more carnival than wake. Whole families came out, with matrons in embroidered dresses and little boys in fatigues and bandannas, young men with pistols and M16s, and girls clutching Arafat balloons. Anybody who had a gun seemed to bring it along, confident that the Israelis would not enter the city that day. Gradually, spectators started crowding the rooftops of the surrounding buildings and hanging out of the windows. Young men shimmied up walls, electricity poles, trees, ladders, and anything else that allowed them to peek over the Muqata'a walls. By midday the dam broke: Hordes of *shebab* started flooding over the walls into the compound, quickly filling the courtyard in a surging mass of humanity. Helpless, the security guards gave up.

Shortly before the two Jordanian helicopters bearing Arafat's coffin and entourage were due to land, a black-clad, masked column of Al-Aqsa Brigades men marched along the street to a drum beat, shooting their M–16s into the air as children ran alongside them. They swept through the gates into the compound and were swallowed up into the crowd. The dark-suited consuls and foreign dignitaries who had been lined up on the tarmac to receive the late Palestinian leader beat a hasty retreat into Arafat's former office. "It was every man for himself," one of them told me later, recalling the chaotic scenes.

In the end, Arafat was laid to rest amid a tumultuous uproar and a hail of gunfire that continued unabated for two hours. The honor guard never got to parade and the band did not get to play; instead they barged into the crowd, trumpets ahead, to try to clear a path for the coffin. By the end of the afternoon, the air thick with dust and with the acrid smoke of gunpowder, it was unclear to many of the mourners whether Arafat's coffin had actually made it into the grave or not. But there was a feeling on the street that the Palestinian leader had been given a proper send-off, a passionate intifada-style final blast by his true heirs, the Palestinian masses.

--⊱⊙⊰--

Less than two months later, in the Tulkarm refugee camp, it is business as usual. Muhammad Taleb, a 37-year-old spokesman for the Al-Aqsa Martyrs Brigades in the camp, meets me in an alleyway accompanied by two flunkies. One, in a woolen cap, is carrying what a local source identifies as an MP5 submachine gun.

Two days ago, in the early hours of December 24—Christmas Eve elsewhere in the world—three youths were shot dead here by an Israeli force, ambushed from behind a low wall. Taleb, a large man with bristly black hair and nicotine-stained teeth wearing a khaki flying jacket, points out the doorway where the latest martyrs fell and lists their names with slow precision, eyeing my notebook as I write each one down: Kamel Abdallah Sabarin, 18; Jamal Khaled Azzem, 15; and Iyad Azmi Ghanam, 20. Israel's Army Radio had called them "armed men" in its routinely brief report on the morning news. Taleb says they were not carrying guns, but a sidekick says one of them was. According to Taleb, the three were out at 1:45 a.m. because they were "guarding the camp" against thefts. Other sources say the three had been up drinking liquor and came out to fire at the soldiers as they drove by in a jeep. When they ventured out again a few minutes later to see where the soldiers had gone, they were killed on the spot. According to a leaflet of the Al-Aqsa Brigades announcing the deaths, the three "brave knights" were killed in an "armed confrontation with a Zionist unit." A photo in circulation of Kamal Sabarin is superimposed with the words "If you weren't a lion, the wolves wouldn't have gathered to kill you."

In these twilight days of the intifada, there is general confusion over whether to present the dead as innocent victims of the occupation forces or as noble warriors. Things are further complicated by the delicate position that Taleb and his comrades now find themselves in. The Al-Aqsa men have pledged their full support for Arafat's successor, Mahmud Abbas, or Abu Mazen, one of the last surviving members of Fatah's "historical leadership." Yet Abu Mazen has openly called for an end to the armed or "militarized" intifada, which has been the Al-Aqsa Martyrs Brigades' sole raison d'etre for the past four years.

Taleb declares that "the intifada will continue, even if all we have are stones and paper, with militarization or without, until we have taken all our rights." But after standing exposed in the alleyway for a few minutes, Taleb suggests it might be safer if we move inside to talk. By his own count, he is one of 17 wanted men left in the camp. He says there are another 25 in the town, and 20 in the surrounding villages. Death could come at any moment.

Taleb leads us into a nearby sports and social hall that has been turned into a temporary mourning venue for the three freshly buried youths. On an outside wall, an intifada poster commemorates two other martyrs from the "Al-Aqsa Brigades Thabet Thabet unit," who are posing with guns. They are Yusuf and Hader Taleb, Muhammad's brothers, killed last year and the year before.

Inside the hall, there are rows of white plastic chairs, mostly empty at this early hour of the afternoon. The walls are covered in pictures of Arafat. Above the door, a plaque in Arabic states that this sports and social center has been donated by USAID, the U.S. State Department's aid and development arm, in order to "further the opportunities of the camp's youth." This probably was not what the Americans had had in mind. Adham Azzem, the brother of the dead 15-year-old, is wandering around looking dazed. Somebody says that he also is wanted, and that the soldiers were probably after him.

Sitting down, Taleb talks in gruff-voiced, laconic formulas. The "armed intifada is now only defensive, not offensive," he says, and its aim is to "get rid of the occupation—that's all." Attacks inside Israel are not planned by the group, but may occur as "individuals' reactions to what the Israelis do. When you see the young bodies lying on the ground . . ." he trails off.

Taleb seems to have a stock answer for everything. Only when I ask him what, if anything, the intifada has achieved, he falls silent, bewildered and at a loss for words. "We've lost so much, we can't talk about achievements," he says after a pause. "Our economy has been destroyed and they've taken our lands to build the wall." He consults briefly with an intellectual-looking young man in round glasses who has come to sit beside him, and who comes up with an answer. The intifada, the young man says, raised the profile of the Palestinian cause. "Even President Bush is now talking about a Palestinian state," adds Taleb, encouraged.

We leave the camp and go to sit in a Tulkarm restaurant run by a man known as Dr. Chicken for the fowl he grills. He is only offering one dish of dried-out strips of turkey *shwarma* today. "This was Arafat's intifada," concludes Abu K., the owner of the grocery store that served as a former drop-off point for the Al-Aqsa funds. "It was personal, revenge for Camp David. He wanted to show who was boss. But he lost control once Hamas got involved. He even lost control of his own Al-Aqsa Martyrs Brigades."

Now, sealed in behind the wall, it is as if Tulkarm is decaying from the inside. By Abu K.'s account, it has turned into a den of hard drinking, drugs, illicit affairs, and crime. He and some friends recently took it upon themselves to close down a brothel opened by a local woman. He tells colorful tales of neighbors' shops that have been torched and men who have been kidnapped in the course of family feuds. Whether Abu Mazen succeeds in reining in and rehabilitating the armed men or not, the once-picturesque market town of Tulkarm, for one, will never be quite the same again.

⊶⊷⟳⊜⟲⊷⊶

Not far away, in the lounge of her sparkling new home back in the Tulkarm refugee camp, Su'ad Sirhan counts her blessings. Around these parts, her son is seen as a hero. The day he died, she relates with satisfaction, 14 babies born in Tulkarm were named Sirhan. She expresses no pity for the children who died in Metzer, a kibbutz not far from here that was dedicated to peace. "They are sad about their children. Are theirs more beautiful than ours?" she challenges.

Burhan, though, is clearly devastated by the episode and is searching for a way, any way, to salvage some shred of humanity from it; to try to make amends. The intifada is officially over, and Arafat is now just a picture on the wall. Burhan asks what the people at Metzer are saying and whether I have the phone number of the kibbutz. Then he asks me to pass on a message to Avi Ohion, the father of the murdered boys. "I saw him on TV. He's thin and dark, right?" Burhan asks quietly. "If you see him, please tell him the following: You lost your children and I lost my son because of this crazy war. We need rationality to stop it. I hope we can work together, if possible, to bring about a just peace between us. I offer you my condolences. Thank you."

5

Right vs Right

When the call for help came from Beit Surik, a village in the wild hills north-west of Jerusalem, it found attorney Muhammad Dahleh in The Hague. It was Tuesday, February 24, 2004, the second of three days of hearings at the peace palace in the Dutch capital, which houses the International Court of Justice. The ICJ was responding to an urgent request by the U.N. General Assembly, at the PLO ambassador's instigation, to provide an advisory opinion on the "Legal Consequences of the Construction of a Wall in the Occupied Palestinian Territory." An international panel of 15 judges had been assembled to hear the case.

Dahleh, an Israeli Arab from the Galilee with a practice in East Jerusalem, was in The Hague as legal counsel on the Palestinian team. Because Israel refused to recognize the ICJ's jurisdiction on the matter of the security barrier it had not sent any representatives, and made do with submitting a terse written brief. As far as Israel was concerned, the ICJ case was politically-motivated and hopelessly skewed from the outset. Even the title riled officials in Jerusalem. For one thing, they insisted, it was not a wall but a fence. More to the point, though, Israel officially considers the territory of 1967 not "occupied" but disputed, its future still to be determined in negotiations.

Israelis have in any case long viewed the U.N. as biased against them, pointing to a long list of lopsided resolutions condemning their actions while omitting any mention of those of the other side. Often, other than the United States, the only ally Israel could count on for support in the assembly was Micronesia, a string of pro-American exotic islands in the North Pacific with a population of 100,000, where in more remote parts the men still wear loincloths and the traditional currency consists of giant stones.

Israel felt its case for the fence had all but been made when a suicide bomber from the Fatah-affiliated Al-Aqsa Martyrs Brigades blew up a No. 14 bus outside Jerusalem's Liberty Bell Garden, a stately park in the five-star hotel area of the capital, at 8:30 on the bright, freezing morning of February 22, the day before the ICJ hearings began.

Among the eight dead were two schoolboys and the brother-in-law of the commercial attaché at the Israeli embassy in The Hague. By chance, Uzi Dayan, the former army deputy chief of staff and NSC head who fathered the fence, was leading a bus full of Jerusalem city council members on a pre-planned tour of the still mostly incomplete barrier around the capital that day in the hope that they would lobby to speed up its construction. Arriving on the scene three hours after the explosion, the road and sidewalks wet from where the fire brigade had washed them down, Dayan declared solemnly to a waiting TV camera: "The war against terror is going on here in Jerusalem, not in The Hague."

Dahleh, a sharp and talented 36-year-old lawyer, had already made a name for himself at home as one of the leading campaigners against the barrier, having represented numerous communities in and around Jerusalem in their battles with the Defense Ministry over its route. On the second day of the Hague hearings, as the judges listened to learned expositions by experts of international law in the peace palace's wood-paneled hall, the desperate caller from Beit Surik told Dahleh that the army bulldozers had arrived to break the ground for the fence around the village, and pleaded with him to come home at once. Dahleh worked the phones and begged his contacts in the Israeli defense establishment to suspend work until his return at the weekend, but the request was denied. Dahleh caught a plane home the following day, and by Thursday, had petitioned the Israeli Supreme Court to examine the legality of the route of a 40-kilometer section of the barrier chosen by the Defense Ministry in the area north of Jerusalem, including the part that threatened to cut Beit Surik's farmers off from most of their land. On Sunday, the court issued an injunction stopping the bulldozers in their tracks.

It was the beginning of a process that would end with a landmark ruling that would require the state to modify much of the barrier route, infuriating the army, challenging the government, and cracking Israel's hitherto almost monolithic national consensus on the fence along the way. Though the Israeli Supreme Court had long ago opened its doors to Palestinians from the territories represented by Israeli lawyers, hearing petitions challenging everything from house demolitions to deportation, Dahleh would squeeze Israel's respected justice system into a tight corner, and attempt to force it to take positions on controversial issues that it has always sought to avoid. For example, the Supreme Court has traditionally evaded ruling on the legality of the Jewish settlements in the territories captured in 1967, always referring authority on the matter back to the politicians. This way, the respected legal institution could avoid going head to head with the government and jeopardizing its position regarding the national consensus, while still maintaining its international prestige.

Dahleh's case would force Israel to redraw its physical and moral parameters, pitting the so-far sacred Israeli right to security against the right of ordinary Palestinians to live a normal life. For while the Jewish state, proud of its democracy and institutions, could dismiss The Hague, it had no choice but to abide by the decisions of its own high court.

All this Dahleh did with the training he received in some of Israel's most esteemed state institutions. Dahleh earned his law degree from the Law Faculty of the Hebrew University of Jerusalem. The original campus on Mount Scopus was off limits from 1949, when the law faculty was founded, an island in Jordanian-held territory until the reunification of the city in the Six Day War. Since 1967 the faculty has been housed in one of the historic stone buildings at the heart of the original campus, now dwarfed by the modernist concrete jungle that has gone up around it. After university Dahleh went on to clerk for two years in Jerusalem's Supreme Court of Justice, the first Arab citizen of Israel to do so in the history of the state. He also has a law degree from American University in Washington, and is a member of the New York Bar Association to boot.

Jerusalem's new Supreme Court building, an elegantly appointed architectural gem, opened in 1992. Its location, on a grassy hill at the peak of the government compound, overlooking the squat Knesset, or house of parliament, next door, is meant to signify the lofty status of justice in the Jewish state. Inside its cool, sleek chambers, sunlit by glass pyramids built into the roof, a venerable team of judges led by Chief Justice Aharon Barak would preside over the case of *Beit Surik Village Council and Others vs the Government of Israel and the IDF Commander of the West Bank* for many months to come. At issue was the fate of a cluster of eight Palestinian villages including Beit

Surik, Biddu, Qatanna, Qubeiba, and Beit Dikku, dotted among the terraced hillsides northwest of Jerusalem, just over the Green Line in the West Bank. The army fence planners had intended to encircle these villages in an enclave, sealing them off from Jerusalem entirely, while letting the barrier contort itself around the neighboring bloc of Jewish settlements including Giv'at Ze'ev, Givon, Givon Hahadasha, and Har Shmuel, in order to leave them on the Israeli side of the divide.

According to the plans, the Biddu-Beit Surik enclave would have one narrow opening in the north, leading in the direction of Ramallah, the PA's administrative capital of the West Bank. Defense Ministry officials charged with "humanizing" the fence, or minimizing its impact on the local Palestinian population in the run-up to The Hague hearings, spoke of plans to build a sunken road that would burrow under the barrier and serve as a short cut to Ramallah, providing the Beit Surik enclave with technical, if not exactly territorial, contiguity. This prompted Dahleh to comment wryly that Israel was building a system that would elevate one people to a higher plane, while burying the other in a more earthly reality down below. Meanwhile the villagers' historic connection with Arab East Jerusalem would be severed, as would normal access to the city's educational facilities, hospitals, and places of worship to which they had always gravitated.

The villages worst affected by the planned barrier would be Biddu and Beit Surik. The fence was supposed to skim the last houses of Beit Surik by just 27 meters and would leave some 76 percent of its agricultural lands on the other side. Biddu, Beit Surik's immediate neighbor, would be separated from 45 percent of its orchards and fields. Ever since 1967, when Israel conquered the area from Jordan and the Green Line opened up, the villagers had been streaming into Israel to work. Since the beginning of the Al-Aqsa intifada, movement across the Green Line had been severely restricted. Once the barrier went up, working in Israel would, for most people, not be an option at all. Many of the villagers assumed they would have to go back to more traditional ways of eking out a living from the land. Yet with the fence route the army was proposing, some families from Beit Surik and Biddu would be left with nothing to farm.

There were plans for four agricultural gates along the 40-kilometer stretch of the barrier northwest of Jerusalem, designed to allow the farmers access to their lands on the other side. But the farmers' gate system, which depended on the granting of special permits and was subject to limited opening and closing times, had already proved unreliable in places where the fence was already up, and was itself the subject of a Supreme Court petition brought by the Association of Civil Rights in Israel on behalf of several Palestinian villages further north.

In February 2004, as the bulldozers started uprooting the olive trees along the projected route of the fence, popular protests broke out in Biddu and Beit Surik. Distraught villagers were filmed by TV crews clinging on to gnarled tree trunks and cleaving to the earth as if for dear life, tears streaming down their faces. While the protesters were unarmed, the local *shebab*, or youth, sometimes threw stones at the security forces protecting the bulldozers, leading them to respond. In one particularly violent confrontation in Biddu on February 26, two Palestinians were shot dead by Israeli border police while an elderly man from the village died later of a heart attack, apparently after having been overcome by tear gas. They were the first "martyrs" in what was being hailed in the villages as a new "popular intifada against the wall."

At the first Supreme Court hearing of the case of *Beit Surik vs the State* on Sunday February 29, the judges asked the two sides—Dahleh and the Defense Ministry—to try to reach an agreement on a compromise route. That was to prove impossible. While the Defense Ministry did make some slight amendments to its original plan for the area in response to the petition, the alterations fell far short of the petitioners' demands.

The first issue the Israeli Supreme Court had to determine, in parallel with The Hague, was whether the state had the right to build the barrier inside the territory of the West Bank at all. The Jerusalem court eventually decided that Israel did have the right, so long as the digressions into disputed territory were for security, not political purposes. At the heart of the case, though, stood the question of just how much diversion into the West Bank could be justified in the name of security. In short, the court was being asked to determine the extent Israeli security considerations should be allowed to override the basic human right of Palestinian villagers to access their own cultivated lands, and whether the security imperative in this particular case and in general justified the barrier's seemingly draconian route.

Dozens of petitions had already been filed by individuals and groups adversely affected by the barrier, represented by activist lawyers like Dahleh and nonprofit organizations, some of which were rejected out of hand and others of which were slowly making their way through the legal process. But this case, coming directly in the shadow of The Hague, and being so clearly defined in nature, immediately took on special significance. Chief Justice Aharon Barak decided early on that the Beit Surik file would establish the legal principles to guide the state of Israel in all future planning and construction of the barrier.

◦⟶≡◦⟵◦

Actually, Dahleh acknowledges, sitting in his smart, certificate-lined East Jerusalem office between hearings, the Beit Surik case, which turned into a courtroom putsch, took off almost by coincidence thanks to Shai the Gardener, a "good citizen" from Mevasseret Tzion, and his "hard-working Palestinian employee" from the neighboring village of Beit Surik.

Mevasseret, a well-to-do suburb of West Jerusalem, sits just within Israel, on the other side of the Green Line right opposite Beit Surik. The history of the conflict, never far below the surface in this ancient land, lurks even here, among the modern boulevards. Mevasseret's middle-class neighborhoods and industrial zone are built around the Castel, an old stone fort and the site of a former Palestinian village. Commanding the strategic high ground above the twisting Tel Aviv-Jerusalem highway, tough battles were fought here in 1948 between the Palestinian legions led by the legendary fighter Abd al-Qader Husseini and the pre-state paramilitary Jewish Haganah. It was here that Husseini met his death, dealing the Palestinian side a serious blow and allowing the Jewish forces to go on to capture West Jerusalem. Today, Mevasseret sprawls along the hilltop, still commanding the road to Jerusalem, but instead of the fort, the yellow neon golden arches of McDonald's at the new mall are the most visible landmark around.

Since 1967, Mevasseret has had a long, almost intimate connection with Beit Surik and the neighboring villages whose men have built the apartment blocks and luxury houses of this Israeli suburb, and who have practically run the place behind the scenes, packing shelves in the supermarkets, staffing the workshops of the industrial zone, and selling pizza at the gas station. It was a relationship based on the solid ground of mutual interest.

Shai Dror has lived in Mevasseret's Rehov Hashalom (Peace Street) for the past 20 years, running a gardening business with hired help from Beit Surik. He receives me after work at his home with typical Israeli informality, clad in khaki shorts and a T-shirt, and introduces his South African-born wife, Gita, a nurse who immigrated to Israel from Johannesburg in the 1970s. The two-story terrace is fairly modest by Mevasseret standards and has no garden to speak of, complying with the old adage that the cobbler goes barefoot.

One day in January 2004, Shai relates, Abed, a young lad from Beit Surik who was helping around the Drors' home with some maintenance work, produced a copy of a map that the army had been distributing in the village showing the route of the approaching security barrier. "I took one look and saw black before my eyes," says Dror. There had been "a kilometer of peace" between Mevasseret and Beit Surik for the past 37 years, he says. Now, the government was "building a ghetto" in his own backyard.

Shai wrote a letter to his fellow citizens of Mevasseret, made two hundred copies, and distributed it in the mall, inviting them all to a parlor meeting at his home in early February. The day before the meeting, he heard that the army had started uprooting olive trees in Beit Surik. He crossed the fields and entered the village for the first time in his life, and joined a demonstration there.

About 15 people showed up to that first parlor meeting, among them Mevasseret mayor Carmi Gillon, a former head of the Shin Bet internal security service. Gillon almost immediately bowed out, saying this was a security issue in which the local municipal authorities could not intervene. So the concerned citizens started taking matters into their own hands. Hagai Agmon-Snir, a Mevasseret resident who works in a center promoting Jewish-Arab coexistence in Jerusalem, and who knew attorney Dahleh from the days they worked together at the Association for Citizens Rights in Israel, started collecting the signatures of Israelis ready to join the Palestinian villagers' petition to the Supreme Court. And the respectable liberals of Mevasseret found some unlikely new allies in a couple of young local anti-establishment activists from a movement calling itself "Anarchists against the Wall," whose supporters had already been involved in anti-fence protests in the north. Among them was Yossi Bartal, a 17-year-old from Mevasseret, who attended one of the first anti-fence demonstrations in Biddu and delivered a speech there in Hebrew stating that Israel should be "ending the occupation, not building walls." As well as participating in the villagers' protests, the anarchists set up a peace tent in a field on the Green Line, between Mevasseret and Beit Surik, where they camped out with some of the local Palestinian youths.

In the end, Agmon-Snir and Dror managed to recruit 30 fellow citizens of Mevasseret to join the Beit Surik case against the state. But standing in court as lone voices opposite the mighty IDF and defense establishment, Shai says, he and attorney Dahleh soon realized the need to recruit some security experts of their own, in order to counter the state's arguments with some credibility. Shai approached some members of the Council for Peace and Security, a lobby group of dovish-leaning retired Israeli generals and security officials headed at the time by Shaul Givoli, a former head of the home-front civil guard. Council members had visited Kibbutz Metzer back when Yoav Ben Naftali and his colleagues were campaigning to change the fence route there, but had declined to get involved. To his frustration, Shai found that now, too, the security brains needed some persuading. When Shaul Givoli got back to him and said he had spoken to a few members and they were not too keen, Shai says he "blew up at them. I told them you've taken us into wars, you say we are right, and yet you won't get your hands dirty. I spoke to him from the belly. He went quiet. Then he said 'I'm with you.'"

In the end, 16 retired Israeli security officials of the Council for Peace and Security agreed to lend their names and expertise, signing an affidavit to the Supreme Court on condition that their role would be confined to the immediate geographical area between Mevasseret and Beit Surik, not the whole 40-kilometer stretch in question, and would be presented as an opinion commissioned by the Mevasseret 30, not Dahleh. The former generals wanted to be portrayed as working for Israel, not Palestine.

In mid March, three Council for Peace and Security members—Asaf Chefetz, a former IDF commander and national police chief, Omer Barlev, a former division commander, and Yuval Dvir, former military governor of the Gaza Strip—presented the high court with the affidavit rejecting the government's route for the fence in the Mevasseret area and suggesting an alternative route that would leave a much larger portion of Beit Surik's agricultural lands on the Palestinian side of the fence. That meant bringing the barrier closer to the Green Line, and by implication, closer to the houses and apartment blocks of Mevasseret; yet in the retired generals' view, such a barrier would still fulfill the primary security functions required of it in the area. When the judges requested a map of the alternative proposed route, it was the retired generals who first turned to consultant Shaul Arieli.

⋅⇥⊃◯⊂⇤⋅

At the end of March, Gen. Moshe Kaplinski, the commander of IDF forces in Judea and Samaria, submitted an affidavit in response to the Council for

Peace and Security that constituted the first detailed public exposition of the defense establishment's justifications for the fence route it had proposed. Kaplinski argued that the area in question had witnessed dozens of "security incidents" in the past three and a half years of the intifada, including shooting attacks on the main Israeli Highway 443 that runs just east of Biddu and connects Jerusalem with the fast-growing Modi'in area to the north, and on to Tel Aviv.

Among the security considerations requiring the barrier to deviate into West Bank territory, Kaplinski cited the need to create broad "security margins" to allow the army time to pursue any terrorists who succeeded in crossing the fence; the need to keep Israeli communities out of range of Palestinian sniper fire; to protect traffic on the main roads; and to control territory that would give the army an advantage in defending the seam area in general and the soldiers patrolling the fence. He also mentioned topographical and other "unspecified" considerations. Throughout the hearings, the state's legal team studiously refused to use the term "Green Line," (*Ha-Kav Ha-Yarok* in Hebrew) since Israel has never officially recognized the 1949 demarcation line as a legal border, only a temporary armistice line. The state attorneys referred instead to the more ambiguous "*Kav Tchum A'yosh*," a vague and ambiguous Hebrew abbreviation that translates roughly as the "Gaza, Judea and Samaria area line." Chief Justice Barak was corrected by the state lawyers at least once for calling the line green.

Accompanying the two young lawyers from the state attorney's office at all the hearings was the IDF fence project head, Tirza. Now a civilian, he wore a dapper navy blazer and dark pants to court, the small crocheted yarmulke on his head denoting his affiliation as a modern Orthodox Jew. Tirza has made his home in a small West Bank settlement called Kfar Adumim, in the desert hills between Ma'aleh Adumim and Jericho. Perhaps because of his penchant for being out in the field, the Palestinians had taken to calling him "Mr. Tarzan." On the "Palestinian" side of the bench sat Dahleh, accompanied by several Arab-Israeli legal colleagues. Of small to medium height, with black bristly hair, Dahleh still managed to cut a dashing figure, especially on days when he rushed in late clutching his briefcase, his black gown flowing out behind him.

As each side was asked again to respond to the other, the Supreme Court case started to drag on. In April, the court lifted its February injunction and allowed the army to resume work on certain portions of the section in question, on the condition that if the court ruled later that the route had to be changed, the scored earth would be restored to its former state and the Palestinians would be compensated for any unnecessary damage to their land. On April 4, the bulldozers returned to Biddu, and the battles started up all over again.

It was a rather motley-looking crew that set out from the parking lot of Jerusalem's Liberty Bell Garden on Thursday morning, April 15. The meeting point had been chosen for reasons of convenience, despite the slight incongruity given the recent bus bombing just across the road. For this minibus was headed for Biddu where the residents, resolutely resisting the bulldozers, had called on Israeli sympathizers and "internationals"—foreign volunteers of the International Solidarity Movement in the Palestinian territories—to join the daily demonstrations against the wall. Arik Ascherman, a Reform rabbi and the American-born executive director of the small but active Jerusalem-based Rabbis for Human Rights group, heeded the call and organized the transport.

Among Ascherman's flock was a large, sweaty, tangle-haired Israeli youth in an orange polo shirt and purple plastic-framed glasses who identified himself only as Laizer. A patch on his grubby satchel read "IDF—Terror Organization" above a cartoon-like illustration of Israeli soldiers looking like Nazi shock troops. Laizer was born into an ultra-Orthodox Hasidic family in Kfar Chabad, the Lubavitcher town near Ben Gurion Airport where the Messiah is always imminently expected. He had rebelled and was now a full-time protester loosely affiliated with the nebulous group of "Anarchists against the Wall." Also on the bus were two slim, softly spoken Israeli women from Beersheba, both named Yael, who do not believe in the Jewish state; a contingent of aging lefties from the northern city of Haifa including a retired Englishman in open-toe sandals who munched on a seemingly never-ending supply of scraped carrots; a new immigrant from Chicago called Daniel; Lucia, his sultry girlfriend from Mexico; and a diminutive left-wing academic from the United States who remained tight-lipped and grim-faced all day.

By the time the bus was ready to leave there was standing room only. Laizer parked himself in the aisle, stuck his earpiece in and listened to some obscure Arabic pop on his Discman. Rabbi Ascherman, a tall, gangly, geeky-looking man with a biblical dark beard and curly hair topped by a colorful crocheted yarmulke, gave a brief pep talk. Although these demonstrations were supposed to be nonviolent, he warned that it was sometimes difficult to control the Palestinian children and stop them from throwing stones. Things could turn nasty. Those who did not want to risk being caught up in violence, Ascherman said, whether as a matter of safety or of conscience, might prefer to stay and protest peacefully outside the Biddu village council building once the rest of the crowd marched off in the direction of the bulldozers.

Rabbi Ascherman's party arrived in Biddu at midday, having abandoned the minibus at the army roadblock, a mound of earth at the entrance of the village, and made the rest of the way in local taxis. The men and boys of the village—bolstered by residents of the neighboring villages, ISM activists, and a number of young, wan-faced Israeli anarchists—were already making their way down the potholed main drag. About 250 meters further along the road, beyond the last house, border police were standing guard at the point where the bulldozers were digging for the fence.

The new arrivals were immediately surrounded by the Palestinian protesters who, with calls of "Hebrew, Hebrew!" swept the Israelis into their midst as they marched headlong toward the security forces clad in khaki and helmets. There was no option of staying behind. The Palestinians hoped that the presence of Israeli civilians would serve as a kind of a human shield: When Israeli demonstrators stood shoulder to shoulder with them, the popular theory went, the border police were more likely to hold their live fire, limiting themselves to rubber-coated bullets and copious quantities of tear gas instead.

Things started cheerfully enough. The Palestinians chanted "Allahu Akbar," the Arabic battle cry of "God is Great," in time to a drumbeat and sang a patriotic song. Young boys, some of whom looked no older than 8 or 9, skipped along impatiently at the back cradling stones in their sling shots, itching for action. It is hard to say whether the stones flew first, or whether they were prompted by the security force's actions, but suddenly the happy chorus came to an abrupt halt, drowned out by a series of sharp booms as clouds of tear gas bellowed out of metal canisters. The column of marchers scattered. In the foggy silence that followed, local men and boys, internationals, and Israeli taggers-on, myself included, crouched by the roadside coughing, spitting, trying to catch a breath, eyes stinging and streaming.

The wives and daughters of the village immediately emerged from the houses lining the street bearing trays of peeled, quartered onions, a strangely soothing popular antidote to the tear gas. Wedges were passed around, held up to noses and inhaled. Soon the protesters started marching again. New rounds of tear gas enveloped them and sound bombs and sudden flashes, the latest weapons in the army's nonlethal arsenal for putting down popular uprisings, scattered them again and again. The carrot man stood in the middle of it all like some Biblical prophet of doom, holding up a homemade placard that read "The Wall shall fall / Sharon shall fall / Bush shall fall / Evil shall fall." Laizer had long since disappeared, having just cadged a ride on the bus and walked over to Beit Surik in search of the peace tent.

Nobody in Biddu was working that day. Defying the wall had become a full-time occupation. Ahmed Mansour, a gray-bearded father of 12, made his way up the road, away from the main flashpoint. His house is the last one before the bulldozers. The army put out a demolition order against it, which Mansour was fighting in a court case of his own. As usual, tear gas had been pouring in through the windows. Spotting my journalists' notepad, he sought me out to tell me, hoarse with desperation, how he and several of his children have had to be taken to the hospital more than ten times. "Where should we go?" he asked. "Bush and Sharon are two faces of the same coin. Bush is a Zionist, not an American," he added, referring to what all Palestinians here saw as the U.S. president's unconditional support for Israel. "They are animals. Animals!" another bearded man spat out as he rushed by, away from the tear gas clouds, anger burning in his eyes. "Bush and Sharon are terrorists."

By 2 p.m., the demonstrators had filtered from the main street down to the nearby olive groves in what had become a well-choreographed routine. The fence was slated to curve down the slope from the end of the main street and run through these orchards, sealing Biddu in from the east. Up on the hill, in the bulldozers' path, stood another lone house marked for demolition. It was here that the February "martyrs" had fallen. By now, most of Rabbi Ascherman's flock had seen enough and had gone back to Jerusalem.

Down in the bumpy soil among the trees, a teenage boy in a baseball cap was urgently seeking help. He said his 10-year-old nephew had been seized by border police who were holding him up on the ridge where a couple of jeeps were stationed and where, he said, the boy was being beaten. Rabbi Ascherman was called, and hastily arranged a "hudna," a 15-minute cease-fire in all stone-throwing activity. Grabbing a megaphone he set out toward the jeeps, moving slowly in the hot pursuit of justice, calling out in heavily American-accented

7. Nobody in Biddu was working that day. Defying the wall had become a full-time occupation: An anti-barrier protest in Biddu village, February 2004. Credit: Avi Ohayon, Israel Government Press Office.

Hebrew: "I am Rabbi Arik Ascherman. I am coming to release the boy. You are beating him and that is in violation of the law."

Ascherman, who grew up in Erie, Pennsylvania, says he wanted to be a rabbi from the age of seven. By the time he reached bar mitzvah, the role models and heroes "that made him cry" were people like David Saperstein, a forward-thinking Reform rabbi dedicated to social action who has since become the Reform movement's mover and shaker in Washington. Ascherman attributes his own acute sense of conscience to his family and his community where, he says, he was raised on stories of Jewish involvement in the civil rights movement and the struggle for social justice. His first real experience of Israel was at the age of 21, when he came for two years on an "Interns for Peace" program and lived in an Arab village in the Galilee promoting coexistence. He officially immigrated in 1984 and joined Rabbis for Human Rights ten years later. Founded by Rabbi David Forman in the late 1980s during the first intifada, RHR has primarily concerned itself with Israeli human rights violations against the Palestinians across the Green Line. About a hundred rabbis in Israel are now associated with the group, including a handful of Orthodox, though the majority hail from the Conservative and Reform ranks. Oddly, donations from North America increased during the Al-Aqsa intifada, despite the fact that Palestinian terrorism had become its hallmark. "You'd be hard-pressed to find an American Jewishly identified person who doesn't want to be seen as pro-Israeli," Ascherman explains, "but at the same time the conscience, the Jewish soul, is at work."

No armchair rabbi, Ascherman is often out in the field, planting trees on Palestinian lands that have fallen on the Israeli side of the new security barrier, standing before bulldozers sent to demolish Palestinian homes, and organizing volunteers to help Palestinian farmers harvest their olive trees that lie close to hostile Jewish settlements or across the fence. For the farmers' benefit, he also sells large cans of Palestinian olive oil out of the organization's offices in West Jerusalem's leafy Rehavia district. "Israel's right to self defense and the Palestinians' right to land and a livelihood are both matters of life and death," he says, adding that the barrier-building enterprise has created a conflict "between right and right."

That afternoon in Biddu, proceeding towards the ridge and the border police jeeps, Ascherman was soon obscured by tear gas. To the delight of the protesters, though, the wind was carrying most of it back in the direction of the troops. The rabbi seemed to get swallowed up, but word soon got out that he had reached the jeeps and been arrested. The cease-fire was off. Palestinian demonstrators splintered into small, rock-hurling gangs playing cat and mouse with ever-multiplying knots of border police. Troops ran up and down the alleyways leading to the orchards, shooting gas canisters sometimes five at a time. The canisters arched through the air leaving trails of smoke like fireworks. At one point the two Yaels, myself, and a couple of other members of the rabbi's group who had stayed on, dangerously sandwiched between a gang of youths spinning their slingshots and border police aiming their guns, dove for cover in doorways and behind cars.

By 4:00 p.m. the remnants of the Ascherman party regrouped, piled into a local-service taxi and headed for the army roadblock. The minibus, a welcome sight, was waiting on the other side of the mound. Ascherman was taken into custody in the police station at the neighboring Jewish settlement of Givat Ze'ev. His lawyer got him out later that night. He had a cut on his nose, the result, he says, of having been head-butted by the commanding officer on the ridge, who also threatened to "rearrange" his face. As for the boy that Ascherman had gone to rescue, a photo of him turned up in the Hebrew daily *Ma'ariv* a few days after the incident. He was Muhammad Sa'id Isa Badwan, aged 13. Looking frightened, he had been tied by a leather belt to the metal grate on the front windshield of one of the jeeps. According to Ascherman, the border police were using the boy as a "human shield" against the rock throwers. Perhaps this was intended as a perverse message to the Israeli leftists and foreigners who had come to shield the Palestinian protesters. After sitting on the hood of the jeep for around four hours, and then inside, Muhammad was released at approximately 7 p.m. that night. A doctor at the Biddu clinic checked him over and said he had bruises on his arms and back, but no further injuries.

The protests went on. Three days after Ascherman's delegation was there, on April 18, Dia Abd al-Karim Abu Eid, 24, was killed in Biddu's orchard of death. A few weeks later his brother Tha'er and his friend Mansour Mansour take me back there and, squatting on the ground among the olive trees, cigarette packs in hand, describe how Dia had been sitting just like this, with two friends, observing a confrontation between protesters from the village and troops stationed on the hill, behind the lone house marked for demolition, about 200 meters away. The friends with him said they did not hear usual sounds of shots being fired, but only a strange buzz as a sniper's bullets "with wings" whirred by. Suddenly Dia grabbed his chest and gasped. He had been shot near the heart.

Tha'er, a car mechanic, is in overalls. Mansour, 26, is in a fashionable black shirt and jeans, and he sports pencil-thin sideburns and a sculpted beard. He used to be a student of radio broadcasting at Bir Zeit University near Ramallah, but he's given up trying to get there since the intifada. Now, he says, he spends his days as an anti-wall activist, coordinating activities in Biddu and liaising with the foreign volunteers, some of whom are living with local families in the village.

As they speak, an orange bulldozer and a dumpster truck are working nonstop up on the hill, leveling the earth for the fence, whining forward and beep-beeping in reverse as a dark silhouette of an armed, helmeted guard patrols back and forth. Retracing Dia's last steps as he stumbled toward a low stone wall, Mansour says he feels he is being closed in, "like in a ghetto or a zoo. Do you expect people to stay quiet?" he asks quietly, coldly, nodding in the direction of the bulldozer. "No. What they build by day, we'll destroy at night."

Mansour describes Dia, the third of 11 children, as a quiet young man who tended to mind his own business and was not politically involved. In the month before he died, Dia had been working at an oriental food restaurant in the picturesque Israeli-Arab village of Abu Gosh. Just within the Green Line near Mevasseret, Abu Gosh is a favorite Saturday lunch spot for Israelis in search of good hummus and grilled meats. Dia had gotten the job because of his excellent spoken Hebrew, honed during the six years he had worked at a building materials store in the industrial zone of Mevasseret from the age of 16.

Dia's relatives say Tzadok Rahamim, the owner of the store, had come to rely on Dia like a son. When Tzadok once took three months off to recover from a kidney transplant, it was Dia who ran the business. He worked from 7 in the morning till 7 at night, his relatives say, bringing home around $1,000 a month, sometimes a little more. Dia did not have a work permit to enter Israel, however, and because the plague of suicide bombings had caused a security clampdown on illegal Palestinian workers in Israel, he had been caught in Mevasseret three times. Threatened with large fines and a jail term, he signed a paper pledging not to enter the town again.

Back at Dia's family home in the center of Biddu, his mother and an uncle, Jamal, show me a copy of a letter Tzadok wrote to the police, offering to pay a bond for Dia and vouching to fulfill any conditions the security authorities could name. Still, no permit was forthcoming. We are sitting in the family's simply furnished lounge decorated with portraits of Dia and another relative killed during the first intifada. Recently, says his mother, sighing through the tears that cloud her startling blue eyes, Dia had been complaining that he was bored. He had bought some text books with the intention of going back to school. He also longed to get married, and spent every spare hour and cent he had fixing up a dream apartment for himself and his future wife on the floor above his parents' home, behind a car accessories store where Tha'er works.

Upstairs, Dia's ghost apartment stands empty like an indictment. The hallway features wooden arches inset with sunken spotlights. A luxury-fitted kitchen has been installed, complete with a steel stove and a smart black marble countertop. And the walls of a bedroom—perhaps a future nursery—have been painted a delightful sky blue. It is unclear whether Dia had already found his bride. Tha'er says his younger brother was waiting, out of respect, for him to marry first.

Standing in the hallway, Tha'er points out that Tzadok Rahamim, whose first name derives from the Hebrew word meaning "justice" and whose second name means "mercy," neither came to the funeral nor visited Dia's family in the days or weeks after his death. He did call one of Dia's uncles a month later and asked if Dia had been a member of any Palestinian faction. They say the uncle replied, "You raised him. You can answer that yourself."

A few days after meeting Dia's family in Biddu, I find Tzadok Rahamim behind the counter of his store in Mevasseret's dusty industrial zone. A bullish looking man in his late 50s or early 60s with close cropped gray hair, Tzadok declines to talk about Dia and asks for understanding. He is still facing prosecution for having illegally employed the deceased youth, he says, and is due to appear in court soon.

As the protests and court case continued, gardener Shai Dror's core group in Mevasseret was working to build a relationship with the immediate neighbors in Beit Surik that would go beyond the one that had existed so far of Israeli employer and Palestinian cheap labor that went home at night. In doing so, Shai had to overcome an unspoken embarrassment: In the past, he acknowledges, he has had a Palestinian lawyer and an accountant from Beit Surik shifting dirt for him for cash. Joint actions were arranged, such as a kitemaking workshop for Mevasseret and Beit Surik children on the Green Line. And Shai's wife Gita started going to the village to meet with some of the women who tended to stay home and had mostly never set foot in Israel. Unlike the men they spoke almost no Hebrew, but Gita thinks she managed to make a couple of girlfriends nevertheless. One of the Beit Surik women, Majida, even called her up once, unsolicited, at home.

On a bright, sunny morning on Saturday May 1, around 150 supporters of the Mevasseret 30 and assorted curious citizens gathered in a parking lot at the end of Mevasseret to join a solidarity walk to the fields bordering Beit Surik. The march had been advertised in the local papers as an opportunity to see where the planned security barrier was meant to go and to hear from some of the Palestinian residents how it would affect them. Sara Bartal, a fifty-something housewifely figure in a floppy floral sunhat, was addressing the crowd.

"These are the kids who woke us up from our slumber," she told the mostly middle-aged, middle-class group, referring to her son, Yossi the anarchist, and his friends. "Instead of saying thank you to these people who built our homes," she continued, now speaking of the Palestinian neighbors, "instead of thanking them for all the years of cooperation and coexistence, we're strangling them."

The party set off, walking up a paved path that promptly turned into a dirt one at the Green Line, then following the trail through the thistle-filled fields and orchards up to a ridge overlooking Beit Surik and Biddu. At the top, in the rugged and beautiful countryside, Yossi, a slightly spotty youth in consciously unfashionable steel-framed specs and a T-shirt that said "Black Sheep," was waiting with a few Israeli and Palestinian contemporaries and a couple of English volunteers from the International Solidarity Movement.

Jaber al-Sheikh, one of Beit Surik's more articulate, Hebrew-speaking representatives, arrived with a few colleagues to explain the Palestinians' predicament. "We've worked in Jerusalem all our lives but now we aren't allowed in," Jaber declared. "We are left with what you see: our olive groves, our vines, our fig and plum trees. This is what our children eat." If the security barrier goes up as planned, preventing the villagers access to both jobs and land, he asked, "How would we survive? They're burying us alive."

After a short tour of the area, during which more Palestinian villagers gathered, including a rowdy group of youths who jeered at the Israelis in

Arabic from a hill above them, everybody retired to a hospitality tent, a black tarpaulin that had just been erected by some of the Palestinian and Israeli activists. Under the shade Shai Dror unfurled his maps and explained the alternative route that was being proposed by the Council for Peace and Security to polite Israeli applause. By the end of the morning, the members of the Israeli bourgeoisie, in sandals and sunhats, were sitting on plastic chairs under the canopy, drinking shots of bitter Arabic coffee poured from copper pots by Palestinian men, smiling at Palestinian grandmothers who had joined them in their traditional embroidered dresses, and signing petitions.

The irony of it all was not lost on Yossi Bartal, still living—or as he says, "mainly sleeping"—at home with his parents, Sara, a former Ministry of Education employee who is still involved in the educational field, and Aharon, who is in the metal business. The family lives in a neat semidetached house in Jasmine Road, overlooking the ruins of the Castel.

I met Yossi later over cappuccino in Tmol Shilshom (Yesterday and the Day Before), a slightly bohemian café-cum-book store in downtown West Jerusalem named for a poem by classic Hebrew author Shai Agnon, and asked him how he got to be an anarchist. He told me that he joined the left-wing Peace Now Youth at 13 or 14, quickly graduated to the Communist Youth League "and just went downhill from there." Yossi describes himself as an "anti-Zionist. I can't judge what Zionism was in the past, or judge the people who came here from Europe," he says. "But we have to recognize the Palestinian *nakba* and the fact that we came to a country where there already was another people."

Yossi joined "Anarchists against the Wall" in the summer of 2003 when a group of radical Israeli leftists, happy to have found a cause, camped out with some "internationals" at Masha, a Palestinian West Bank village north of Modi'in that also stood to be divided from much of its lands. It was a kind of Israeli equivalent of Woodstock. "A link was created between people on the margins of Israeli society," Yossi recalled. "Anarchists, punks, gays, and lesbians—nobody had to hide." He acknowledged that the Masha village sheikhs, who were trying to protect their own patriarchal society and conservative mores, were not entirely delighted with the presence of these new arrivals, though they managed to stay put for five months, forging links with local Palestinian leftists.

In the event, the diverse peace campers were unable to stop the bulldozers at Masha or prevent the barrier being built, but they later succeeded in drawing at least some sympathetic attention to themselves from the Israeli mainstream when soldiers shot at them from the other side. During a demonstration at Masha in December 2003, when the protesters were engaged in an action to cut the wire and sabotage the new fence, for the first time an Israeli participant, Gil Na'amati, was shot by army live fire. Na'amati, 22, had himself recently completed three years of military service in the artillery corps. He was hit in both knees and lost dangerous quantities of blood before reaching the hospital. Unlike Dia, he survived. In their defense, the soldiers said they had not realized that Na'amati was Israeli, the implication being that had he been a Palestinian, the incident would not have gained attention, and certainly would not have created any shock. A minor public furor ensued. Na'amati's father, Uri, a regional council head of a group of Negev communities, told Army Radio, "Today they shot my son, tomorrow they'll shoot yours." And while he stressed his support for the security fence, he also defended the legitimacy of protesting against its route, capturing the essence of Israel's eternal grappling with the competing and even conflicting principles of defense and democracy.

Yossi, reveling in his radicalism, said he was "invited in" for a chat by the Shin Bet, the Israeli internal security service, in the spring of 2004. Still a minor, he refused to go. "My father went to sit with them in a café instead. He's more of a security-minded Zionist," he says. "They told him I was the Anarchist ringleader of northwest Jerusalem. Actually we have no hierarchy and no leader, but they can't deal with a non-hierarchical movement. They told my father I was being bugged and followed."

At the age of 18, a healthy Israeli like Yossi would normally be drafted but he told me he had reached an agreement with the army. "They don't want me and I don't want them. They know who I am and I know who they are. We decided together." Instead, he was planning to travel abroad for a while, following the modern Israeli convention, then return for a year of national service doing community work for a little known nonprofit social welfare organization called "Revolution."

The alliance that was forged between Yossi and his comrades, his mother and her bourgeois friends, the retired generals of the Council for Peace and Security, the Israeli-Arab lawyer and the Jewish gardener, the rabbi from Pennsylvania, and the Palestinian farmers, must have been one of the more extraordinary and eclectic coalitions that Israel had ever seen. Yet there was something in it for everyone. The generals offered the anarchists a modicum of respectability and credibility, while the young rebels in turn provided the dovish-minded Israeli establishment with a human bridge to Biddu and Beit Surik.

It was this coalition that raised Dahleh's hopes for a landmark ruling. It is well known, he told me while the case was still on, that Israel's Supreme Court judges are never keen to cast themselves as supreme generals on questions of security. Nor, he noted, do they like to go against the national consensus, which had so far been unquestioningly in favor of the fence project. Now, though, the case showed there was no total consensus, and a new dynamic had been introduced into the "power game" he said he was playing between the government, the court, the Israeli public, and The Hague. This was the first case, Dahleh added, in which the "clients of the wall"—the Israelis in Mevasseret—had joined its "victims," the Palestinians living across the lines.

Even so, the Israeli participation was not without qualms. Gita Dror says she sensed a certain reticence on the Palestinian side, an unwillingness to socialize with the Israelis any more than was necessary. It was always Shai and the other Israeli activists on the phone pushing the Palestinian village representatives for the next meeting, she complains, and never the other way around. Gita wanted them just once to come and say, "We need your help."

Perhaps it was unnatural to try to forge instant friendship between the middle classes of Mevasseret and the "foreign laborers" who used to clean the streets. The Drors also soon realized that unlike them, the villagers were not only opposed to the barrier's route, but were fervently against the construction of any fence at all. Shai says he tried to engage them in dialogue about the logistics of the day after, even offering to organize Israeli volunteers to care for the Palestinians' fruit trees stuck on the Mevasseret side of the fence. The villagers refused.

The anarchists' peace tent didn't last long either. The more conservative Palestinian villagers were far from delighted with the presence of long-haired Israeli youths like Laizer and New Age females in spaghetti-strap tops with their midriffs exposed, smoking illegal substances till the early hours then bunking down. The young Palestinian activists had taken to hanging around the tent, but this was not the kind of coexistence their Palestinian elders had had in mind. Before long, the Israelis were asked to leave.

The day after the peace walk, on May 2, 2004, the judges sat for the last hearing in the case of *Beit Surik vs the State of Israel.* By 9 a.m., formality had already gone to the wind in the Supreme Court as the judges, lawyers, members of the public, and the press all got up and crowded on tiptoes around two 3-D models of the Mevasseret-Beit Surik area, one made by "Bimkom," the Israeli alternative urban planning NGO for the Dahleh team, and another simpler one by the army. The models were complete with miniature houses and colored lines depicting the various routes for the barrier—blue for both the Dahleh and Council for Peace and Security routes, which differed slightly, adding to the confusion; red for the army; and yellow for the small sections the army had already altered.

Tirza took the stand to try to justify the state's route one last time. After him came Yuval Dvir, the reserve general from the Council for Peace and Security, suntanned and sporting a casual blue polo shirt, who made a pragmatic argument based on Israeli interests. "We moved the fence away from the Arab houses," Dvir declared from the stand, "because otherwise every kid could reach out and touch the sensors and set off the alarms without even leaving his home!"

Sara Bartal was there, sitting on the public benches alongside uniformed members of the border police and army. So were Rabbi Ascherman, Shai Dror, and various members of the Council for Peace and Security. Yossi had made a brief appearance too, but had had to leave early. During a recess, Sara explained to an Israeli reporter that "each family in Beit Surik has a small plot of land. They grow wheat, take it home, and grind it. From that they make their bread. We're taking away their bread!" The reporter stuck his microphone closer into her face and asked whether she was not afraid that her son would end up in trouble. "I'm scared of what might happen from our side," she said, uttering words that were strange for Israel's Supreme Court, for a society so proud of its democracy where everybody's brother or neighbor is a soldier. "Our kids stand with nothing. It's the army that has the guns."

"Shouldn't you keep him at home then?" the reporter persisted, confronting her with a question usually reserved for the crying Palestinian mothers of martyrs to the cause. "Listen," she replied softly, "I brought him up to have humanistic values."

Finally, on June 30, 2004, the Supreme Court issued its verdict. The route of the barrier would have to be changed. The judges accepted the state's argument that the barrier was being built for security, not political purposes, and therefore may be constructed inside West Bank territory. But they vetoed six of the eight army land-seizure orders for the fence northwest of Jerusalem, pertaining to 30 kilometers of the 40-kilometer stretch in question. The parts of the barrier that were planned to skirt around Biddu and Beit Surik were sent back to the drawing board. Chief Justice Aharon Barak, in a detailed exposition, ruled that the route that had been proposed by the defense establishment violated international and human rights law, causing disproportionate harm to the local Palestinian population in the name of security.

"Our task is difficult," Justice Barak declared in his eloquent, agonized epilogue. "We are members of Israeli society. Although we are sometimes in an ivory tower, that tower is in the heart of Jerusalem, which is not infrequently hit by ruthless terror. We are aware of the killing and destruction wrought by the terror against the state and its citizens. As any other Israelis, we too recognize the need to defend the country and its citizens against the wounds inflicted by terror. We are aware that in the short term, this judgment will not make the state's struggle against those rising up against it easier. But we are judges. When we sit in judgment, we are subject to judgment. We act according to our best conscience and understanding. Regarding the state's struggle against the terror that rises up against it, we are convinced that at the end of the day, a struggle according to the law will strengthen her power and her spirit. There is no security without law. Satisfying the provisions of the law is an aspect of national security."

The judges then ordered the state to pay the petitioners' court costs to a tune of roughly $5,000.

A triumphant Muhammad Dahleh praised the courage of the court. Dany Tirza called the judgment a "black day" for Israel and suggested that the responsibility for the next suicide bombing would be on the judges' heads. Tirza had effectively been given marching orders to move the rest of the planned barrier as close to the unmentionable Green Line as possible.

A week later, on July 9, the International Court of Justice in The Hague issued its own advisory opinion, ruling unsurprisingly, by 14 judges to one, that "the construction of the wall by Israel in the Occupied Palestinian Territory is contrary to international law." The Hague decision stipulated that all parts of the barrier that fall inside the 1967 territories, including in and around Jerusalem, should be dismantled "forthwith."

As predictable as the outcome was the Israeli establishment's immediate rejection of it. Israeli officials and jurists objected most vocally to the international court's failure to address the context in which the barrier was being built: the plague of Palestinian terror. The only such reference in the whole 64-page document came in Article 116, which stated reservedly, "For its part, Israel has argued that the wall's sole purpose is to enable it effectively to combat terrorist attacks launched from the West Bank." Moreover, the ICJ had rejected Israel's claim of a right to build the barrier in the West Bank on grounds of self-defense, arguing that the U.N. Charter "recognizes the inherent right of self-defense in the case of armed attack by one State against another State." Israel, the ICJ found, "does not claim that the attacks against it are imputable to a foreign state" because Israel exercises control in the "occupied Palestinian territory" from where, by Israel's own account, the threat originates.

The only dissenter was American judge Thomas Buergenthal, who voiced his reservations about the court's "sweeping findings" reached "with regard to the wall as a whole without having before it or seeking to ascertain all relevant facts bearing directly on issues of Israel's legitimate right of self-defense, military necessity, and security needs."

Particularly riling for the Israeli officials was the fact that the president of the ICJ who delivered the verdict was none other than Chinese judge Jiuyong Shi. After all, his country, whose own Great Wall is visible from space, and others that had helped make the case against Israel, such as Sudan, Cuba, and Saudi Arabia, were hardly world champions of human rights themselves.

Prime Minister Ariel Sharon immediately determined that the ICJ decision was "purely political" and ordered the fence builders to follow the rulings of Israel's own Supreme Court, not The Hague. But the Justice Minister, Tommy Lapid, warned that The Hague verdict, though not binding, could constitute a "first step in turning Israel into South Africa," raising the specter of it becoming an increasingly alienated, pariah state. And Attorney General Meni Mazuz issued a report saying that it was "difficult to minimize the negative repercussions" of The Hague decision, adding that it created a "new legal reality for Israel in the international arena that can be used as an excuse or catalyst to take different actions against Israel, including sanctions."

Six months after the verdicts in February 2005, I am sitting in Muhammad Dahleh's law office again. On the second floor of a tastefully renovated old stone house in one of downtown East Jerusalem's more pleasant backstreets, it is a couple of blocks away from the fortress-like Israeli Ministry of Justice building which moved to the commercial Salah al-Din Street once the city was reunified in 1967. Dahleh's desk is piled so high with papers and files that at one point a chunk of them slides off onto the floor. On the walls are

Dahleh's graduation photos and framed certificates, and lining the walls of the corridor outside are newspaper clippings of recent interviews he has given in English, Arabic, and Hebrew. Dressed in a dark suit, white shirt, and striped tie he is warm and friendly, but clearly on a mission.

It is 5:30 in the evening, and the energetic Dahleh, a married father of two young children, is probably only halfway through his day. Since his victory in the Supreme Court, he has not let up. Though the route of the barrier has been quite radically revised in the wake of the June 2004 Supreme Court ruling—in certain areas, notably in the southern West Bank, it has been moved to correspond more or less with the Green Line—Dahleh is still representing Palestinian villages at various points along the route including Shukba, near Qibya, A-Ram north of Jerusalem, and several communities along Highway 443. Most annoyingly for the Israeli establishment, though, he is also back in court on behalf of the villagers of Biddu and Beit Surik. "The army started calling me to show me the new maps in October," he relates. In November and December, military orders were issued to seize the land needed for the construction of the barrier. For legal reasons the seizures, like the fence itself, are defined as temporary though the period is undefined. In January, Dahleh filed a new petition to the Supreme Court, this time in the name of Biddu council, to distinguish it from the Beit Surik case before it.

Dahleh spreads out maps he has acquired from the army, showing the old fence route and the new. The main changes come at the northern end of the revised section, at Beit Lakiya near Modi'in. "They have also made the prison bigger at Beit Surik," Dahleh allows, pointing to where the new route now runs much closer to the Green Line, lying exactly on it at parts and even a jutting a tiny bit over into Israeli territory for topographical reasons at one point near Mevasseret. One of this cluster of West Bank villages, Beit Iksa, is to be placed altogether on the Israeli side of the fence because it looks right over Highway 443, putting Israeli traffic within sniper range and making it too dangerous to leave in Palestinian hands. "There are minor changes by Biddu," Dahleh continues, "but a lot of the village lands are still slated to end up on the other side. We cannot accept such a wall."

In response to the new petition against the state, the defense establishment has noted that if originally it was claimed that some 500 dunams (125 acres) of Beit Surik land was to be seized for the construction of the barrier, and 6,000 dunams (1,500 acres) of its fields and orchards stood to end up on the Israeli side, the revised route required the seizure of 360 dunams (90 acres) for the construction of the barrier and would leave only about 729 dunams (182 acres) of privately owned farmland on the other side. As for Biddu, the defense establishment now notes, only 69 dunams (17.25 acres) of privately owned land will lie across the newly routed barrier, 18 of which contain olive groves and the rest of which are uncultivated, the implication being that this inconvenience to the Palestinians is surely proportionate to Israel's security needs.

Dahleh admits that things are not going too well. The Supreme Court, in a sign of impatience, almost immediately lifted a stop order on work along most of the route northwest of Jerusalem. "Generally, I'm not optimistic. I see what's happening on the ground," Dahleh states glumly. "I see the true face of the occupation every day in my work." Despite the death of Arafat, the election of Abu Mazen, and the dramatic decline in intifada violence, he complains, "it's business as usual. Even more than usual. Under the cover of the international community's optimism, Israel is doing whatever it wants in terms of land confiscation, settlement expansion, and the wall—all the evils, you might say."

I ask Dahleh what he thinks of the Supreme Court's principle of "proportionality"—the need to find the balance between security and human rights as established by the case he brought for Beit Surik. "The Supreme Court is part of the Israeli establishment," he replies. "That's the maximum it could get to, the most it could interfere. Anything else would have meant total confrontation with the government on such hot potatoes as the settlements and annexing land."

This time around, though, Dahleh is surprisingly frank about his real agenda, an ambitious one designed to rock the Israeli justice system's foundations. "The new Biddu case is based more on The Hague," he declares. "I am trying to implement The Hague ruling through the Supreme Court of Israel. I am trying to push the limits." If the Supreme Court were to accept The Hague ruling, essentially barring any construction in the territories Israel occupied in 1967, that would be a huge victory, Dahleh says, though he doubts it will. "If it doesn't, and goes against The Hague," he continues, "that would undermine Israel's democracy and legal system"—thus shamelessly declaring his intention of exploiting the state institutions which nurtured him in order to delegitimize them. "Listen," he responds, when I ask about the ethics of such actions, "if you visit those villages and feel their pain, and weigh that against undermining the system—it's not my job to protect the Supreme Court from being embarrassed at home or abroad."

A precursor came in September 2005 when the Israeli Supreme Court reached a verdict in the case brought by the Association for Civil Rights in Israel on behalf of the Palestinian villages stuck inside the Alfei Menashe enclave. It ruled that the Jewish settlement should remain on the Israeli side of the fence, contrary to the opinion of the International Court of Justice in The Hague, on grounds that Israel was bound to provide security for the Israeli citizens there. But it also accepted ACRI's claim that life for the Palestinian villagers inside the enclave had become intolerable, and the court ordered the state to reexamine alternative routes that would leave the villages out, on the West Bank side of the fence.

Both sides claimed a degree of victory. Alfei Menashe Mayor Hisdai Eliezer confirmed the Palestinians' fears by declaring that the ruling effectively ensured his settlement's de facto annexation to Israel. Only the Palestinian villagers themselves were left confused, unsure about whether they had won or lost. Eighty or ninety percent of the men still earned a living by sneaking illegally into Israel to work. Being on the West Bank side would make that virtually impossible. The villagers' restored dignity would cost them their livelihood.

Dahleh is driven to distraction by the fence and wall. He works his hands and eyes, searching for the words to express the depth of the affront. "I went out with the army today along the Biddu section," he tells me. "They were telling the people if anyone has a specific request regarding their property and the route, to come forward. The people were saying it's not about bypassing one tree or another—they don't want the wall at all. It was crazy. One old man from the village was just sitting on a rock, staring in silence. I know what he was feeling. I come from a village in the Galilee. I have worked the olive harvest. I know about the attachment to the land. I am part of this culture." Israel wants to put the Palestinians in prison, he says, and "not even have to pay for their meals."

Dahleh had not tried approaching his former partners from Mevasseret and the Council for Peace and Security for support this time, recognizing that "It might be easier to push the limits alone." That is because for Palestinians, Israeli democracy stops at the Green Line. The Supreme Court has opened its doors to cases concerning Palestinian residents' rights in the West

Bank and Gaza Strip arising from the occupation, Dahleh says, but "it has not opened its heart or mind. It helps, but sometimes it is even dangerous in that it merely sweetens the pill, not more than this."

Dany Tirza calls Dahleh a lawyer from a small-time East Jerusalem firm who has made an international name for himself on the back of the barrier, and says that he is working directly for the Palestinian Authority. Dahleh denies direct links to the PA, saying that he "represents the villagers," but he acknowledges there is "a common interest." Asked who pays him for the efforts that have taken over his life for the past three years, Dahleh will only say that the Palestinian village councils "get him the money." Dahleh, for his part, accuses Tirza of being "a settler in spirit who symbolizes what this wall is about: the settlement enterprise," charging him with keeping as many settlements on the Israeli side as possible.

Muhammad Dahleh is a one-man walking seam zone. His working of the system shows up both the strength of Israel's democracy and its limits at the same time. Blurring the lines between Israel and Palestine, he embodies the point where the two meet, and the point where they fundamentally part.

6

The Holy Seam

Hidden away behind the Mount of Olives, on the seam between Jerusalem and the Palestinian village of El-Azariya, where the green hills of the capital give way to the Judean desert, there is a rest home for nuns set in a secluded, tranquil garden. The garden has a swimming pool where the nuns can relax in privacy, away from the troubles of the world and from prying eyes. At least they could until the wall went up, part of the "Jerusalem Envelope" security barrier that, once completed, will seal the holy city off from the West Bank. An 8-meter-high section sits right opposite the nuns' garden, across a narrow dirt track. And to the chagrin of the bathing sisters, it includes an equally tall round gray watchtower where Israeli soldiers sit on guard, observing all movement in the area through window slits that together provide a panoramic view. So as to avoid offending the nuns with the possibility of Israeli soldiers observing them out of their habits, the window slits on the convent side have been blacked out.

Dany Tirza points out the blackened windows with vague amusement as we tour the muddy back roads and dirt paths of the Jerusalem seam in his compact silver four-wheel drive. Tirza, the reserve colonel and head of operations for the security fence project, seems more comfortable behind the wheel charting the rough terrain than he does in the rarified atmosphere of the Supreme Court, where he has been appearing to defend the route of his barrier on an almost daily basis of late. Trim and clean shaven, in civilian clothes and with dark hair that is thinning on top, Tirza would not stand out in a crowd. But he turns out to be an engaging guide, something of a raconteur with a story to illustrate almost every point along the way, his soft but confident delivery spiked with a hint of wry humor. He certainly commands the respect of two young soldiers accompanying him, who sit quietly in the back seat of the car.

Tirza has just come from a meeting with the Palestinian mayor of El-Azariya, a village of 16,000 inhabitants that falls just beyond the city boundaries in the West Bank, and will therefore remain outside the wall. El-Azariya is the ancient Bethany where, according to the gospels, Lazarus lived and was resurrected from the dead. Today, a mosque covers Lazarus's tomb, while two churches, one Roman Catholic and the other Greek Orthodox, stand like sentinels on either side. The area between the Mount of Olives and El-Azariya is known as the "monastery district," where 17 Christian holy sites and institutions, each with their own grounds and attached to different denominations and countries, are interspersed with Muslim cemeteries.

For a year, Tirza has been unable to finalize a route here due to the religious and political sensitivities, explaining the many gaps in the wall. To generate some consensus, he called the heads of all the churches to a meeting in a Jerusalem hotel where they came to an agreement on a line that "causes the least damage." When the Muslims got wind of this, rumors started circulating that the Christians had "closed a deal" with Israel, aggravating underlying tensions between the ever-wary members of the two communities. The Palestinian Authority mayor of El-Azariya, a Muslim, heard that trouble was brewing, so Tirza took his maps and went to meet him and other key figures on the other side. He hopes to "close" with them too. "I see it all the time," he says, "when you come down to the people on the ground, there's always a solution," even if it means going centimeter by centimeter, house by house. "By the way," he adds, speaking of both the Muslims and the Christians, "they all want to be on the Israeli side." It befits Jerusalem that an observant, yarmulke-wearing Israeli Jew could play a role in preventing Muslim-Christian strife. Then again, it is Tirza's barrier that was the potential cause of it in the first place.

Walling Jerusalem, one of the most hotly contested religious and political centers on earth, was always going to be a challenge. Any unilateral attempt to physically delineate the city's political boundaries is almost doomed to fail. "It's like walking on eggs," says Tirza, who has been tasked with negotiating this spiritual minefield to build a profanely functional barrier that will keep the terrorists out.

Though only 5 to 6 percent of the 600-kilometer-long security barrier between Israel and the West Bank will in the end consist of concrete wall rather than wire fence, the majority of the 30 kilometers of concrete will be going up around the capital for reasons of both space and security, in parts cutting through densely built Palestinian residential neighborhoods that straddle the Jerusalem seam zone. Though the Jerusalem Envelope is less than half finished by the time I go out for my tour with Tirza in February 2005, massive stretches of gray wall are already visible from prime locations in the center of Jerusalem, coursing along the once-picturesque hills to the east and casting a menacing shadow over the city of gold.

Tirza is casually dressed in a coarse, mustard-colored shirt, dark canvas pants and sturdy brown leather walking shoes that are spotlessly clean. It is always worth treading carefully in Jerusalem, the ancient stomping ground of prophets and kings, and today a volatile powder keg. At the heart sits the Old City fortified by the thick stone walls that the battle-victorious Turkish sultan, Suleiman the Magnificent, started building in 1536. Like a repository of antiquity, it contains the Church of the Holy Sepulcher, the traditional site of Christ's crucifixion and tomb; the Western, or Wailing, Wall, the last remnant of the Second Temple and revered by Jews all over the world; and the Temple Mount / Haram al-Sharif itself. The incendiary nature of the Temple Mount was underlined by Sharon's visit there on September 28, 2000. For three years after that, Jews were barred entry to the site. Once it was reopened, Israeli security officials expressed their concerns that radical opponents of Sharon's disengagement plan might try to derail it by blowing up the mosques on top. And with a strong dose of historic irony, given Sharon's insistence on visiting the Mount in 2000, providing a trigger for the second intifada, in the spring of 2005 the authorities banned four right-wing Knesset members, including two from Sharon's own Likud party, from entering the mosque compound for fear they would spark a third one.

Because of its acute sensitivity and importance to the three great religions, Jerusalem, according to the United Nations Palestine partition plan of 1947, was to become a *corpus separatum*, a separate body to be administered by an international regime. In reality, the U.N. made no efforts on the ground to safeguard the city, and after the 1948 war Jerusalem was split into two halves, with Israel claiming sovereignty in the west and Jordan controlling the Old City and the eastern sector abutting the West Bank. The Jordanians expelled all the Jews who had remained inside the Jewish Quarter of the Old City during the hostilities, while Palestinians abandoned their homes in the west of the city and were forbidden by Israel to return. Those houses were taken over by the Israeli Custodian of Absentee Property and leased or sold to the government housing agency for use by needy Jewish immigrants, social institutions, and senior employees of the state.

After 1948, the eastern and western halves were divided by concrete walls that ran across roads, barbed wire fences, barriers of various shapes and sizes, and swathes of empty no-man's-land. Under the armistice agreement with Jordan in 1949, Israel retained a small enclave on Mount Scopus in the northeast corner of the city containing the old Hebrew University campus and the original Hadassah hospital, but entry was limited to a set number of policemen. Despite the terms of the agreement, Jews were denied access to the Western Wall to pray.

All this was to change. The emotional peak of Israel's victory in the 1967 war came at 10 a.m. on June 7, when the paratroopers seized control of the Old City and General Motta Gur's voice crackled over the radio announcing that "Temple Mount is in our hands." The walls and barbed wire came down between the east and the west and in the euphoric days following the conquest, a special committee of Israel's ministers sat and mapped out expanded municipal boundaries for the newly liberated, united city amid pledges that it would never be divided again. The old Green Line, the pre-1967 border that had run through the heart of the city, had left the western Jewish sector vulnerable to Jordanian sniper fire. The guiding principle in redrawing the capital's boundaries was that even in the event of a peace deal involving an Israeli withdrawal from the West Bank, the high ground around Jerusalem would never fall into enemy hands again. The new city limits extended to the outskirts of El-Azariya and neighboring Abu Dis in the east and to the outer edge of the village of Sur Baher in the south. To the north, the limits were originally meant to end at Mount Scopus and French Hill, but Mayor Teddy Kollek insisted that the municipal boundary should take in the small airstrip at Atarot. That meant also incorporating Kafr Aqab, the village on the hill overlooking the runway, on the approach to Ramallah.

In 1967 Israel effectively annexed the eastern half and extended Jerusalem residency rights, though not automatic citizenship, to the 78,000 Palestinians who fell within the new city limits, and who then made up about a quarter of the capital's population. Since then the Palestinians of East Jerusalem have had a special status, different from that of the residents of the West Bank. They hold blue identity cards, like Israelis, allowing them free movement throughout the country and making them eligible for national insurance and other social benefits. They have the right to vote in Jerusalem city council elections—which they traditionally boycott, in protest against East Jerusalem's occupation—but they cannot vote for the Knesset.

Soon after the war, Israel also set about building a dozen huge Jewish suburbs on the newly won high ground, neighborhoods such as Gilo in the south, East Talpiot in the southeast, and Pisgat Ze'ev in the far north, all wedged between the outlying Arab suburbs and creating a Jewish-Palestinian patchwork with the aim of obliterating the pre-1967 line and making it impossible to divide the city between east and west again. In 1980, the Knesset passed the Basic Law on Jerusalem officially extending Israeli jurisdiction to the eastern half of the city, confirming the annexation in the face of international nonrecognition.

Today the Palestinian residents of Jerusalem number some 250,000, and constitute almost a third of the city's population. Around 180,000 Jewish residents live in the new neighborhoods east of the old border—the area the Palestinians demand as the capital of any future state. Nobody conceives of the new neighborhoods ever being removed, but Israel's demographic reshaping of the city map has been only partially successful in laying the groundwork for the preservation of Jerusalem as an eternally united capital. While it is no longer realistic to talk about dividing the city along the old Green Line, it is generally assumed that if there is ever an Israeli-Palestinian permanent settlement, Jerusalem will have to be shared. Most peace initiatives, including the Clinton proposals at Camp David, now focus on a mosaiclike principle whereby the Arab neighborhoods would be ruled by the Palestinians, and the Jewish ones by Israel, with roads, bridges, and tunnels providing links and national contiguity. Control over the Jewish, Muslim, Christian, and Armenian quarters of the Old City would also likely be split between the parties. No solution acceptable to the two sides has yet been found for the issue of sovereignty over Temple Mount.

Tirza's Jerusalem seam tour starts in the Jewish neighborhood of Gilo on a windy outcrop overlooking Beit Jalla, the Aida refugee camp, and Bethlehem in the West Bank. Behind us is another gray watchtower with a commanding view placed on this southernmost tip of Jerusalem, and a small orchard of olive trees. Tirza, who is intimate with every detail along the barrier route, points out the two Arab houses on the edge of Gilo to which most of the trees belong. "To us the olive tree symbolizes peace; to them, *sumud*," he remarks pointedly, referring to the Palestinian ideal of steadfastness on the land. A section of security fence cuts through the valley directly below us before coming to an abrupt stop at another disputed area, near Rachel's Tomb, a once-charming domed Jewish pilgrimage site on the Jerusalem-Bethlehem road, now obscured by hideous concrete fortifications.

In the early months of the Al-Aqsa intifada, Palestinian snipers from the Aida camp were in the habit of taking over houses and rooftops in Beit Jalla, formerly a quaint and prosperous Christian village, and would fire into Gilo, a distance of 700 meters away. A border policeman was critically injured and several residents were also wounded as a result of the random shooting. Neighboring Bethlehem, the cradle of Christianity, is now three-quarters Muslim, most of the Christian population having migrated abroad over the decades. Caught between the militants from the camp and the Israeli army retaliation, many of the last Christians of Beit Jalla packed their suitcases as well, and left with no intention of returning.

Though Beit Jalla was the responsibility of the Palestinian Authority, the PA did hardly anything to prevent the sniper fire, forcing Israel to take measures of its own. "First we spoke to the PA, then we put two tanks here, and in the end we had to take over Beit Jalla," Tirza recounts, describing the efforts to bring the shooting to a halt. Should the shooting resume again, the wire fence below us will do nothing to prevent it. A row of low concrete panels have been placed further up the hill behind us, to shield Gilo's residents as they walk in the streets as well as to protect a nearby kindergarten. Students have painted the Gilo side of the blocks with scenes of rolling hills. In another measure against the gunmen, the southern-facing windows of apartment buildings on the neighborhood's edge have been fitted with bulletproof glass.

The purpose of the fence is to stop the human bombs that turned Jerusalem into a capital of death during the intifada. The walk from Beit Jalla to Gilo takes just seven minutes, Tirza says, and to illustrate the ease with which infiltrators have so far been able to enter the city from the West Bank he describes an incident in June 2002. On the night of June 17, two young Palestinian men took a taxi from Bethlehem's Deheisheh camp, also visible from where we are standing, to Aida, where they met a contact who used to work in a Jerusalem restaurant. The contact gave out instructions and handed over two bombs. In the morning, the pair crossed the valley and climbed up this slope toward Gilo. As they were walking, an army jeep passed by. One took fright and ran back into the West Bank. The other boarded a crowded 32A bus at a stop along the main road. A few seconds later, at 7:50 a.m., he blew himself up, killing 19 passengers. Seventeen of them were residents of Gilo, including a 15-year-old and an 11-year-old on their way to school.

I had been driving my own son to a school nearby when the bomb went off. Within minutes, ambulances were screaming past us on the road. Half an hour later, when I went back to the scene of the attack, the bodies were lined up along the roadside in black bags, awaiting a visit by Prime Minister Ariel Sharon. The bus was a burnt-out hulk of twisted metal with most of its roof blown off. A van directly in front of it had stopped in its tracks, its windows blown out and its seats littered with shards of glass, traces of blood, and debris from the bomb itself—the nails, bolts and ball bearings that had been packed around the device to maximize the damage. There were two schoolbags left by the driver's seat.

During the four years of intifada, terrorists like this one struck all over Jerusalem, carrying out some 90 attacks. Over 30 of them were suicide bombings targeting the city's crowded buses, shopping centers, bars, and cafés. One bomb left in a bag in the Frank Sinatra cafeteria on the Hebrew University's Mount Scopus campus, reopened after 1967, killed nine in the summer of 2002. A suicide bomber who pushed his way past the guard at the door of the elegantly glass-fronted Café Hillel on Jerusalem's fashionable Emek Refaim Street in September 2003 killed seven. Among the dead were Dr. David Appelbaum, 51, who headed the emergency room at Jerusalem's Shaare Zedek hospital and his 20-year-old daughter Nava. She had been due to marry the next day.

Despite the carnage, the Israeli project to seal off the capital has been marked by particular sluggishness, with pressure groups, foreign interventions, and court injunctions stopping the bulldozers almost every step of the way. Following the "tunnel riots" of May 1996 and the outbreak of the Al-Aqsa intifada in late 2000, the Israeli authorities are themselves keenly aware that given the religious and political tensions in the capital, any change in its delicate status quo is liable to cause a conflagration. Tirza acknowledges that the Jerusalem episode of the barrier project has been the most problematic. "Nobody wanted to touch it," he says.

8. *The suicide bombers proved a particularly potent weapon. They posed an existential threat to the Israeli way of life: The remains of the bus blown up near Gilo in June 2002, killing 19 passengers. Credit: Avi Ohayon, Israel Government Press Office.*

With the Green Line no longer relevant in the capital, Israel essentially had three options in planning the route of the Jerusalem Envelope. None offered a perfect solution. One possibility was to have the barrier on demographic lines, weaving between the Jewish and Arab neighborhoods of the capital, keeping the Jews "in" and the Palestinians "out." This was rejected on legal grounds. "Although division along demographic lines might be right for a political solution," Tirza posits, "it cannot be right for this. I cannot differentiate between Jews and Arabs. A blue ID is a blue ID."

Alternatively, the barrier could have swept out into the West Bank and enveloped all the Arab suburbs that are symbiotically attached to Jerusalem—villages such as El-Azariya, Abu Dis, and Al-Ram that in Jordanian times were considered part of the Jerusalem district, but fell beyond the new city limits after 1967. Aside from avoiding severing these populous suburbs from the capital, this option would also have solved the problem of tens of thousands of Jerusalem Palestinians who have moved to these outlying areas over the years in search of cheaper housing, but who want to maintain their residency rights and lives in the city. Tirza says it was rejected because it would have cut tens of thousands of West Bank Palestinians off from the West Bank. It would also have effectively annexed them to the Arab population of the capital, with the added security risk that would have entailed, and defeating the object of the barrier in many Israelis' eyes.

The third option, the one chosen, was to build the barrier more or less along the expanded municipal boundary—more or less, says Tirza, "because the reality is more complicated than the maps."

A classic example of this complex reality has played out in Sur Baher, a village of blue card-holding Palestinian Jerusalemites in the southern rolling hills opposite Bethlehem in the West Bank. The post-1967 city limits encompassed Sur Baher, though for many years the boundary remained largely academic and invisible, nothing more than a line on a map. On the ground, there was nothing to mark the border where Jerusalem ended and the West Bank began other than the odd yellow fire hydrant placed by City Hall. With the separation fence now set to run along it like a steel vice, however, it became apparent that the village had in the meantime outgrown its official boundaries. In the 1970s, a fifth of Sur Baher's lands were expropriated for the new Jewish neighborhood of East Talpiot. Land inside the village became scarce and building permits from the municipality were hard to come by, so residents started constructing homes to accommodate their growing needs on what was left of their ancestral lands across the municipal border, in the valleys of Wadi al-Ain and Wadi al-Humus, pastoral areas rich with mature olive trees that feel far from the urban bustle.

By the time the bulldozers arrived to prepare the ground, there were 70 buildings housing some 150 Sur Baher families in these valleys, all slated to fall outside the barrier and be cut off from work, schools, stores, close relatives, and friends in the main part of Sur Baher, and indeed, from the rest of Jerusalem. Residents of Sur Baher mounted a year-long legal campaign against the Defense Ministry, demanding that the fence route be moved a few hundred meters back into the West Bank territory so that the two valleys would remain joined to the village. They lost.

I visited Sur Baher one fall morning and stood above Wadi al-Ain as a bulldozer flattened and re-flattened the same patch of earth, preparing the ground for the approaching fence. Two dozen olive trees uprooted along the way had been unceremoniously replanted in a patch of fresh soil out of the bulldozer's path. Sticking out tenuously at odd angles, they looked like they had not yet decided whether to take to their new environment or not. A column of women and children suddenly appeared from the valley, mostly in conservative Muslim garb, demonstrating against the approaching fence and chanting slogans like *Allahu Akbar* (God is Great). A jeep full of armed border police rushed up to observe the proceedings while a score of children clambered up onto the bulldozer that had been stopped but left with its engine running to pose for a couple of Palestinian press photographers who had shown up. Miraculously, nobody was hurt and the demonstrators marched off, chanting their slogans as they went.

Next a bearded young man whose dark eyebrows met in the middle came huffing and puffing up the hill, sweating profusely from under his baseball cap, his eyes bulging with fury or despair. He introduced himself as Salah Dabbash, a native of Sur Baher. The barrier was about to ruin his life. Dabbash lived up in the main part of Sur Baher, well within the Jerusalem limits, but two of his seven brothers, his parents, his land, and his olive trees were all in Wadi al-Ain. After an acquaintance of a few minutes, however, he got around to articulating the real source of his angst: Namely, that he had a wife with two children at home in Sur Baher, on what would be one side of the fence, and another wife pregnant with her fourth on the other.

Once the barrier starts closing in, the residents of Wadi al-Ain and Wadi al-Humus will either have to rely on gates in the fence or move back into Sur

Baher. In other areas where the Jerusalem Envelope divides East Jerusalem Palestinians from those on the West Bank, countless other such problems arise. This, together with the decades of Jewish building across the 1967 lines, leads Daniel Seidemann, a West Jerusalem lawyer who often represents Palestinians from the east, to conclude that there is simply "no appropriate route" in Jerusalem's case. He calls the insistence on building the barrier on the municipal boundary the "Olmert principle," alluding to Ehud Olmert, the influential Likud politician and former mayor of Jerusalem. Olmert obviously did not want a barrier that added more Palestinians to the population of the eternal Jewish capital. But he also rejected any territorial concessions to the Palestinian Authority, determined to maintain every inch of Jerusalem's integrity and to prevent any Clinton-like division of the city in the future.

But Olmert's principle was already broken in the earliest stages of the Jerusalem Envelope project. One of the first parts of the barrier to go up around the capital was a short section in the north, skirting the runway of the tiny Atarot Airport which had been out of use since the outbreak of violence in 2000. The village of Kafr Aqab, home to some 20,000 blue ID-holding Palestinians and a tax-paying part of municipal Jerusalem, landed out of the fence on the insistence of the army because of its proximity to the Qalandia refugee camp and Ramallah, and the security problems that including the village would pose. Adding to the confusion was Olmert himself, who in the meantime became an outspoken supporter of Sharon's disengagement plan, and suggested that perhaps Israel did not need to keep all the populous Palestinian neighborhoods that fall within the current city limits as part of its eternal capital after all. He named Sur Baher as one in particular that would not be missed.

The next stop on the Tirza tour is Checkpoint 300, the crossing point between Jerusalem and Bethlehem, where the construction of a vast new passenger terminal is underway to regulate the traffic between the two cities once the barrier is complete. In peaceful times, some half a million Christian pilgrims visit the Holy Land in a year. To get from Jerusalem to Bethlehem's Manger Square, a few kilometers away, they will now have to pass through a gate in a colossal 9.5-meter-high concrete wall that is almost Herodian in scale. Beyond it lies the Shepherds' Field of Beit Sahur, where, according to

Christian tradition, the Christmas angel appeared to the shepherds keeping the night watch and sang of peace on earth and good will to all men.

In an apparent attempt to soften the appalling sight before us, Tirza explains how everything possible has been done to make this $2 million terminal user-friendly for the Palestinian permit holders and tourists who will pass through. The inspection area will be roofed and air-conditioned. Advanced technology will be used to detect explosives, avoiding direct contact between the Israeli supervisors and the people being checked. "Dogs are best" at detecting explosives, Tirza remarks, "but that's very inhumane." The terminal will have the capacity to process some 1,500 people per hour. There are also plans to replace the soldiers who ordinarily control the checkpoints and crossings with a civilian force in an effort to lower the friction and provide a higher level of service, "just like in the airport," Tirza says.

A solid wall is deemed necessary here to prevent Palestinian snipers from firing into the terminal. The height compensates for the lack of breadth—it takes time to scale nine meters, and more time to get down again, giving the army the opportunity to spot would-be infiltrators. In addition to the cylindrical watchtowers, a 45-meter-high metal pylon with cameras on top, one of several going up on the outskirts of Jerusalem, will survey a radius of eight kilometers. Altogether there will be 11 crossings between Jerusalem and the West Bank to accommodate the tens of thousands that will need to make the trip each day. An even larger terminal is going up at Qalandia, at the entrance to Ramallah.

In a further attempt to camouflage the bleak look of the security facility, the terminal buildings have been painted in light pastels. "We put a lot of thought into this," Tirza says. The sidewalks are paved with decorative small bricks made by the Ackerstein cement company, the same one that produces the pillbox guard towers and the slabs for the wall. Tirza says Ackerstein won the contract for Jerusalem on condition that it continued molding the wall panels in its factory in Yeruham, a poor development town in the south.

The aesthetics of the Jerusalem wall are obviously a cause of concern to Tirza, particularly since the most accessible part, on top of the Mount of Olives near Abu Dis, has become a popular tour bus stop. There might be a joint Israeli-Palestinian children's project to paint it, Tirza says, which he would encourage and even help fund. There had been an idea to cover the wall with a facing of Jerusalem stone, the dolomite limestone that characterizes the capital and gives it its light golden hue, but tests showed that the textured surface would be too easy to climb. On a remote dirt track on the seam near El-Azariya, there is a section of wall where experiments have been made with different facings. It appears that none has been found suitable yet.

Continuing the tour along the southeast perimeter of the city, we arrive at Ras Mukaber, a lookout point above the Arab village of Jabal Mukaber offering a stunning view of the Mount of Olives and Mount Scopus, the Old City, and the glistening Dome of the Rock. When the Jews could not get to the Old City, Tirza relates, they would stand here and pray. "I think it's a marvelous place, amazing," he says, breathing in the startling beauty and history of the whole area, known as the "holy basin," which is stretched out before us.

To the right is Abu Dis, the native village of Palestinian Authority prime minister Ahmed Qurei, better known as Abu Ala, which some Israeli negotiators once touted as a possible compromise location for the capital of the Palestinian state and where the Palestinians were constructing a building to house their parliament. Gray wall now separates the West Bank village from Jerusalem, the unfinished parliament building peeping over it. Alongside the parliament is the main campus of Al-Quds University, whose soccer pitch became the focus of international attention for a while in the fall of 2003 after Al-Quds president Sari Nusseibeh caught on to the fact that the separation wall was planned to run right through it. The university is partly built on land that was once Jewish owned, Tirza explains, and some of it, including the soccer pitch, technically falls inside Jerusalem. "No one bothered before," Tirza continues, "but when we came to build the wall, the pitch was the best place for us. It was flat."

Nusseibeh was having none of it. He activated his considerable contacts and launched an international campaign, getting as far as Condoleeza Rice, then America's National Security Advisor. Tirza, taken aback by the international storm the soccer pitch was causing, agreed to meet with Nusseibeh— again, in a Jerusalem hotel—to sort out an acceptable route for the barrier around the campus. The Israeli colonel was surprised when the U.S. consul in Jerusalem walked in on the meeting, indicating the interest the U.S. took and the influence Nusseibeh had. In the end, the soccer pitch was saved.

Less easy to resolve is the controversy looming over the area beyond El-Azariya and Abu Dis, where the beige hills of the Judean desert are dotted with the red-roofed Jewish settlements of the Ma'aleh Adumim bloc. Ariel Sharon has pledged to include the city of Ma'aleh Adumim and its satellites, with a population of around 30,000, inside the barrier. In early 2005 it also became public knowledge that he had given the go-ahead for construction of 3,500 new housing units in an empty expanse between Ma'aleh Adumim and the capital, reviving a long-standing Israeli plan to physically join the two. Both the fence route and the building plans met strident opposition from the American government, Washington having always supported the Palestinian position that any attempts to join Ma'aleh Adumim to Jerusalem would violate the territorial contiguity of the West Bank, almost severing the northern half from the south. The temporary solution, as with Ariel, is to leave a gap in the barrier several kilometers wide. Tirza happily points out some biblical connections to the desert area having to do with the animal sacrifices made in the Temple days, but he becomes uncharacteristically noncommunicative, even curt, when I broach the subject of his own home in Kfar Adumim, one of the smaller settlements in the bloc.

As we continue through the Arab neighborhoods of the Kidron Valley along steep, potholed roads, Tirza points out two houses on the edge of Abu Dis, a few meters inside the separation wall, that were taken over in the summer of 2004 by radical Jewish nationalists, the first arrivals in a settlement project called Kidmat Zion (East of Zion). On the slopes of the Mount of Olives itself, not far from the ancient Jewish graveyard in the Arab neighborhood of Ras al-Amud, another 37 Jewish families live in a large purpose-built apartment complex funded by American Jewish casino tycoon Irving Moskowitz, a patron of the right-wing associations dedicated to Jewish settlement in the Arab parts of East Jerusalem. In the Arab neighborhood of Silwan down below, just south of the Old City walls, several more Jewish families are living in homes that were acquired from their Arab occupants secretly and by sometimes questionable means. In one case reported in a local Jerusalem newspaper, a Silwan home was purchased from the Palestinian owner while he was allegedly drunk. Dozens more Jews live in the Muslim Quarter of the Old City, and there are grandiose plans for more projects, including one already being marketed as "Zion View," an exclusive gated Jewish complex abutting Jabal Mukaber.

The trend of Jewish families settling in Arab areas of East Jerusalem was started in the early 1990s with the aim of placing further obstacles before any political solution involving a redivision of the city in the future. Tirza, a more moderate settler, calls it "disorder." The guiding principle of keeping the peace in Jerusalem and maintaining the city's delicate equilibrium has always been one of separate quarters. Arabs would live among Arabs, and Jews would live among Jews, in neighborhoods that catered to the customs and lifestyles of each population, with each having its own schools, community centers, and places of worship. Teddy Kollek, the legendary mayor who was first elected in 1965 and stayed in office for 28 years, was a strong adherent of the principle, seeing in it the seeds of a possible political solution for the capital based on a borough system of neighborhood autonomy. In later years peace negotiators took the notion further, floating ideas of shared sovereignty in the capital split along similar lines.

This is not a vision that has been shared by Ariel Sharon, who has frequently declared his commitment to an eternally united Jerusalem under Israeli sovereignty. Rather, some of the clues of who encouraged the "disorder" lead straight back to him. The settlers' acquisition of houses in Arab neighborhoods beyond the Old City walls started in early 1992, when two buildings were seized in the middle of the night by Jewish activists in Silwan. It transpired that the government had claimed the houses by a twisted and draconian application of an old law that allowed for the transfer of property of East Jerusalem Palestinians who were not in the city on June 28, 1967, to the state's Custodian of Absentee Property. The custodian admitted he had been taking his orders for a while from the Israel Lands Authority, then under the aegis of the Housing Ministry, and the settlers had leased the buildings from the government housing agency Amidar. Unsurprisingly, the housing minister at the time was Ariel Sharon. Already in 1987, as a demonstrative act, Sharon himself had rented an apartment in the Muslim Quarter of the Old City from a radical Jerusalem settlement organization. The considerable cost of guarding the apartment still comes from public funds, though Sharon has rarely set foot in the place since.

Jerusalem has a tendency for contradictions. So while the Palestinian leadership demands the eastern half as the capital of its future state, the Palestinian inhabitants themselves, wary of losing the benefits that come along with Jerusalem residency and a blue identity card, prefer to remain on the Israeli side of the fence. It was therefore entirely predictable that once the separation bulldozers got to work, thousands of East Jerusalem Palestinians who had moved outside the municipal boundaries over the years to the cheaper suburbs around the periphery would seek to move back in. Danny Seidemann warned

9. *While the Palestinian leadership demands East Jerusalem as the capital of its future state, the Palestinian inhabitants prefer to remain on the Israeli side of the fence: Palestinian residents climbing through a gap in the temporary barrier at Abu Dis, January 2004. Credit: Moshe Milner, Israel Government Press Office.*

from the start that Jerusalem would soon be "bursting at the seams." Other Jewish critics, such as leftist academic Menahem Klein and researchers at the Jerusalem Institute for Israel Studies, a prestigious think tank in the capital, warned of the economic boomerang effect of cutting East Jerusalem off from its metropolitan hinterland in the West Bank. A population explosion in the already crowded neighborhoods in the eastern half of the city would only add to the rampant poverty and crime, it was argued, hardly contributing to Israel's security.

While East Jerusalem's Palestinians did not participate in the Al-Aqsa intifada for the most part, beyond the opening days, there have been exceptions. One would-be suicide bomber who tried to blow himself up in the capital's Café Caffit came from Jabal Mukaber. The attack was thwarted by a young waiter who pushed the bomber out the door and wrestled him to the ground after his bomb switch malfunctioned. A Hamas cell from Silwan organized the Hebrew University bombing and had reportedly been plotting to get a Palestinian kitchen worker to poison diners at a popular downtown café. An Islamic Jihad cell discovered in Sur Baher had supposedly planned to shoot down the prime minister's helicopter over Jerusalem, and two East Jerusalem brothers got seven life terms for providing a suicide bomber with an explosive belt and transporting him to Café Hillel.

Mostly, though, the Palestinians of the city kept out of trouble and stood by, feeling increasingly abandoned to their fate as Israel plugged ahead with the de facto amputation of East Jerusalem from the West Bank. Yasser Arafat had repeatedly threatened to lead a million martyrs on the road to Jerusalem and pledged to defend the mosques of the future Palestinian capital. Yet in another sign of failure, as the walls closed in, the silence from the PA was deafening. On the first day of the hearings against the barrier at The Hague, in February 2004, Prime Minister Abu Ala had delivered a rousing speech at a demonstration behind the wall in Abu Dis. Immediately afterwards, when the protests degenerated into rioting and clashes with the Israeli security forces, I took refuge in Abu Ala's office for over an hour until things calmed down enough for me to be able to extricate my car and drive back home. It was peaceful in the prime minister's office: During the time I sat there with him, the phone on his desk hardly rang.

The death of the popular and charismatic Faisal Husseini, the son of the 1948 Palestinian militia commander Abd al-Qader al-Husseini, in 2001 had left Jerusalem's Palestinians bereft of any strong political leadership or representation. Sari Nusseibeh was appointed to replace Husseini in an official capacity within the PLO, but in practice he kept a low profile. Some saw it as indicative that his campaign against the wall was largely limited to the bit that threatened to cut off his soccer pitch.

The ever-pragmatic Nusseibeh, sitting in a protest tent at the Abu Dis campus days before he reached his agreement with Tirza, explained to me that he was merely dealing in the art of the possible. "We are not superpowers," he said. "Nobody has any illusions about stopping this wall from being built. All we can do is to try to minimize the damage. When the bulldozer is coming, all you can do is get out of its ruinous path." Nusseibeh blamed the PA leaders in Ramallah for not having done enough as Jerusalem was being taken away from under their very noses and the borders of the expanded Israeli capital were being cast in concrete. "I think they woke up too late," he said. "People have been left to their own devices. Each neighborhood and village has had to get its own lawyer."

There is little doubt about the national identity of Pisgat Ze'ev, a soullessly modern neighborhood spread over several hills in the north of Jerusalem on the way to Ramallah. The roads have names like Moshe Dayan Boulevard, Air Force Way, The Gunner, The Sixth Battalion, and The Scout, all an urban paean to the glory of military conquest. This is the capital's newest and fastest-growing Jewish neighborhood in a far-flung corner well over the 1967 lines. It started going up in the early 1990s, and now, a decade or so later, is home to over 40,000.

A few blocks from the Mr. Cheap supermarket, in a side street named for another heroic battalion, Sami and Suzanne (not their real names), a retired couple in their late 60s, quietly moved in to a small ground-floor apartment in February 2005. A pair of homely grandparents living on an Israeli state pension, they appear harmless enough and can hardly be classed as subversive. The evening I meet them, Sami is sitting in slippers and a dressing gown watching light entertainment on TV while Suzanne clucks over her grown son, Michael, making sure he eats enough at the tiny kitchen table. But their very presence here is another example of what Tirza might term disorder. For unlike all the other residents in the block they are not Jewish. They are

Christian and Palestinian, pioneers of a new trend afoot in the capital, a still marginal but ironic and politically significant process of settlement-in-reverse.

As the separation walls and fences started going up around Jerusalem, the predictions about thousands of Palestinian Jerusalem ID cardholders streaming back into the capital soon proved true. Hard numbers were difficult to come by since Palestinians who had left the city limits in the first place tended to keep their moves off the books for fear of losing their Jerusalem residency rights. According to anecdotal evidence, however, once the concrete barrier started going up along the middle of the Jerusalem-Ramallah road in the north of the capital by Al-Ram, a moving van would cross into the city every half an hour, carrying Palestinians' household goods to the western side of the wall. The Palestinian neighborhoods inside Jerusalem, particularly those in the north such as Beit Hanina, quickly became crowded while property prices shot up with demand.

There had been talk of a trickle of Palestinian families opting for nearby Pisgat Ze'ev instead, since it offered more spacious accommodation at a better price, and incomparably better municipal services to boot. Rumor had it that Muhammad Dahleh, the maverick Palestinian Israeli lawyer, was encouraging the trend. He himself had made a point of purchasing a home in the Jewish half of the Abu Tor neighborhood which straddles the 1967 line. Since the newcomers to Pisgat Ze'ev shunned media exposure, however, the story seemed more like an urban legend—until a friend put me in touch with "Michael."

Michael is not his real name either. Like his parents, Sami and Suzanne, he lives on the edges of Israeli and Palestinian society and prefers to keep his head down in both. "The Jews and the Muslims have their conflict," he explains when I ask who or what he is afraid of. "As Christians, we are with neither. We are small in number and weak. Everyone is on our case anyway, so why give them any extra excuse?" I first meet Michael at the small business he runs in Mahaneh Yehuda, the colorful Jewish market area of West Jerusalem filled with produce stalls known for low prices and crowds, the latter having historically made it a prime target for terrorist bombings. It is a stronghold of the capital's Jewish working class, Sephardic immigrants from Arab countries like Morocco and Iraq who traditionally vote Likud. Michael speaks about "the Arabs" in a derogatory manner, the way some of his more bigoted Jewish customers might.

To the Jews, of course, he is an Arab himself. In a way Michael is like a composite character, a flesh and blood embodiment of Jerusalem's cultural, national, and religious kaleidoscope. His parents, Israeli Arabs who hail from Nazareth in the Galilee, came to live in Jerusalem, on the Israeli side, in 1957. They moved from Jewish neighborhood to Jewish neighborhood until they settled in an ultra-Orthodox area not far from the wall that then separated the Israeli side of the city from the Jordanian-held east. They remained there after the reunification of the city in 1967, while Sami worked for 32 years as a jack-of-all-trades for a large Israeli company. As the children became young adults, Sami wanted to provide more space so that the family could stay together, in traditional Arab style. In 1989, he took all his savings and capital from the sale of a property in Nazareth and bought a plot of land in Al-Ram, where he built a family compound including a ground-floor apartment for himself and Suzanne and two spacious apartments upstairs, one for each of his sons. A daughter who was already married had previously moved to Al-Ram and lives in a large house on an adjacent plot. In 1990, Michael married a Christian Palestinian girl from Beit Hanina, and once the new building was finished they relocated to Al-Ram.

An unattractive conglomeration of houses and apartment blocks with a shopping street down the middle, Al-Ram falls just beyond the Jerusalem city limits in the West Bank. The city boundary—and now an 8-meter-high concrete wall—runs right up the middle of the main road bordering the Palestinian neighborhood. Of Al-Ram's estimated population of 60,000, about half are thought to hold Jerusalem ID cards. Only a tiny minority of Al-Ram's residents, perhaps a quarter of a percent, are Christians, says Michael, adding that the vast majority are "Hebronites"—Muslim Palestinians who migrated to Jerusalem from the Hebron area in decades past, commercial types who have the reputation of being less sophisticated and less cosmopolitan than the city's native Palestinian aristocracy.

Back in 1990, there were no checkpoints or physical obstacles between Ramallah and Jerusalem at all. Jammed between the two, Al-Ram offered slightly cheaper housing than the established Arab neighborhoods of East Jerusalem further south along the main road. Michael and his family did not think twice. With the outbreak of the intifada, however, an army road block went up at the entrance to Al-Ram on the Jerusalem-Ramallah road, controlling all traffic in and out of the capital and causing Michael delays of an hour or more on his way to work. Getting to the Catholic church and community center in nearby Beit Hanina also turned into a lengthy business, as did getting his four young children to and from their French Catholic school. Once the wall around Al-Ram has been completed, the only way into Jerusalem will be through the notoriously chaotic Qalandia checkpoint. Israel is planning to turn it into a modern terminal with an even bigger capacity than the one at the entrance to Bethlehem. But with many thousands of Palestinians expected to need to pass through Qalandia every day, nobody can say yet how it will work.

Michael is dressed fashionably in black, his long dark hair pulled back in a pigtail, when I go to his store in a small street off the main Mahane Yehuda market. There is a dollar bill stuck on the wall that a religious Jewish customer once brought him for luck from the late Lubavitch rebbe, a revered rabbi in New York. "It hasn't worked," Michael notes. Since the intifada, a lot of his Jewish customers have stopped coming in. Indeed, during the hour we sit talking on a weekday afternoon, nobody enters the store.

A few days later, on a Friday afternoon, the eve of the Jewish Sabbath when the market closes down, Michael finishes work early and we meet in Al-Ram. We tour the nearly deserted streets as he points out the closed-up houses and abandoned buildings left behind by the hundreds, if not thousands, of families who have moved back into the city. A supermarket on the main Jerusalem-Ramallah road, now facing the blank wall, is boarded up, its windows broken. Unfinished apartment buildings, built in the post-Oslo boom, look half derelict, their owners unable to sell or rent the properties out. Many businesses inside Al-Ram are shuttered up as well. Only a few grocery stores, butcher shops, and a couple of hair salons seem to be still open. Michael assures me that before the wall, at this time on a Friday, the streets would have been teeming.

Down a narrow alleyway off Al-Ram's shopping street, just wide enough for a car to pass, is Michael's family compound, a large two-story building faced in Jerusalem stone. An electric gate opens onto a driveway with covered parking of which his father, Sami, is particularly proud. A minaret rises up over a rooftop a block away. Sami and Suzanne's ground-floor apartment remains just as they left it, with icons and crosses on the wall, a tapestry clock embroidered with the legend "God bless our home," over stuffed couches with richly colored striped fabric, and a spacious and luxurious cherry wood kitchen.

The stairs up to Michael's apartment are white marble with black trim. Inside, his wife Rula, a petite woman in skin-tight jeans and pointed stiletto boots, is sitting at the kitchen table smoking a narghile with her mother-in-law Suzanne, who comes every Friday to cook dinner, and the household help. Sami is watching TV as his grandchildren scamper around. It is a comfortable nest, furnished in Western style. Michael stresses the investment he has made in his no-expense-spared home, and repeatedly mentions the "mini central" air-conditioning system he has put in. All of this has a lot to do with why he and Rula are in no hurry to leave. For one thing, they say, it is impossible to sell anything in Al-Ram nowadays at a decent price. Renting the apartment out is not an option either since there is no law enforcement here by either Israel or the Palestinian Authority, making it impossible to get tenants out. What's more, Rula has a senior position in a company in Al-Ram that she would probably have to give up if they moved to the other side of the wall. In the meantime, they have decided to sit tight.

"All my friends are asking what we are waiting for," says Rula. "They say 'Pack your things and move back.' Of course I'm afraid about what might happen, but I want to wait until the very last minute. Maybe something will change and the wall won't get finished. Or maybe the Qalandia terminal won't be so bad."

Sami and Suzanne, however, are taking no chances. The flat they have bought in Pisgat Ze'ev is like a family insurance policy, "so the children won't end up in the street." Less than half the size of the one they have left behind, it is cozily cramped with large new sofas covered in a cherry-colored fabric. The only visible reminder of Al-Ram is the narghile half hidden away behind an armchair in the corner.

It was not so easy to buy in Pisgat Ze'ev. Sami and Suzanne felt several times that agents were stalling. "It could be that they don't like to sell to Muslims," says Suzanne, a plump woman with a wide face like a cat. "They have a different mentality." Whether it was because of their Christian faith or the market, they made a purchase in the end. Michael's parents at least feel safe that they will not wake up one day to find themselves out of the borders, belonging to somewhere else. I ask why they chose Pisgat Ze'ev over, say, Beit Hanina, the nearby Arab neighborhood where their church is and where their daughter-in-law is from.

"Who knows what will be," Suzanne replies in broken Hebrew, a language she has never learned to read or write. "Maybe next they'll give back Beit Hanina too." Sami and Suzanne estimate that at least 14 families that they know have moved in to north Pisgat Ze'ev. Michael says he went to the

Pisgat Ze'ev shopping mall on a recent Saturday night and was surprised to see it was "90 percent Arab."

According to one Talmudic legend, by the time the Messiah comes, Jerusalem will be ringed by seven walls, "walls of gold, silver, ruby, emerald, pearl, fire, and jasper" whose brilliance will shine to the ends of the earth. Archeologists have already found the remains of three ancient city walls, all heading off in slightly different directions. After Suleiman the Magnificent's, Dany Tirza's wall makes five. He knows his barrier is far from perfect and may not last the test of time. In fact, he stresses, the concrete panels can be easily and quickly moved, for "it is clear that the borders in a political settlement will be different to those of today." In the meantime, he is trying to create some order out of the holy space. And Jerusalem, which defies definition, seems to be getting increasingly mixed up.

7

The Big Prison / Gaza Syndrome

I first met Ihab al-Ashkar a few weeks before Yasser Arafat made his triumphant return to the Gaza Strip in the summer of 1994 to head the embryonic Palestinian Authority after nearly three decades in exile. Ashkar, a shady-looking character with pockmarked skin and a shadow of a beard in his early 30s, was sitting smoking in a typically gloomy and inactive office belonging to the Fatah-affiliated Health Services Council in an alleyway in Gaza city. He seemed to have little actual employment at this historic juncture, despite his impressive nationalist credentials.

Ashkar had made his name as a leader of the first intifada that started in late 1987 and officially ended with the signing of the Oslo agreement in 1993. The rioting first broke out in the Jabalya refugee camp north of Gaza City, rapidly igniting the whole of the Strip and then spreading across to the West Bank. A purely domestic revolt against the Israeli occupation, the outbreak of the first intifada had taken the PLO leadership in Tunis by surprise. And when five men from different Palestinian political factions gathered in Gaza at the founding meeting of the Unified Command, the underground leadership formed to coordinate the popular uprising in the Strip, Ashkar was among them. A student leader of the Shabiba, or Fatah youth organization, at the time, Ashkar's home was the Shati' (Beach) refugee camp, a low-rise mud-colored slum sprawling along Gaza City's then garbage-strewn Mediterranean shore. He served as a popular leader of the intifada in the Strip, and spent part of the next five years in and out of Israeli jails.

With Oslo, the Israeli army withdrew from nearly 80 percent of the Gaza Strip, only remaining in the area of the Gush Katif Jewish settlement bloc in the south and in and around a few isolated settlements in the middle and north of the Strip. The PA arrived to take over the newly autonomous, or liberated, Palestinian areas. Askhar, however, was offered no role in the governing administration. At the time he claimed that he was happy to sit on the sidelines, believing that anyone who went in at this early stage would only "get their hands dirty." In any case, he was hardly one of Arafat's favorites: When Ashkar had visited PLO headquarters in Tunis in 1993 to ask Arafat to commit himself to Palestinian elections, he got slung into prison for two days by Arafat's bodyguards who beat him black and blue. According to one version of the story, the brutal treatment was revenge for an interview that Ashkar had given to Israel TV prior to his trip in which he had implied that Arafat, a notorious autocrat, would have reason to fear if he brought his old non-democratic and corrupt ways with him to Gaza. Another version was that Ashkar had cursed one of the guards.

Either way, Ashkar was not banking on a career in politics. Rather, he said he was setting himself up with a job at the Trust insurance company that had just opened up shop in Gaza. Trust International, then owned by several wealthy diaspora Palestinians, had its head office in Bahrain and branches worldwide, from England to Venezuela. Luckily for Ashkar, a business-savvy uncle of his, Ghazi Abu Nahl, also a Shati' camp refugee now living abroad, was chairman of the board.

In the summer of 1995 I went to visit Ashkar again. Arafat had been back a year, accompanied by his young, blonde wife Suha. Though 30,000 babies would be born in Gaza that year, theirs was not one of them. Pregnant, Suha had just left the Strip for Paris, her favorite shopping destination, to await the birth of the first daughter of Palestine. Meanwhile most of Gaza's million-plus residents were still living in poverty, with unemployment reaching alarming levels which some put at over 50 percent.

I found Ashkar at his desk at the Trust International Insurance Co., behind an unassuming whitewashed façade in an old building in Gaza's mostly dingy city center. Inside was a different world. The carpets, desktops, and even the files lining the walls were all the same shade of cool mint green. A mineral-water dispenser in the corridor offered an Israeli brand which advertised itself as "nature's champagne." A spiral staircase led up to the director's bureau, with its ultramodern lighting and a green triangular table custom-made to fit the sharp angles of the room. This was where Ashkar sat.

Ashkar had no regrets about having left the revolutionary life behind. "I feel good that I did my bit, but why not go off and build my own house?" he said. Though Trust was equipped to insure everything from shipping to life itself, the only thing that people were insuring in Gaza, with its dire economy, was cars. Ashkar would insure any car licensed by the PA. As for those obviously stolen from Israel, he said, he would only provide insurance against personal injury, not comprehensive, in a prudent management of risk.

Ashkar's own BMW was parked outside. Life was clearly treating him well. Having recently moved out of the Shati' camp into the city "to live nearer work," he said he had come to the conclusion that "the homeland isn't a piece of land. It's self respect. Everyone's home is his palace," he added, "a man can be a zero but still be king to his kids." In Gaza, Ashkar felt like royalty.

There was a catch, though, for Ashkar's palace was also a cage. Even before Oslo, Gazan Palestinians working in Israel, seeking to visit the West Bank or traveling to other countries, needed permission from Israel to come or go from the Gaza Strip, an oblong patch of land on the Mediterranean all of 40 kilometers long and six to ten kilometers wide. The Israeli army had built its first 60-kilometer defensive fence around Gaza on the Green Line in 1994, following the peace accords and the repeated attempts of extremists to derail them by perpetrating terror attacks inside Israel. That fence was only partially successful, though, and early on in the second intifada, a more sophisticated one went up. Designed by the IDF's Southern Command, the new barrier included a fence equipped with high-tech sensors, a bulldozed security buffer zone, barbed wire, and ditches. It soon became the model and inspiration for Israeli military personnel and officials looking for ways to plug the flow of terror from the West Bank.

The Gaza fence indeed provided an answer to the suicide bombers. Its effect on the psyche of the Palestinians inside, however, may need to be studied for years to come, as might its impact on the Israeli-Palestinian battlefield. For one thing, the economic effects of being closed in, and the growing impoverishment and despair of the local population, are generally considered to have led to increased support in Gaza for the terror organizations—a pattern, Palestinians warn, that is bound to repeat itself in a fenced-off West Bank. For another, the success of the smart fence around Gaza led the militant factions there to seek ways of bypassing the physical hurdle from above and below, tunneling beneath it to smuggle in weapons and ammunition across the Egyptian border and developing crude missiles to fly over it into

Israel. On the eve of Israel's withdrawal from the Gaza Strip in the summer of 2005, even as the bulldozers worked on completing the barrier between Israel and the West Bank, the recently retired army chief of staff Moshe Ya'alon bleakly predicted that the Palestinians would soon resume their campaign of terror, and that it would not be long before rockets started flying across from the West Bank into Kochav Ya'ir and Kfar Saba.

Squeezed between the Israeli city of Ashkelon and the Egyptian border, the Gaza Strip is said to have one of the fastest-growing populations in the world, with an average of six children born into each household. Two-thirds of Gaza's population are refugees, or the descendents of refugees, from 1948. Half of them still live in the camps, where over the decades residents have added rooms and floors, higgledy-piggledy, onto their original U.N.-supplied cinderblock homes. Jabalya and Shati', which have turned into teeming urban slums, are counted among the most densely populated areas on earth.

Given the difficulties of controlling the area but the ease of controlling access to and from it, most Israeli peace plans have started with "Gaza First," meaning that the Strip would serve as a test of the Palestinian ability to maintain security and create the institutions of state. The Gaza Strip is considered so undesirable an asset, its Palestinian residents often note wryly, that even the peacemaker Prime Minister Yitzhak Rabin reportedly wished publicly in 1992 that it would just "sink into the sea."

Israel first started curtailing the movement of Gazans into Israel in the late 1980s, during the first intifada, instituting a magnetic card and exit permit system that became more sophisticated and restrictive over time. The first extended closure was imposed on the Strip during the Gulf War of 1991; for two weeks, nobody came or went. The method was repeated following terrorist incidents and in 1995, as a result of a series of Hamas suicide bombings in Israel in which 30 people were killed, the Gaza Strip was closed off almost entirely for several months. It was a vicious circle: Many Palestinians argued that the economic hardship brought on by the closures only fuelled further attacks. While some 80,000 Palestinians used to cross on a daily basis into Israel from Gaza to work through the Erez checkpoint at the northern end of the Strip, by the mid-1990s the numbers had dwindled sharply. According to the terrorist profile built by Israel's intelligence services, unmarried men under the age of 30 were deemed security risks and were not allowed into Israel at all. Anyone with any kind of security record was also barred.

For Ashkar, by then a successful and respectable businessman, traveling to Tel Aviv or even the West Bank, both less than an hour's drive away, had become an almost impossible feat. He described how he had recently had to pull an inordinate amount of strings with people he knew on both sides of the Israeli-Palestinian military liaison committee in order to secure a permit for a single day out. By the summer of 1995 Ashkar was suffering from a strange complex, a particularly Gazan syndrome that combined personal upward mobility and national claustrophobia. "After work, where can I go?" he complained, "to the beachfront to smoke a narghile? Then what? That's my life. As soon as I want to breathe a little more air, I run into problems."

Ironically, as the Oslo peace process progressed, it did little to ease Gaza's isolation. In some ways, things appeared to get worse. Gaza's international airport opened with great fanfare in late 1998, inaugurated by President Clinton during his historic visit to the Strip. Proudly perceived by the Palestinians as an early symbol of sovereignty, it handled 120,000 passengers the following year. Most Gazans, however, could not afford to take to the skies. Meanwhile the implementation of the West Bank-Gaza "safe passage" promised under Oslo—a 40-kilometer land corridor across Israeli territory linking the two halves of the new Palestinian entity—was chronically delayed. The road link finally opened in October 1999, but even then, Palestinians had to apply for permits to use it and complained that their cars and buses were subjected to lengthy security checks.

The sea was closed too other than for bathers and Gaza's fishermen, who could operate within a limited area off the coast. It took Israeli and Palestinian negotiators until September 20, 2000, to finally come to an agreement allowing the building of a seaport in Gaza. Days later, the second intifada broke out and the plans went with the tide. The only other way out was via the tightly controlled Egyptian border crossing in the sandy town of Rafah at the southern end of the Strip. From there, it is a six-hour drive to Cairo through the Sinai desert.

At the beginning of the Oslo process there had been high hopes for Gaza. With the right mix of political stability, foreign investment, and Palestinian entrepreneurial spirit, Israeli and Palestinian pundits imagined, the Strip had the potential to become the Singapore of the Middle East. Instead, Gaza's "inmates" were now referring to it as "the big prison."

In spite of the limitations, Ihab al-Ashkar's rise in the world was by no means an isolated case. For when over a million people find themselves

largely confined to a narrow strip of land between Israel, the Egyptian border, and the sea, the only way to go is up. Before Oslo, Gaza City looked like
a third-world backwater, reminiscent of a neglected Egyptian province. It
had no traffic lights, one hotel—the faded two-story Marna House in which I
once spent two nights as the only guest—and no skyline to speak of. The
poor stuck close to the ground in cramped, often rickety quarters, while the
small clique of wealthy Gazans from established, aristocratic stock, like the
Shawa and Abd al-Shafi families, inhabited a few elegant though unostenta-
tious houses in a small mansion district of the city.

Yet within a couple of years, some 160 high-rise apartment blocks of 10 stories or more had sprung up like mushrooms after the rain. Palestinians who had
earned good money abroad remained wary of investing in business ventures in
the Strip, put off by the political uncertainties, the corruption, and the lack of
free movement for people and goods, but they were eager to help build the
homeland in bricks and mortar. From late 1995 to late 1996, the private sector
had put more than $600 million into construction, according to PA Planning
Ministry indicators at the time. Building seemed a safe bet given the influx of
thousands of Palestinian exiles who had come back with Arafat to take up jobs in
the PA, and who needed homes. There was no shortage of skilled labor either,
many Gazans having acquired years of experience on construction sites in Israel.

One such developer was Tawfiq Shahada, an orphan who, like Ashkar,
grew up in the single-story cinder block homes of the Shati' camp, but unlike
Ashkar, was still living there. He and some associates who had made a lot of
money in the Gulf were building a residential project called Al-Fairuz, named
for Shahada's late mother. I met Shahada at the building site, just beyond the
Shati' camp, where the four-tower, 160-apartment complex was going up, in
February 1997. "The idea of building towers is a national thing," Shahada told
me. "People want to build, to prove to Israel and the world that this is our
homeland." The apartments, priced at $50,000 for a "super-deluxe" three-
bedroom unit, were said to be selling at a rate of two or three a day.

New hotels also went up along the coast, and once spruced up a bit,
Gaza's Mediterranean shoreline was revealed in its pristine sandy glory.
Chalets and restaurants were built along the beach and soon became the hub
of Gaza's revived social life. After the dour years of the first intifada, during
which the Israeli army imposed a nightly 8 p.m. curfew on Gaza, even the
relative freedom was to be savored. At the peak of Oslo, curious Israeli
tourists came to stay on weekend package tours.

Among the Gazans who made good was one in particular: the consummately smooth, talented and ambitious Muhammad Dahlan. Dahlan was born in 1961 in the Khan Yunis refugee camp in the southern Gaza Strip and made a name for himself, like Ashkar, as a student leader of the Shabiba, or Fatah youth, in the early 1980s. Dahlan's nationalist activity earned him a few stints in Israeli jails until he was deported by the authorities in 1986 and found his way to PLO headquarters in Tunis. There he became the protégé of Khalil Wazir, better known by his nom de guerre Abu Jihad, Arafat's dear comrade and the brain behind the Palestinian resistance, who was assassinated by Israeli agents in his villa in Tunis in 1988. When the first intifada spontaneously broke out in the territories, flummoxing the PLO in exile, Dahlan became useful because of his intimate knowledge of the Strip. By the time he returned to Gaza in 1994, he was considered one of Arafat's close acolytes and bore the rank of colonel.

Appointed to head Gaza's powerful Preventive Security apparatus, the PA's plainclothes internal security agency which employed thousands of men, Dahlan soon won the confidence of Israeli and American officials. Seen as a reliable peace partner, Dahlan's security network became a main recipient of CIA funds, training, and equipment for use in subduing Hamas. He had the reputation of someone who could deliver, having led a PA crackdown against Hamas in 1996. And when a Hamas suicide bomber blew up an Israeli army jeep escorting a school bus from the Jewish settlement of Kfar Darom, days after the PA and Israeli Prime Minister Benjamin Netanyahu signed the Wye River interim accord in October 1998, Dahlan's men rounded up 200 Hamas suspects within hours of the attack. Dahlan became one of the key Palestinian negotiators opposite the Israelis, and at the Camp David summit in July 2000, he was viewed by his Israeli interlocutors as one of the more pragmatic members of the young generation, one who seemed ready to strike a deal.

As a Palestinian Authority VIP, Dahlan was able to move in and out of Gaza with relative ease. His position afforded him many other privileges besides, including financial opportunities. Dark and handsome, with full lips and thick black hair always perfectly coiffed, Dahlan took to designer suits and limousines like a duck to water. He ended up buying one of Gaza's most desirable residences, the classic mansion of the late Rashad Shawa, a long-time mayor of Gaza who was considered almost royalty in the Strip. Dahlan's loyal deputy, Rashid Abu Shbak, another Shabiba graduate who would later take over from Dahlan as Gaza's Preventive Security head, moved into a new luxury penthouse with an unobscured sea view.

Still, for most Gazans, the revamping of the Strip was a cosmetic and superficial affair. At ground level life was a grind, and a suffocating one at that. The lid burst with the outbreak of the second intifada in late September 2000. As in the West Bank, Palestinians converged in anger on the Israeli army positions and checkpoints such as the one dissecting the main north-south Gaza road near the Jewish settlement of Netzarim, just south of Gaza City. That is where 12-year-old Muhammad al-Dura was killed in crossfire on the second day of rioting. Caught on film crouched behind his desperate and helpless father before falling to the ground, his death inflamed the territories even further and quickly became one of the most emotionally devastating images of the intifada.

In the Gaza pressure pot, the meltdown of the Palestinian Authority, and the meltdown of the boundaries between the official security apparatuses and the armed militias, was swifter and more pronounced than in the West Bank. Perhaps more than anything, the metamorphosis of Muhammad Dahlan epitomized the slide toward chaos in the Strip. As the Al-Aqsa intifada raged, Dahlan, never short of political smarts, saw the way the wind was blowing and changed tack. He began to disassociate himself from the PA peace process regime and opted instead to go with the popular flow, reverting to his original Fatah powerbase and roots. Members of his Fatah-dominated Preventive Security apparatus were soon being accused by Israel of playing an active role in shooting attacks and laying roadside bombs. In an attack reminiscent of the Hamas 1998 incident that sparked a round of arrests by Dahlan, another bomb targeted a school bus just outside the same Kfar Darom settlement in November 2000, killing two adults and maiming several young children. But this time, Israeli security sources were accusing Dahlan's deputy, Abu Shbak, of being behind the attack, making Dahlah responsible by association, as head of the apparatus. The new Gaza Preventive Security HQ, an impressive white building with columns, curved staircases, and large windows, was bombed in an Israeli retaliatory raid while Likud opposition head Ariel Sharon reportedly suggested that Dahlan should be liquidated and the CIA temporarily cut its ties. As prominent Palestinian political analyst Khalil Shikaki remarked at the time, "Once the Camp David process failed, Dahlan understood it was a matter of survival. He was willing to make the sacrifice. He probably learned that lesson from his boss, Arafat. If there's going to be a revolution, lead it."

With the violence, the safe passage to the West Bank was shut down altogether and Israeli army bulldozers ripped up the runways of the airport. In what may have been either a demonstrative act of defiance or an impulse to break out, the original Gaza perimeter fence was largely demolished by Palestinians from the inside during the first two months of the intifada. Major General Doron Almog, then the head of the IDF's Southern Command, stated that nearly 30 kilometers of the barrier were dismantled and stolen, and the rest was heavily damaged, representing a total loss to Israel of approximately $25 million.

Within a few months, the IDF's Southern Command had come up with the new model for an improved, multi-component barrier system around Gaza. It was constructed in 2001. "The resultant synergistic effect," Almog later wrote in a paper for the Washington Institute for Near East Policy, "helped the military achieve the previously unreachable goal of 100 percent prevention of terrorist infiltration. Indeed, hundreds of attempted infiltrations were thwarted inside the buffer zone before the terrorists ever reached the electronic fence. In only eight instances between June 2001 and June 2003 were terrorists able to penetrate the fence for short distances before being intercepted by the IDF." Intercepted usually meant getting shot dead, even when the infiltrators were not terrorists, but unarmed Palestinians in search of work.

A notable failure came in March 2004 when two 18-year-old suicide bombers from the Jabalya refugee camp made their way out of Gaza, hidden in a false compartment of a cargo truck, and penetrated the Ashdod port, one of Israel's most sensitive strategic locations, killing ten. Had the bombers exploded the huge bromide tanks at the site, Israeli security experts warned, the country would have suffered its first mega-terrorist-attack. Nevertheless, the Gaza fence was enough of a success for many in the security establishment to hail it as a perfect model to be replicated along the seam between Israel and the West Bank.

In the meantime, the Erez crossing point at the northern end of the Strip became more and more of a regimented border with Israel. If, in the early 1990s, Erez was a dusty, rowdy marketplace where Israeli and Palestinian traders congregated and a couple of soldiers manned a few cement blocks marking the 1967 line, a decade later it had become a full-blown border crossing with computerized passenger terminals and X-ray machines.

It also became increasingly deserted. After four years of intifada, in 2004, the number of workers and merchants still allowed into Israel from Gaza fluctuated between a high of 2,000 and zero. No men between the ages of 15 and 35 were allowed to exit the Strip. Since it was so hard to get out of Gaza, Erez itself, like other checkpoints and crossings, had become a target for local suicide bombers who hid their explosives on their bodies, sewn into vests, trouser legs, and even underpants, and blew themselves up among the soldiers there. Erez would close down completely for days or weeks following such incidents, and the security measures on reopening would become even tighter. The few workers who had day permits to enter Israel had to pass through clanging iron turnstiles and metal detectors and, most humiliatingly, they had to lift their shirts to reveal their bare bellies to nervous soldiers who peeped through window slits in fortified positions and barked barely intelligible orders through crackly loudspeakers.

A solution for explosive underpants had not yet been found. Sometimes specially trained sniffer dogs would rummage through bags checking for explosives, scattering their contents on the ground. VIPs, foreign aid workers, journalists, and the like were spared the shirt-lifting, but the metal detectors were so sensitive that on one occasion as I tried to leave Gaza I had to squeeze my thin gold wedding band off my finger and remove my tiny stud earrings in order to get through.

The difficulty in mounting suicide attacks outside the Strip led the Gaza terror gangs to adapt and innovate. The sandy earth lent itself to tunneling, so a seemingly never-ending supply of ammunition and weapons were smuggled into the Strip—along with toilet bowls, song birds, and anything else in demand—from Sinai, beneath the Egyptian border. Tunnels were also dug to allow militants to worm their way under Israeli army installations and blow them up. Terrorist infiltrations into the Gaza settlements, which usually proved to be suicide missions, continued, but other methods of attack were developed too. First mortar shells were lobbed into the settlements from nearby Palestinian towns and refugee camps, and then Hamas came up with the Qassam 1, a primitive, locally produced rocket with a small explosive warhead and an initial range of three kilometers. It was named, like the Hamas underground itself, for Izz al-Din al-Qassam, a Syrian-born Muslim preacher and guerrilla leader who was the first to organize against the British and the Zionists in Palestine in the 1930s and whose death sparked the Arab Revolt of 1936–39. At first the rockets were used against the settlements, and usually

caused minor damage. By the time the Qassam 4 model was coming out of the
local lathes, though, the range of the rockets had increased to some 10 kilometers and the missiles began flying over Gaza's perimeter fence into Israel.

The Palestinian town of Beit Hanun, in the northeast corner of the Gaza
Strip, just a kilometer or two in from the Erez crossing point, looked like it
had been struck by some natural or supernatural force this August morning
in 2004. Once-green fields were now barren expanses dotted with piles of
dirt, rubble, and twisted metal. Houses shaded until recently by fruit trees,
vines, and jasmine bushes now stood out starkly against the scorched earth.
Parked outside the door of one family home was a flattened red car. The few
asphalted roads in this agricultural town of 30,000 were cracked down the
middle, cleaved apart as if by an earthquake. It did not matter too much,
since transport in these parts was mostly by foot or donkey anyway.

The Qassam country, one of the optimal launching pads in the Gaza
Strip for the home-made rockets of Hamas and, by now, of other militant
factions as well. Beit Hanun's proximity to Gaza's eastern border made it an
attractive site from which to fire the missiles over into Israel, its houses and
orchards providing the militants with cover. A favored target was the Israeli
working-class town of Sderot, which lies only three kilometers or so across
the perimeter fence.

The Qassam gangs usually came at around 5 or 6 in the morning, Beit
Hanun residents said, in a van, their faces masked. They set up in orchards
and courtyards, behind mosques, on sandy rises, on rooftops, and they often
used timers to delay the launch for five minutes, by which time they could be
back at home base in the Jabalya camp or well on their way back into the
thick of Gaza City.

The Qassam rockets are unreliable and inaccurate. Launching them is
a notoriously hit-or-miss affair; some just fizzle out, while others backfire.
But a few weeks earlier, on June 28, one had landed outside a Sderot
kindergarten, killing a 49-year-old man and a four-year-old boy, and seriously injuring the boy's mother. In response the army launched a sweeping
military operation inside Beit Hanun, the second in a year. It lasted 37
days, from June 29 till August 5, during which, according to residents, the
army "shaved" nearly 4,000 dunams (1,000 acres) of land, uprooting citrus

orchards, demolishing hothouses, and flattening crops, in order to expose the Qassam launchers' former hiding places.

Altogether, some 8,200 dunams (2,050 acres) of Beit Hanun's 11,000 dunams (2,750 acres) of farmland had been destroyed in the past year. This time, the army bulldozers and tanks also destroyed 21 houses, damaged 17 wells, ripped up roads, and ruined parts of the electricity and sewage systems. Seventeen Palestinians were killed during the incursion; six were said to have been ordinary civilians, one a mother of seven.

A few days had passed since the army moved out, and the small compound of the Za'anin clan, a farming family, was still more or less intact. The walls of the large, square whitewashed house, where 25 adults and children live, were pockmarked by bullet holes but it was still possible to sit out under the old, twisted vine heavy with both green and black grapes and sip thick black coffee while chickens clucked around in the dirt among the sheds. The orchards out back had been flattened, as had the hothouses where the family was growing tomatoes and cucumbers. Only a couple of metal skeletons remained. A 27-year-old son of the Za'anin family, who asked not to be identified because he "didn't want problems with Hamas," described how he tried to protect his property once last year when a Qassam gang came to fire from the yard where we were sitting. He asked them not to, fearing that the house would become a target for Israeli retaliation. The Hamas militant "pointed his gun at my chest. He was probably younger than me," the farmer noted, since it added to the insult, "then he fired the Qassam anyway." Following the launch, Israeli soldiers at a position to the west started firing machine guns at the source of the rocket fire and the farmer hit the ground to avoid getting shot. The Qassam never even got anywhere, he remarked scornfully, describing the surreal scene as if it were an everyday occurrence, which it was in Beit Hanun.

The farmer felt nothing but disgust for the so-called heroes of Hamas's Izz al-Din al-Qassam Brigades and their ilk. "We were stuck in the house with tanks in the front yard for a week. We couldn't even open a window. Where were their suicide bombers then? Where were the Qassam people? Sitting on the beach smoking narghiles?" He said he was even convinced that the Hamas rocket men were in cahoots with the wood dealers who came to clear the chopped-down trees following the Israeli incursions, and were sharing the profits. He could swear he once saw a Qassam gang counting up the trees in a particular orchard they were using for cover *before* the rockets were launched. Having lost so much faith in the purported Palestinian resistance, the farmer no longer knew where to turn. Perhaps the Israeli Sderot and the Palestinian Beit Hanun could become twin towns, he suggested wryly, enemies standing together against the curse of the Qassams.

Palestinian officials protested the massive destruction wrought by the Israeli army in the wake of the Qassams. Compared with the deadly power of a single suicide bomber ripping through a crowded city bus, PA foreign minister Nabil Sha'ath told me on one occasion, the rockets were mere "pinpricks." In Sderot, however, the pinpricks had created an atmosphere of trauma and fear. People could not sleep at night. A few had sent their children away or packed up and left town. For, incredible as it seemed to the frustrated residents of the town, the mighty Israeli army had so far failed to come up with an answer to the flying iron tubes. Even while the army was sitting in Beit Hanun, the Qassams did not cease. The militants simply moved up to a sandy hill known as Tel Za'atar, a little further back from the border and on the edge of the Jabalya camp, and fired them into Israel from there. Following the death of two more young children in Sderot at the end of September, the army mounted an incursion into Jabalya itself that lasted 17 days and killed over a hundred Palestinians— mostly militants, the army said.

As the intifada dragged on and became less popular, largely as a result of the massive Israeli retaliation for the militants' actions, Dahlan, like a chameleon, changed his colors again. There had been bad blood and rivalry in the past between the Gaza strongman and Abu Mazen, the PLO No. 2 official. But by the summer of 2003, the suave colonel had fully aligned himself with Arafat's future heir. Arafat had been forced, under intense external pressure, to appoint Abu Mazen to a new post of prime minister, and Abu Mazen was tasked by Israel and the international community with trying to restore order in the territories. Dahlan became Abu Mazen's minister for security affairs, despite the bitter opposition of Arafat who, in the meantime, had started to consider Dahlan a threat. However, constantly challenged by Arafat and receiving little in the way of practical support from either Israel or the Americans, the government proved short-lived, lasting only four months before Abu Mazen resigned.

Both Abu Mazen and Dahlan fell out with Arafat until his last days. For well over a year, Abu Mazen boycotted even those Palestinian political institutions that he himself headed, having gone off in pique to his family in

Qatar. Dahlan used the time-out to improve his English and manners at Oxford, and to quit smoking. "He is grooming himself for something," a Gaza journalist commented at the time, "but nobody knows for what."

Anarchy grew in the Strip to the point where, in the summer of 2004, rival gangs from competing PA security agencies, including the Preventive Security apparatus, started physically attacking and abducting each other and the ruling Fatah movement, riddled with internal divisions and jealousies, started collapsing from within. In one incident, henchmen loyal to Dahlan and Abu Shbak were said to have stuck the head of a particularly unpopular police chief, Ghazi Jabali, down a toilet. Dahlan strongly rejected the accusations, according to the *Jerusalem Post*. Adding to the mayhem, unruly Fatah-affiliated masked militiamen temporarily took over some PA installations under the slogan of fighting corruption. On one occasion, members of the Fatah-affiliated splinter group called the Abu Rish Brigades, from the Khan Yunis refugee camp, briefly took four French aid-workers hostage before releasing them unharmed.

Having thrown his lot in with Abu Mazen, Dahlan was, as usual, one step ahead and perfectly positioned when Arafat unexpectedly took ill and died in November 2004. With Abu Mazen at the helm, he slipped easily back into the PA hierarchy as the new leader's right-hand man. The accusations of Dahlan's association with terror seemed to have been forgotten, as if they had never existed. In Abu Mazen's interim government, Dahlan was appointed minister for civil affairs, the portfolio responsible for liaison with Israel. And once again, Israeli hopes were pinned on the Gaza security czar and his loyal men for restoring law and order after Sharon's historic disengagement from the Strip and the evacuation of all 21 Jewish settlements there, in August of 2005.

⋆⇒◯⇐⋆

The day that Arafat died, Gazans say, a thick, black cloud hung over the Strip as mourners burned tires as a sign of respect. By the next day the pall had lifted, and with it, the Strip seemed to gain a new lease on life. "It's over. *Khalas*. We must have a new leadership," said one local journalist. "But we'll suffer for years from Arafat's dirty policy of supporting one rival Fatah gang against another. It is even said he was paying money to Hamas's Iz al-Din al-Qassam!"

A couple of weeks later, Um Ahmed Minshawi is home in her second-floor apartment in the Fairuz complex, the project built in the 1990s by Tawfiq Shahada on the sandy lot behind the Shati' refugee camp in Gaza City. It is raining, and the road outside is muddy and unpaved. The lobby and stairwell are reasonably clean though not exactly "superdeluxe." The apartment is spacious and well appointed by Gaza standards, with a comfortable lounge and open-plan fitted kitchen.

Life has not been a picnic for Um Ahmed, but at 45 she seems to have landed on her feet. A husky-voiced smoker with strong-featured classic Middle Eastern looks and a dry humor, she is dressed like a modern matron in black slacks and a loose dark brown top. When she goes out, she ties a black headscarf over her thick, dark hair. Her story is one of resilience, intricately tied up with the Palestinian cause. And in this case, Gaza is the happy end.

Born to a family of refugees from Haifa, she grew up in Lebanon, moving between the Sabra, Shatilla, and Tel al-Za'atar camps around Beirut. She trained and worked as a Red Crescent nurse, and married a son of refugees from Acco, a Fatah fighter who was "martyred" in the vicious fighting known as the Camps War between the Shi'ite Amal militia and the PLO in 1986. Her father had earlier been killed in the Sabra and Shatilla massacre of 1982.

By the age of 27 Um Ahmed was widowed with four young children, three boys and a girl. Clearly a practical woman, she took the family to Tunis, where they all went to live in an orphanage for the children of PLO martyrs, sponsored by the wife of the Tunisian president Habib Bourghiba. There were about a hundred children there, she recalls, all of whom had lost either one parent or two. Five children from Sabra and Shatilla who had lost both parents were formally adopted by Yasser and Suha Arafat. The other 95 or so were also known as "Arafat's children," or, alternatively, as "*ibna' al-sumud*" (the sons of steadfastness). Um Ahmed says that her children, like the others, considered their father to be Arafat, whom she refers to by one of his more affectionate nicknames, *Al-Ikhtiyar*, a word denoting the chief or old man of the tribe.

The family album consists of a pile of photographs taken at the orphanage. In photo after photo Arafat is seen dropping in on the orphanage like Santa Claus in a checkered kaffiyeh and fatigues, an expression of utter delight on his face. In many of the pictures Arafat is eating with the children or feeding them out of his hand. Um Ahmed's youngest son Jamal, a cute three- or four-year-old at the time, had a particular knack for ending up by his side. As Um Ahmed passes the pictures around, the room is filled with peals of laughter and watery eyes, the kind inspired by nostalgia and happy reminiscence of a dearly departed relative. "Now we feel we are orphans," Um Ahmed says, looking at me with a sigh and taking a long drag on her cigarette.

The Old Man brought 75 of the children, aged 7 to 19, with him to Gaza in 1994. They all flew out of Tunis together in a Saudi cargo plane. At first, the children, Um Ahmed, and the other accompanying adults who served as house mothers moved into a building on the Gaza shore, near Arafat's headquarters by the new Cliff Hotel. Arafat would come by to visit the orphanage, where he made a point of breaking his Ramadan fast, and the extended family would come visit him at the office. After three years, the landlord wanted the building back for development. It later reopened as the Grand Palace Hotel. Arafat's children were split up between apartments that were purchased for them. Um Ahmed moved into her new home in the Fairuz high-rise with her own three sons, Ahmed, Faisal, and Jamal, and took in one of the parentless orphans from Tel al-Za'atar, Esam. Her daughter had married in the meantime and moved to Jordan.

Amid the chaos of Gaza of the past four years, Um Ahmed has created an island of domestic order. None of her charges, the steadfast "sons" of Arafat, has joined a militia. Esam works in the PA's Ministry of Interior. Ahmed is a computer net-designer in the Ministry of Economy and Trade. Faisal, now a hip 22-year-old with gelled hair, sideburns, and baggy shorts, is a student of journalism, public relations, and administration at one of Gaza's universities. As a hobby, he raps in the year-old Gaza band RFM, which stands for members Rami (aka Romeo), Faisal (aka Fuds), and Muhammad. Alternatively, Fuds says, it can stand for *Rab Fi Medinati*, the band's new name which means Rap in My City. Fuds sings of revolution, but performs mostly in his bedroom. "You know the situation in Gaza," he says, referring to the morbidity and danger of the intifada years that have not exactly lent themselves to parties. His bedroom walls are adorned with English and Arabic graffiti saying things like "Love for Evere" (sic) and "Play with the Best, Die like the Rest." An Eminem banner is draped over a cupboard door. Here, on the new-looking computer, Fuds composes his patriotic Arabic raps that try to sound angry, the latest an ode to "Abu Ammar," nom de guerre of the recently deceased Arafat. The screensaver is a scanned-in photo of Fuds's girlfriend, a pretty Gaza teen with a dark bob now studying in Jordan. (Ahmed's room is a more staid affair, with a small framed picture of Arafat on the dresser and a PLO emblem on the wall.)

The youngest Minshawi, Jamal, is still at school. Um Ahmed, for her part, works in the President's Office as a secretary for Force 17, the PA's elite presidential guard. Um Ahmed's journey has been long and not uneventful. When I ask her where is home, she replies in her usual laconic, no-nonsense tone, without hesitation. "Any part of the homeland is our home." I ask Fuds, or Faisal, who was born in a Beirut camp, moved to Tunis aged three, and to Gaza at 12, the same thing. "Coming to Gaza was like coming home. It was always a dream for me to come home," he replies with a soft innocence that belies the cultivated rapper image. Faisal had better like it, because he could be stuck here for some time to come. He says he was invited to perform in Germany by the Palestinian community there, but being a male between the ages of 15 and 35, he was not given permission by Israel to travel. Um Ahmed says that after the Israeli withdrawal, Gaza will be a big prison. Faisal quips that it already is Alcatraz, then has to explain to his puzzled mother what that means.

Soon after she arrived in 1994, Um Ahmed got a permit for a one-time visit to her native Haifa. The port city in northern Israel is dominated by the ever-green Mount Carmel and was her refugee parents' home. Were it not for the checkpoint at Erez, it would be a straight two-hour drive up the coast from here. Not one to describe her feelings, she simply says of the experience: "I can live in any liberated spot of Palestine, but I will always have a special nostalgia for Haifa." At the same time, she stresses, the Palestinian refugees' demand for the right of return to their original homes, strenuously rejected by Israel, is a cardinal principle that must be addressed as part of any solution, "a red line for anybody."

The pointed message is directed at Abu Mazen, who is just in the process of taking over from Arafat. Um Ahmed will not say a bad word about the deceased leader, whom she obviously adored. At the same time, even she seems to exude a sense of relief that the Old Man's time is up. "Palestine without *Al-Ikhtiyar* has no taste," she says, but adds that people are pleasantly surprised by how smooth the transfer of power has been. Even in war-torn Gaza, or particularly in Gaza, there is a strong sense that the people are ready to move on.

Abu Mazen has made his first priority a dialogue with the militant factions in Gaza, particularly the fundamentalist Hamas, to reach understandings on a temporary cease-fire with Israel and, specifically, to bring an

immediate halt to the firing of Qassams. But the anarchy is never far away.
There is a reminder of that just outside Um Ahmed's door: Across the hallway, at the entrance of the apartment opposite hers, there is a "martyr's
poster" marking the death of the neighbors' son, one of two Force 17 men
killed a few days earlier when masked gunmen arrived at the Gaza mourning
tent for Yasser Arafat and started shooting during a visit by Abu Mazen and
Muhammad Dahlan. They were said to be members of a gang affiliated to
Fatah who wanted to scare, not assassinate, the new leadership, but to this
day it is not entirely clear who they were or what they wanted.

Barely two weeks after Abu Mazen was elected to the post of chairman of the
PA in the historic January 9, 2005, elections, only the second election ever
held in the Palestinian territories, the Qassam rockets stopped flying daily
over Gaza's border. Their most recent victim, a 17-year-old girl called Ella
Abukasis, had died of her wounds a couple of days before the unofficial temporary truce came into effect. She had been struck by shrapnel from a Qassam on the streets of Sderot as she shielded her 12-year-old brother with her
body. Still, whenever a terror cell or splinter group had a personal account to
settle with either Israel or the PA, even after Israel's August 2005 withdrawal,
the mortars and rocket attacks would flare up again.

The vulnerability of Sderot raised obvious questions about the useful-
ness of the $2 billion barrier under construction along the length of Israel's
border with the West Bank, where Palestinian and Israeli population centers
hug either side. Should Abu Mazen and the cease-fire fail, and the intifada
start up again, it would only be a matter of time, Israel officials warned, before the Qassams would make the hop over from Gaza to the West Bank.
Occasional intelligence reports indicated that a few had already been found
in "terror labs" in the northern West Bank city of Nablus; and in early
March 2005, the army announced that in a raid on a Hamas terror lab in a
village near Jenin, it had found a made-up Qassam that was ready for
launching. Once the West Bank fence has been completed, the suicide
bombers will have a hard time getting out. The militants will be looking for
other options. And as Tel Aviv University Jaffee Center strategic analyst
Mark Heller points out, most of Israel is within short rocket range from
somewhere or other along the Green Line. In the built-up and populous

residential centers of the coastal plain, even low-tech Qassams could have a potentially devastating effect.

Fence architect Major General Uzi Dayan argues that it is stupid to dele-gitimize the security barrier on such grounds. When asked such questions, Dayan snaps impatiently that to stop building the barrier because of the Qas-sams would be like refusing to take antibiotics for an infection because it will not wipe out all disease. Nevertheless, it appears that for now, as in Gaza, the effectiveness of the security fences and walls is less in the hands of rational people like Abu Mazen and Um Ahmed, and more in the hands of unpre-dictable elements like Abu Harun.

Abu Harun, an unsophisticated 27-year-old Gazan with a short black beard, has taken on the unenviable task of spokesman for the notoriously undisciplined Abu Rish Brigades, a Fatah-affiliated armed militia that operates mostly out of the Khan Yunis refugee camp in the southern Gaza Strip. We meet in the Gaza City apartment he is renting with his young wife and two daughters, Assia and Aya, aged three and one. It is a few days in to the unofficial truce, but having spent years on Israel's wanted list, Abu Harun still carries a revolver and instinc-tively takes a good look around before leaving a building and stepping into the street, fearing assassination. "Israel has seized many men they thought were Abu Harun," he says, stressing that he is a "military man." As such, prior to the Is-raeli withdrawal, his movements are confined to Gaza City—traveling to Khan Yunis would require passing through an Israeli army checkpoint and risking capture. Abu Harun has named himself for Harun al-Rashid, Islam's 8th century "rightly guided" caliph of the *Thousand and One Nights* who achieved success on the battlefield and greatness among the Arabs. But the neighbors refer to him simply as Abu Rish, after the late leader of his armed gang.

For now, Abu Harun's home is a small, modest apartment on the sixth floor of a neglected building on the seafront. The window offers a splendid ocean view though you can not see any of it when you are sitting down on the couch. The furnishing is simple, typical of a rented place. On the wall behind me is a framed photograph of Yasser Arafat with some comrades, and oppo-site, a bright blue picture of a waterfall. Since Abu Harun sticks to the con-servative Muslim mores of keeping his wife out of the sight of strangers, he has to carry in the trays of tea and coffee from the kitchen himself. It is not quite the glittering, harem-filled court of Baghdad where his namesake used to preside. As a female, I am later invited into the apartment's gloomy inte-rior to meet Abu Harun's wife, a slim woman wearing tight jeans.

Abu Harun's left eye always stares straight ahead, the result of an injury from an Israeli bullet during the first intifada, when Abu Harun was a 10-year-old child participating in the confrontations in the alleyways of Khan Yunis. Indeed, the Abu Rish Brigades has its origins in the first uprising and is named for its leader in the camp, Ahmed Abu Rish, who was assassinated by Israel in 1994. His successor, Amr Abu Sitta, was hunted for 15 years by Israel until he was finally killed in Rafah from the air in July 2004. The Abu Rish Brigades played a role in the anarchic events of that month, and were responsible for the brief abduction of the French aid-workers. Abu Harun was quoted in a local paper after the event, apologizing and explaining that the kidnappings were "a means, not a goal," meant to draw attention to Gaza's suffering.

Today, says Abu Harun, the Abu Rish Brigades supports Abu Mazen and may agree to a *hudna* (truce), so long as it is mutual between the Palestinian and Israeli sides. "Now we have a quiet *hudna*," he volunteers. "There is resistance work going on, but it is very light. We are still shooting at the hot spots like the checkpoints and settlements of Gush Katif. But only a bit."

Until recently, he points out, the Abu Rish gang was firing its own home-produced rockets at Sderot and the settlements. It is a source of annoyance to him that the Israelis only ever referred to them as Qassams, using their Hamas name. The Abu Rish rockets, he says, are called Sumud (Steadfastness), but they were never given proper credit. The support for Abu Mazen is, meanwhile, conditional and will largely depend on how the PA protects or treats the likes of Abu Harun, who Israel would expect to see at least disarmed, if not in prison or dead. There is a militia man in every Gaza home, Abu Harun says, with an implied warning for Abu Mazen should he harbor any thoughts of a confrontation or showdown. "They are of the people, and the people stand with their sons." Abu Mazen has to "love the fighters" like Arafat did, he continues, adding, "If not, he'll fail. He'll lose the people. They will turn against him."

Abu Harun went with other militants to meet Abu Mazen in the southern town of Rafah, by the Egyptian border, before the January election. "He promised to solve our problems and told us he respects us," Abu Harun recounts. "We told him 'If your program works, we're with you. If not, we'll fight you.'"

Problem is, it is difficult for Abu Harun to articulate just what kind of program he would support, or where his gang members' loyalties truly lie. Asked what he and his comrades will do if the war is really over, he says they will go back to their regular day jobs, adding, "Most of us are family men."

Abu Harun is employed by the administration of Gaza's Al-Quds University. As for the idea floating around that the armed men may be folded into the official PA security apparatuses, Abu Harun notes that "Most are already working in the PA, in security." In Gaza, it is not unusual to find policemen moonlighting as militants and vice versa. It perhaps goes some way to explaining the difficulty of restoring order in the Strip according to Abu Mazen's election motto of "One law, one authority, and one gun."

Abu Harun's own political agenda is equally vague, to say the least. He says this intifada was the result of the last ten years of negotiations "which brought us nothing." He complains that under Oslo, he had to cross an army checkpoint to get the few hundred meters from Khan Yunis to the sea. The checkpoint was there to protect the neighboring Jewish settlement of Neve Dekalim, the largest in Gush Katif. "Our principle is no peace with occupation," he declares. At the same time, he is far from committed to the solution espoused by Abu Mazen for two states, one Israeli within the 1949 borders, and the other Palestinian in the territories of the West Bank and Gaza with its capital in East Jerusalem. To Abu Harun, as to many Palestinians in their hearts, that would only constitute a stage in the struggle. "We can fight Israel another 30 years because this is our land. We'll fight until we are free and we hope that the state of Israel will be finished. It's written in the Quran."

At this point, he brings out an Arabic copy of the Quran and opens it at Surat al-Isra', the chapter describing Muhammad's night journey to Al-Aqsa (the furthest) mosque and that some interpret as predicting the destruction of Israel. It was Arafat's favorite Quranic verse, a couple of Abu Harun's friends in the room note with amusement. "I won't forget my home from 1948 in Beit Daras," Abu Harun goes on, referring to his ancestral village near Ashdod. "One day we'll get there. We prepare to return. I believe Israel must be finished. The Israelis can go to the United States or Cyprus," he continues, allowing that those who came before 1948 "can stay." Yet a moment later, when I ask whether his thinking is not more in tune with that of Hamas than Fatah, which is supposed to have adopted the two-state solution, Abu Harun says, "We can make peace and live with them, but we won't forget our original land." Then he adds, "No empires last forever. Look at the British. Look at the Pharoahs. I'm not afraid of death. I'm a Muslim. God promised us Paradise."

Abu Harun is a fervent believer. He would like me to believe too, and makes me promise to think about Islam, and, essentially, about heaven and hell, when I lay down at night. He is equally passionate when he talks about only one other thing: the perceived cruelty of the Israelis. I first came to Gaza in June 1992 following a two-week closure of the Strip. That came in the wake of the fatal stabbing of a 15-year-old Israeli schoolgirl, Helena Rapp, at a bus stop in Bat Yam, near Tel Aviv, by a 19-year-old from Gaza. Rumors were circulating in Gaza City that the Israeli occupying forces had left out cartons of poisoned orange juice in the streets for the children. What struck me was how easily the ordinary people here believed that the Israelis could be capable of such a horror. Here, on this narrow strip of land that even Ariel Sharon, the father of settlement, no longer wants, Israel had gained the reputation of a monster.

In this context, the shootings, stabbings, bombings, and random firing of rockets therefore seem entirely justified to the Gazans; Israeli soldiers are the barbarians who must be kept at the gate. "I want to save my daughters from the Jews," says Abu Harun, injecting a tone of urgency into his usually quite monotonous voice. "The soldiers are trained to shoot at the heads of children. They have no humanity. They kill with precision from Apache helicopters, including innocents. All Israelis are the army," he continues, referring to the policy of conscription. "Israel has no civilians."

The day that Abu Harun and I meet, PA police carrying light arms as permitted under the Oslo accords are spreading out in the south of the Strip for the first time since the start of the intifada, a signal from Abu Mazen to the militants that from now on, attacks will not be tolerated. A few days earlier, the police had taken up positions in the north, including around Beit Hanun. Abu Harun stresses, though, that the rockets only stop when the fighters decide to stop, and not as a result of Abu Mazen's policemen. "We are not scared of them. We are stronger than the Authority. We are the people. We have better weapons than they do," he crows.

Abu Harun claims that the Abu Rish Brigades has plenty of Sumud rockets left, and that his colleagues are now developing one against aircraft. "We want to shoot them before there's a solution!" he exclaims, probably only half in jest. "They are 100 percent a local product made in Khan Yunis with local expertise," he states proudly. "One day they will reach Tel Aviv."

➻⫶⊜⫶➼

The same day I meet Abu Harun, I decide to look up Ihab al-Ashkar once again. He is not in his office at Trust. His secretary says he has taken a few days' vacation, which he is spending at home. Reached on his cell phone late in the morning, Ashkar says he is out of politics and does not give interviews anymore, but I am welcome to come over for coffee. He gives me the address of his new home in the exclusive "Haidar Abd al-Shafi neighborhood" of Gaza City, a couple of streets of villas named for the eponymous elder states-man of Gaza who headed the Palestinian delegation to the Madrid peace conference in 1992, and whose bay-windowed residence, a Gaza landmark, sits on the corner by U.N. Square.

My taxi driver, looking for the house, says that Ashkar is a "good man" who is liked by Muhammad Dahlan and is in with Rashid Abu Shbak. Then the taxi pulls up in front of a high wall with an ornate iron gate. A new gold Lexus is parked on the quiet street. Responding to the buzzer, a gray-haired butler-cum-security-guard in a khaki safari jacket graciously asks me in. The gate opens to reveal a palatial, pinkish-stoned mansion with gables and a cou-ple of new four-wheel-drive jeeps parked in the pathway. I follow the butler through the small landscaped front garden, along a rustic path paved with small stones that look like they have come from Tuscany. We head past a pink marble-paneled wall into the back garden, where Ashkar is sitting with three cultured Palestinian friends. There is a small swimming pool, empty of water on account of it being January, even though it is an unseasonably warm and sunny day. Ashkar, with the same pockmarked face and close beard, and dressed in a beige T-shirt, jeans, and sneakers, is smoking a Cuban cigar. Small glasses of thick Turkish coffee are served from the bar in the corner of the garden. His friends are all in suits. One is the wealthy owner of a success-ful Gaza media production company, another is an American-educated chemistry professor from Gaza's Islamic University, and the third works for the United Nations and has just returned from a lengthy stint in Iraq.

Ashkar has progressed to what he calls the "assistant general manager of Trust forever." His uncle, Ghazi Abu Nahl, is now the sole owner. Ashkar is welcoming and in good humor, though as he warned, he is hardly gushing with sound bites or eager to pour out his soul. Married with two little daugh-ters, he built this house and moved in three months ago. It is a source of great personal pride. "You are the new Gaza," I say, complimenting Ashkar on his new home. "You're right," he says with all seriousness, placing a hand on his chest in thanks. "The good life is possible in Gaza, because we want to live. Palestinian leaders throughout history promised death, not hope. This is not acceptable in my eyes."

Now, after four years of intifada and with Arafat gone, Ashkar says he hopes to see the steady cultural and economic development of the Strip. Abu Mazen has done well up until now, he thinks. "He's not a strong politician, but he has an affinity for establishing strong institutions, and he's consistent," he says. "Abu Mazen was the first in the PLO to construct any kind of formal building." Ashkar does not need to say how glad he is that the Arafat era is over. It's obvious. He jokes that he is now "planning with some big business friends to buy the whole PA. I'll manage it myself, and get together some Israeli businessmen willing to do the same on the other side!"

Though a product of a Gaza refugee camp and of the first Palestinian uprising, like Abu Harun, Ashkar clearly has little truck with the methods of this Al-Aqsa intifada. He remains diplomatically silent when I ask him about the violence. But Abd al-Salam, the perfectly groomed, mustachioed media company owner who looks like a young Omar Sharif, answers in his place. "We've lost half of Rafah, half of Khan Yunis, half of Beit Hanun. The fact is we lost everything. If it is between possessing the Al-Aqsa mosque or my son, I'd rather have my son."

Ashkar may be enthusiastic but he is not naïve. He says he is "positive that Sharon has a global idea for peace. I believe he will withdraw from Gaza, for sure, and from the large cities of the West Bank. But the withdrawal itself is not the point. The concern is over giving the Palestinians their historical rights there." On its own, Gaza is a small place. The last time Ashkar was allowed to leave was almost six months ago, in August of 2004. It is hard to be closed in, he says. It is like a constant knocking somewhere in his body. He is embarrassed to say exactly where. And after the Israeli disengagement from Gaza in the summer of 2005, Israel made it clear that the freedom of movement of people and goods in and out of the Strip would be entirely conditional on the level of security that the weak and largely dysfunctional Palestinian Authority managed to impose inside.

Despite the palatial surroundings Ashkar now finds himself in, being born in Gaza is like a life sentence. Many Palestinians fear that with the new security barrier going up, a similar fate awaits the residents of the West Bank. And they are certain that in the long term, national claustrophobia will hardly contribute to peace. After all, as Ashkar concluded years ago, the homeland is not a piece of land. It's self respect.

8

Beyond the Pale

Perhaps this murder was also part of God's plan, though for what purpose is not yet known. Dr. Shmuel Gillis, a gifted 42-year-old hematologist, had finished a long day's work at Jerusalem's Hadassah-Ein Kerem Hospital and was driving home to his family in Karmei Tzur, a religious Jewish community at the bottom end of the Gush Etzion settlement bloc, about 20 kilometers south of the capital in the West Bank Hebron hills. As his green Peugeot rounded a dark bend in the Jerusalem-Hebron road by the Al-Arroub refugee camp, Shmuel was ambushed by Palestinian gunmen who shot him in the neck and chest, killing him on the spot. He left my cousin Ruthi widowed with five children aged from 13 to three.

Thousands turned out the next day for the funeral, which set out from the hospital courtyard and ended at the small cemetery in Kfar Etzion, at the center of the Gush. In an unprecedented salute, thousands of the area's Jewish residents came out and lined the route. That Friday morning Ruthi stood over the fresh grave, under a clear sky, eulogizing her late husband in a strong, unwavering voice. Shmuel loved the rain, she said. Maybe tomorrow there will be rain. By the end of Shabbat, the rain started to fall. It continued on and off for days, building up by the last night of the *shiva*, the seven-day mourning period, into a thunderous, gushing storm, like a blessing for the parched land.

Shmuel was a modest man with a shy, lopsided smile, devoted to family, home, Torah, and work. He had no borders. He was a bridge, said Ruthi, between fellow human beings, regardless of their religion, nationality, or creed. At Hadassah, Shmuel had treated Jews and Arabs, religious and nonreligious, leftwing and rightwing, with the same compassion. His patients, suffering from leukemia and lymphoma, came not only from Israel, but from Gaza, Ramallah, even Jordan and Egypt. As the doctor of an elite army unit, he had cared for the welfare of prisoners as well as for his men. And though Orthodox, he would often spend hours on the phone to the hospital on the Sabbath, and when necessary drive in, the deed of saving a life superceding the sanctity of the holy day of rest. An Arab woman that Shmuel had been treating before he left for home on his last night told the newspapers that an angel had been taken away.

By the graveside, the head of the Gush Etzion council, Shaul Goldstein, a leading member of the YESHA Council for the Judea, Samaria, and Gaza District Communities, promised that Shmuel's death would be met with "a Zionist response"—code for the establishment of a new neighborhood within a Jewish settlement, or of an outpost some distance away from an existing one, to further the religious Zionist goal of settling the whole land of Israel. The settler initiative of building illegal outposts in the conquered territories, creating new facts on the ground ahead of official authorization, had proliferated after Ariel Sharon, as foreign minister, had urged the settler youth to "grab the hilltops" in protest of prime minister Benjamin Netanyahu's compromises with the Palestinians in 1998.

The killing of Shmuel Gillis resounded throughout the country. During the *shiva*, thousands of well-wishers passed through Ruthi's home, including politicians, dignitaries, top army brass, rabbis, colleagues, former patients, local and foreign TV crews, and complete strangers who simply felt a pressing need to be there. The same week, several mobile homes were moved to a site a few hundred meters away from the main settlement on a ridge overlooking a dramatic ravine, offering commanding views of Halhoul, a Palestinian village on the outskirts of Hebron. Ruthi named the new foothold Tzur Shalem, *tzur* (rock) being one of the names attributed to God, and *shalem* (a word with connotations of wholeness and peace) made up from the letters of Shmuel's name. Five young families moved in.

Shmuel was murdered four days before the February 2001 elections in which Ariel Sharon trounced Ehud Barak. When Ruthi got home from the funeral, Sharon was on the phone. "He spoke kindly," she recalls, "He told me he knows what it is to lose a spouse. He apologized that because of his schedule, he would not be able to make it to the *shiva*. I told him I was very worried about our situation here. He said 'That's why I am running for office.' He indicated that we could trust him. I wished him luck and success in his endeavors. But he obviously isn't too worried about us," says Ruthi, sitting at the dining table of her plain stucco home in Karmei Tzur four years on. "Now look. We're out of the fence."

Just a couple of weeks before, in February 2005, the Sharon government in Jerusalem had finally approved the route for the rest of the security barrier. What had long been expected was now official. Most of the Gush Etzion settlements would be included on the Israeli side the barrier, but Karmei Tzur, a ten-minute drive south of the main Etzion junction, was to be left out.

For Jews, physical exile and exclusion from the community is a particularly cruel punishment. Now it was as though the fence was creating a new pale of settlement in which Jews would be permitted to live, a century after the Russian Revolution did away with the one established by the czars. Those insisting on remaining beyond the pale—literally, the stake in the ground marking the boundary—would by implication find themselves outside the bounds of acceptability. The message that Sharon's fence drove home was that Karmei Tzur, Tzur Shalem, and dozens more settlements throughout the land of Israel were no longer considered essential or worth preserving. The isolated settlements found themselves cast out from the Israeli "national consensus," if they were ever truly in, delegitimized by the very father of the "hilltop youth." Ruthi thinks Sharon has "gone crazy."

Ruthi and Shmuel came to Karmei Tzur from a densely built residential neighborhood of West Jerusalem in 1991 when their third child, Neta, was a month old. The settlement had been established six years earlier; the Gillises were the thirtieth family to move in. It has since quadrupled in size, to 115 families. "We loved Jerusalem but the apartment and the surroundings were cramped," relates Ruthi, a wholesome breakfast of bread, cream cheese, and green olives before her. "We started looking for a place in a small community that would be close enough to the hospital for Shmuel. We looked in the area north of Jerusalem and at lots of places in Gush Etzion. We were looking for a place with simplicity and modesty and we found it here. The houses are plain, functional. We came for a spiritual quality of life which we found among the people and their ideology. We also moved from a small apartment into a house which, though small, was in much more spacious and pleasant surroundings."

Karmei Tzur is an archetypal Jewish settlement consisting of a few neatly ordered rows of red-roofed single-family homes on a hilltop in Judea. Karmei means vineyards, and Tzur refers to Beit Tzur, the ancient community that once existed nearby and was the scene of the priestly Hasmoneans' last battle on the way to Jerusalem. To the north lies Beit Umar, a sprawling Palestinian agricultural village, and just beyond it, the cement-gray close-packed houses of the Al-Arroub refugee camp. A few kilometers to the south sit Halhoul, Hebron, and the adjacent urban Jewish settlement of Kiryat Arba.

The slopes leading up to Karmei Tzur are planted with vines, gnarled and dry in the winter, that belong to the Palestinian farmers of Beit Umar. Karmei Tzur is not an agricultural community; most of its residents either work in their professions in Jerusalem, as Shmuel did, or as teachers in the many Jewish educational institutions in the area. A somewhat dour and austere-looking place to an outsider, the forbidding atmosphere is accentuated during the winter months when the settlement, at well over 800 meters, is often whipped by the wind and wrapped in swirls of cloud.

In keeping with the values of modesty, Ruthi is dressed in a long black velvet skirt, a loose corduroy jacket, sturdy brown platform shoes combining outdoor practicality with settler style, and a black crocheted cap with a colored border that covers most of her short light brown hair. A pink scarf and dangly silver earrings add adornment to her round, open face and penetrating light brown eyes. Ruthi often wears robes trimmed with rich turquoise or purple, reminiscent of the hymn of praise to the *eshet chayil* (woman of worth), which appears at the end of Proverbs and is sung in religious homes on the Sabbath eve.

The living room is sparsely furnished with a few cushioned round cane chairs—the kind Israelis used to go to the West Bank markets to buy. There is a dining table and a white Formica cupboard with Shabbat candlesticks and jars of honey and olive oil on top. Everything here has meaning: The honey was a gift from Dror Weinberg, a commander of the Hebron Brigade who was killed in November 2002; the oil came from Shmuel's unit. One wall is taken up with the shelves of holy books and scriptures that are to be found in every religious home. The other ornaments, decorative pieces made from blue glass and silver trim, are Ruthi's handiwork. The most prominent feature of the room is an arched window in the lounge, fitted with a blue-cushioned window seat, looking out onto the houses of Beit Umar straggling down the opposite hill.

"I used to sit for hours at this window, studying the village, watching, wondering what was going on inside," Ruthi says of Beit Umar, a place she has never entered. "I didn't come here to 'occupy' and conquer. I thought it could really work, that we could be neighbors. On our first Independence Day here, the *mukhtar* [village notable] of Beit Umar came to join us round the bonfire." There was a man from Beit Umar called Muhammad who used to work in the apartment block of Ruthi's grandfather in Jerusalem. "He called when we built our house here, and he used to come over, sometimes with his wife. We'd sit for hours talking in the yard."

It was not coincidental that Ruthi became a settler. She was born in Jerusalem into a religious Zionist family and grew up in Bnei Akiva, the nationalist pioneering youth movement whose graduates laid the foundations on which the ideological settlements were built. Like many, Ruthi's philosophy of Jewish strength and survival is built on the notion of her people's redemption from persecution and its rebirth from the ashes of the Holocaust. She says "Most people want a normal life. They [the Arabs] are people no different from us. And yet we can never forget who we are. We are the remnants of the millions who aren't with us. This is our identity. This is our place. It's our only option and it's not up for discussion." Ever since she accompanied a youth group on a visit to the extermination camps in Poland in 2003, Ruthi has been lighting an extra two candles on the eve of every Sabbath in memory.

"I believe we have to live in the land in every place. We have to settle every single part of the Land of Israel," she continues. "There are rules of course. It says in the Bible that when we came into the land, we were commanded not to hurt the *gerim*, the strangers in our midst. But nor should their presence here disturb ours. It would doubtless be more convenient for us if there was no village over there, just empty hills. But we have to live with the reality."

Most, though not all, the settlers abide by this commandment. There are also those who fit the stereotype of the gun-toting messianic Jewish settler chopping down Palestinian olive groves, vandalizing Arab property, and stopping at nothing to ensure Jewish domination of the land. A few days after I visited Ruthi in mid-March 2005, some forty yeshiva students on the settlement of Nahliel, near Ramallah, used clubs and stones to attack a group of

Palestinian laborers legally working there, injuring five. In an extreme case, three men from Bat Ayin, a settlement in Gush Etzion, were convicted in a Jerusalem court in September 2003 of attempted murder after they were caught leaving a trailer filled with explosives set to go off outside a girls' school in a Palestinian neighborhood of East Jerusalem. Their purpose, they said, was to avenge Jews who had been killed by Palestinians. And members of a Jewish underground who had allegedly murdered at least six Palestinians in the West Bank during the intifada were still on the loose by the time Abu Mazen declared the war over in early 2005.

Such conduct is about as anathema to Ruthi as Palestinian violence itself. She stresses that she is perhaps more "accepting" than others in the Greater Israel movement, but she adds that most of her own community is behind her. Karmei Tzur is known as a quiet place that keeps to itself, and villagers I have met from Beit Umar confirm that they have had "no problems."

In the Palestinian lexicon, however, a well-meaning settler is a contradiction in terms. If the first uprising of stones left some neighborly relationships between Jewish and Palestinian residents of the West Bank intact, the armed second intifada has turned the struggle for control of the West Bank hills into a cruel, existential, zero-sum game. "I remember when the intifada broke out," Ruthi recounts. "It was Succot," the Feast of the Tabernacles, which fell in early October 2000. "We had been out on a trip with the community. On the way back the road was closed and we waited at Etzion junction for three hours. When we finally got through, we saw that the whole way between Al-Arroub and Beit Umar was strewn with broken glass and smoldering tires. The air was gray and thick with smoke. We understood there'd been a wild disturbance. The feeling was that everything had changed."

Three months later, Shmuel was killed. After that, Ruthi often asked herself whether they would have come to live here if they had known that Shmuel's death was going to be the price. The reply came a year on when she found herself outside the Hamashbir department store in King George Street in downtown Jerusalem, just minutes before a suicide bomber went off there, killing three. This confirmed to her the ideological-settler credo that Palestinian aspirations do not stop at the Green Line, but rather include the destruction of all of Israel. "It doesn't make any difference where you are. It's not about where you live. It's because you are a Jew, and you could be anywhere," she says of the Palestinian terror campaign. On the other hand, she adds, "there's a feeling in Israel as if the attacks on settlers have some legitimacy, as if we deserve it because we shouldn't be here. But that's a distortion of what is really going on. We are part of the nation. We serve in the army and pay taxes. Who's got the right to decide who belongs and who doesn't?"

⊷═◉═⊷

There must be a certain comfort in a belief that is sturdy like a rock, that cannot be shaken even when tragedy strikes for a second time. For that is what happened shortly after 2 a.m. one Sabbath in June 2002 when Palestinian gunmen attacked the outpost of Tzur Shalem. Ruthi was not home at the time. She was with her children at the Dead Sea on a weekend organized by One Family, a charity helping the victims of Palestinian terror. She heard only the following afternoon that two terrorists had climbed up from the valley below and started shooting at the mobile homes where about 11 families were by now living. A married couple in their early 20s, Eyal and Yael Sorek, who were married at the time that Ruthi was sitting *shiva* for Shmuel, were killed along with a 35-year-old reservist, Shalom Mordechai, who arrived at the scene of the attack and engaged in a firefight with the two gunmen. Eyal was a combat soldier due to be discharged a week later. Yael was nine months pregnant. One of the gunmen was killed by a soldier, and the other fled in the direction of Halhoul.

For Ruthi this was a blow, but still not one strong enough to shake her conviction. "It was a very, very bad feeling that it happened there. That you put something up in someone's memory, and it takes such a heavy price. And in general, it added to the feeling of insecurity here. Till today, when I have a houseful here over the Sabbath, I breathe a sigh of relief when morning comes and everybody's OK." The frosted-glass front door of the Gillis home has been replaced by a more solid one with security locks, Ruthi notes, as protection "not against thieves, but murderers. It's a life of worry. Any unexpected knock on the door gives you a fright. And you can't stop along the road if you see an old Arab man or woman standing there who needs assistance. Fear doesn't let you help."

Walking in the area is now impossible, except for the annual memorial march for Shmuel from Karmei Tzur to the Etzion junction, for which the army closes the road for two hours and nervously patrols the fields and orchards lining it. Ruthi travels to and from Karmei Tzur in a heavy bullet-proof pickup truck. She is the only one on the settlement to have a plated

car, and constantly questions whether to keep it or not because of the pro-
hibitive cost of maintenance and gas. There would be nowhere to meet
Muhammad, the family acquaintance from Beit Umar, any more, even if he
were to call: Since the murders, Palestinians are no longer allowed past the
settlement's gate.

If the settlers had previously been harboring any self-doubt about their
mission, even privately within their own souls, the Palestinians, by taking
their suicide bombings and shootings over the Green Line into Israel proper,
eliminated any possibility of the Jewish ideologues even considering the conflict as a territorial issue. For mainstream Israelis too, each consecutive attack
served to blow away the credibility of the intifada leadership's claims that the
goal of the struggle was limited to the liberation of the lands occupied in
1967, the removal of the Jewish settlements, and the establishment of a
Palestinian state there. Rather, the indiscriminate bloodshed tallied more
with the ideological settlers' conviction that the Israeli-Palestinian conflict is
not about turf, but about the Arabs' historic and irreconcilable hatred of Israel and all Jews, an eternal contest that will not be resolved by ceding the
biblical heartland of Judea and Samaria.

"They want to see the Jews in the sea. Gush Katif won't satisfy them,"
says Ruthi, referring to the soon-to-be-evacuated Jewish settlement bloc in
the Gaza Strip, "and nor will Karmei Tzur." Most confounding for the settlers, though, is that just when they feel most vindicated in their belief that
the Israeli-Palestinian conflict is not about territory, they find mainstream Israel, led by the arch-settlement-builder Ariel Sharon, turning its back on the
biblical heartland and putting the vast majority of it beyond the barrier, or
pale. For Ruthi "it's a very painful thing. I mean personally, as well. This was
after all a Zionist enterprise. True, not all the nation was behind it. But now
we are being made to feel illegitimate, as if *we* are the enemies of the people—the obstacle to whatever, though nobody can say exactly to what."

As I sit with Ruthi, fateful decisions are being made. Prime Minister
Sharon intends to send the police and army in to remove all 8,000 Jewish settlers from the Gaza Strip and to remove hundreds more from four isolated
settlements in the northern West Bank, by force if necessary. Here too there
are personal implications for Ruthi, as her younger sister married a kind man
who grew up in Gush Katif from the age of five and who has invested his life
and soul there, in agriculture. They and their children, now third-generation
residents of Gush Katif, will be among the evacuees.

The settler population and their supporters in Israel have been protesting for months, holding rallies, prayer meetings, and forming human chains, plastering the cities with posters proclaiming that Sharon is tearing the nation apart. The most radical opponents of disengagement, meanwhile, have been sitting in back rooms plotting more provocative and shocking ways to thwart it, or at least to ensure that this withdrawal is so traumatic that it will be the last that any Israeli government will have the stomach to undertake.

It is clear, however, that this partial disengagement will not be the end of the story. Sharon is under increasing pressure from Washington to remove the unauthorized outposts, like Tzur Shalem, that sprung up on the initiative of the settlers and without government permits, but which have received significant ex post facto financial and logistical backing from government ministries and the state companies providing utilities like electricity and water. In March 2005, a lawyer commissioned by the prime minister's office, Talia Sasson, produced a report on the illegal outposts, which she counted as numbering at least 105, and recommended criminal proceedings against state employees who had facilitated their establishment. The outpost scandal, Sasson argued, was a potential threat to Israel's democracy and rule of law.

The ideological settlers and their supporters on the right counter that by that standard all of Zionism was an unauthorized enterprise; that without the daring and initiative of the early pioneers, from the illegal immigration under the British Mandate to the buying of land for the first settlements, modern Israel would simply not exist. When it came to the land conquered in 1967, Gush Emunim's tactics of forging facts on the ground ahead of government permission proved themselves again and again, whether in Sebastia, Hebron, Beit El, or Ofra. All these were flagships of Gush Emunim's pirate settlement enterprise, which subsequently gained government approval; but now the settlements find themselves outside the fence. "No government took the initiative and set up new settlements, other than in the Golan and the Jordan Valley," Yisrael Harel, one of the settler movement's intellectual leaders, once told me, "Not even the [Likud] governments of [Menachem] Begin or [Yitzhak] Shamir." Harel, the founder of the YESHA Council, was among the early settlers of Ofra. He acknowledged that Ariel Sharon did help greatly during his years as agriculture minister in the Begin government from 1977 on. Still, he insisted, "It was all our initiative, and now it's our children's initiative."

Another veteran settler, Dov Weinstock, a bear-like resident of Gush Etzion and a former lands-inspector for the regional council, echoed Harel as he careened through the green hills with me in his jeep one day in 2002. "State apparatuses work slowly," he explained. "No government initiated anything. If we'd waited for them . . ." He trailed off, but the implication that nothing would have happened is clear. Weinstock went on to describe the new pioneers' rule of thumb. "As soon as we saw a signal, we moved in. Then they'd have to get us water, urgently, and so on. Get it?"

The runaway settlement-building effort carried on through the Ehud Barak years, preceding the premiership of Sharon. "Whenever we wanted to set up a settlement, Barak didn't stop us," noted Harel. Barak was, by all accounts, merely trying to buy himself some domestic political quiet on the right, smug in the knowledge that much of what was being built would anyway be taken down once he struck a final peace deal with the Palestinians. The deal, of course, was never made.

At the same time, the settlers argue that everything they do gets government approval in the end, even if only after the fact. "Do you think we did this all ourselves?" Ruthi asks me, "And all this infrastructure? Shimon Peres was here when Karmei Tzur was founded and Fuad [Labor's Biyamin Ben Eliezer] was minister of defense when Tzur Shalem went up. The state doesn't know what it wants. They even built a road to Tzur Shalem."

The access road to Tzur Shalem is a perfect example of the state's equivocating ineptitude when it comes to making decisions about the West Bank. Newly asphalted, it winds down the hill to the dozen mobile homes that make up the outpost. It is so narrow, though, that when two vehicles need to pass in opposite directions, one of them has to edge off the road into the dirt. Tzur Shalem exists in a twilight zone. Prime Minister Sharon promised President George W. Bush in 2004 that, in accordance with stage one of the U.S.-backed peace plan known as the Road Map, he would remove all the outposts that had gone up since March 1, 2001, when he came into office. Tzur Shalem, founded in February 2001, falls just short of that category. Its status, according to Defense Ministry sources, is "frozen." Sasson argues that there is no legal distinction to be made between outposts that went up before or after March 1.

The Sharon government's March 1, 2001 outpost-removal cutoff date is news to Ruthi, giving her hope that Tzur Shalem will survive. "It's a place that doesn't harm anyone," she says. "If it was built on private [Palestinian] land I'd understand, but it's not. It's built on state land." In fact, on Defense Ministry maps, the outpost, referred to as Tzur Shalem-Gillis, is listed as being on *adamot seker*, land of unclear ownership whose status is to be determined. Such land has the potential of being declared government owned at the end of a checking process. In the Talia Sasson Report, meanwhile, Tzur Shalem-Gillis is listed as one of over 30 outposts established on land that is of mixed status, being part state-owned, part *seker*, or part privately Palestinian owned. To Ruthi, the community is fulfilling a crucial mission. "The whole settlement is so isolated, the government should encourage us to expand in any way we can," she continues. "If we weren't here, the whole area between Gush Etzion and Hebron would be an abandoned no-man's-land."

As if on cue, the sound of a muezzin drifts over from a Beit Umar mosque calling worshippers to midday prayers. It serves as a reminder that even if Tzur Shalem is built on bona fide state land, the real question is whose state. As far back as 1937, the Peel Commission, appointed by the British then controlling Palestine, concluded that the small area between the Jordan River and the Mediterranean Sea, which is subject to competing claims, should be partitioned into two states, one Jewish, the other Arab.

It is clear that unbridled Jewish settlement in the West Bank endangers any real possibility of implementing a two-state solution to the century-old conflict, a solution based on partition of the land. This is something deeply worrisome to many Israelis. Without dividing the land into two separate states of Israel and Palestine, Israeli opponents of the settlement enterprise argue, the very survival of Israel as a Jewish and democratic country is at stake. Sooner or later, with their high birth rates, the Palestinians in the West Bank and Gaza Strip, together with the Palestinian citizens inside Israel, will make up a majority of the population in the land despite current disputes over the exact numbers. The settlers' appetite for expansion, the critics warn, and the government's failure to set firm, logical borders for a consolidated Israel will eventually, indeed inevitably, result in a single, binational Jewish-Arab state between the Jordan River and the sea. For once the Palestinians are the majority, or almost the majority, it is assumed, they could well drop the demand for a separate, independent state and call for one man, one vote instead. The beleaguered Jewish state, ruling over a non-Jewish majority, will struggle to maintain supremacy and control. Without divine intervention, Israelis of lesser faith than the settlers fear, it could be a recipe for Armageddon.

For Ruthi, two states is no solution anyway. She is not about to give up the Jewish birthright in the West Bank, just as she assumes that her adversaries, the

Palestinians, are not going to give up on their own dream of returning to re-
deem the destroyed villages and abandoned homes left behind in 1948. Her
reasoning reaches into the very core of the conflict, touching on its most sensitive nerves. Just as Israel has returned to the Biblical landscapes of Judea and
Samaria, Ruthi points to the Palestinians' yearning for the coastal cities of Jaffa,
Haifa and Acco, and for their former homes in what are now the leafy, exclusive
Jewish neighborhoods of West Jerusalem.

In this historical equation of rights, Gush Etzion plays an illustrative, in-
trinsic role. Originally founded in the 1940s, Kfar Etzion was one of four
kibbutzim that made up the original Etzion bloc. In the 1948 war, the Etzion
settlements fell with the rest of the West Bank to the Jordanian Arab Legion
and Palestinian militias. The women and children had been evacuated, but
the men fought a heroic battle to the end. Scores were killed. Only four survived and were taken prisoner.

In the immediate aftermath of the June 1967 war, a group consisting
mostly of the sons of those killed in 1948 asked permission to go back to the
mountain. The land had been held by the Jordanian custodian as enemy
property, and was empty. The prime minister, Levi Eshkol, promised in a
cabinet meeting to review the request within a month. The same day, pre-
empting the government, the settlers moved in. Government approval followed, and by September, Kfar Etzion had become the first official Jewish
settlement in the conquered territory of the West Bank.

Today, in the community center auditorium of the rebuilt Kfar Etzion, a
sound and light show tells the history of the Etzion bloc and ends dramatically and chillingly when the screen is raised to reveal the original bunker
where the last fighters met their deaths. I was alone in the auditorium on a
weekday morning as the dry-ice-produced smoke swirled up into the mar-
bled memorial hall built around the bunker, its walls inscribed with the
names of 240 Jews killed in the various battles for the Gush. Their progeny
have pledged never to forget.

In the minds of the ideological settlers, 1948 and 1967 are significant
dates, but only milestones in a long and ancient history. They do not expect
the Palestinians to forget either. "Kfar Etzion was already settled in 1948.
And from the Biblical perspective, this is Eretz Yehuda, the land of Judea,"
says Ruthi. "OK, there was the 1948 war. But those who weren't satisfied
were the Arabs, and there's a price to pay for that. It is our right to live here.
What difference is there between here and Tel Aviv? There are abandoned

Arab houses in Jaffa and Talbieh," she challenges, pointedly choosing the West Jerusalem neighborhood where I live, once a mansion district for wealthy Palestinians who fled the 1948 war and were not allowed back. "It is only a matter of time. What if there's an intifada to return to the houses in Talbieh? Where's the limit, where's the border? If you don't have a fixed ideology, everything is open to argument."

Not surprisingly, Ruthi does not believe that fences and walls will solve anything either. "This fence is not something that came out of peace. It'll just be the starting point for new problems, the departure point for the next war." Sooner or later, she predicts, the Palestinian mortars and rockets will come flying over the fence. "Then what, should we build a higher wall?"

The demographic argument does not sway her. The populations are already so mixed up, she asserts, referring to the 1.2 million Arabs that still live within the Green Line as citizens of Israel, that the demographic problem will merely pop up somewhere else, in a different form. "In the Galilee perhaps, inside the wall," she says, pointing to an area in northern Israel where the population is already over 50 percent Arab, "Or over the wall. The demographic issue is not the point."

There will be no genuine separation, Ruthi contends, unless there is a wholesale transfer of all the Arabs to one side of the barrier and all the Jews to the other—a scenario that she neither advocates nor sees as happening.

Nor is she impressed by the potential danger to Israel as a democratic state. Pointing to opposition to the Gaza withdrawal within Sharon's own Likud Party, Sharon's political machinations to create a majority in the cabinet in favor of the disengagement plan, and his refusal to countenance a national referendum on the contentious issue, she says she is not sure if "we are even living in a democracy today. If there is to be no national referendum at a time like this, then Israeli democracy is finished for me."

Strangely, Ruthi's words echo the thinking of a small but growing sector of the Palestinian avant-garde made up of academics and political activists like Muhammad Jaradat, a refugee "right of return" campaigner from Bethlehem, who would prefer to see a binational country for Arabs and Jews in all the land rather than a truncated Palestinian enclave state in the West Bank and Gaza Strip, bisected by Israel down the middle. Essentially, this is a revival of the PLO's old goal of a single democratic state in all of Palestine, the agenda that preceded the organization's formal adoption of the two-state solution in 1988. The fundamentalist Palestinian organizations like Hamas subscribe to the same one-state goal based on historically determined Islamic hegemony, though they would rather it had no Jews at all.

Muhammad Jaradat works for the Badil (Alternative) Resource Center for Palestinian Residency and Refugee Rights, a Bethlehem-based Palestinian NGO that advocates the right of return for all Palestinian refugees. He is an ardent believer in a binational solution for the Israelis and Palestinians. "The Palestinians will never forget Haifa or Jaffa," he posits, affirming Ruthi's point. "Even as a nonrefugee from Hebron I feel these places are mine. And how can I tell the Israeli Jews that the Ibrahimi Mosque [the Tomb of the Patriarchs, the traditional burial place of the biblical patriarchs Abraham, Isaac, and Jacob, and matriarchs Sarah, Rebecca, and Leah] in Hebron is not theirs?"

Indeed, much of the inter-Palestinian debate about the desirability of independent statehood revolves around the refugee issue and the longstanding Palestinian demand for the right of return. The Palestinian demand is based on U.N. Resolution 194, passed in 1948, which stipulates that the "refugees wishing to return to their homes and live at peace with their neighbors should be permitted to do so at the earliest practicable date," and that compensation should be paid for the property of those who choose not to return. In Palestinian lore, this has become a sacred individual right that cannot be conceded. The roughly 700,000 Palestinians who became refugees in 1948 are now estimated, through natural growth, to number over 4 million. Counting those not registered with the U.N. and other displaced Palestinians, PLO officials put the figure as high as 6.5 million. The majority live in the West Bank, the Gaza Strip, and the neighboring countries of Jordan, Syria, and Lebanon, about a third of them in camps.

The refugee experience resulting from the 1948 *nakba* (catastrophe) forms the core of the Palestinian narrative and identity. It is one of the most sensitive issues to be dealt with if the Israeli-Palestinian conflict is ever to be resolved. But there are no magic formulas. Since the total population of Israel proper stands at just over 6.5 million in 2005, with Jews making up 80 percent of it, no Israeli government could conceivably agree to grant the refugees free entry for fear that the country would be swamped and cease to exist as a predominantly Jewish state.

In late 2001, Sari Nusseibeh, the Palestinian philosophy professor and Al-Quds University president, broke a Palestinian taboo and publicly stated what his countrymen knew but would not acknowledge: that the inherent logic of a two-state solution implies that the refugees should "return" to the new state of Palestine, not Israel. That notion formed the basis of the Destination Map, the document of principles for a final status agreement drafted by Nusseibeh and former Israeli Shin Bet head Ami Ayalon in 2003. Nusseibeh himself has often declared that he would have preferred a single, democratic state where Israelis and Palestinians share equal rights. His conviction that the Jewish state will never willingly self-destruct by allowing this to happen in the foreseeable future has led him to support the alternative solution based on two states.

Since Nusseibeh's position remains controversial and unacceptable to many Palestinians, others still committed to the two-state solution—including the current PA leadership under Abu Mazen—have sought a semantic middle way to try to resolve what they perceive as the historic wrong. PLO officials and negotiators adhere to the principle of return but express a willingness to be flexible on the implementation, on the pace and scale of repatriation. According to Diana Buttu, a young expert in refugee issues and international law at the Negotiations Support Unit (NSU), a technical arm of the PLO's Negotiation Affairs Department, "the Palestinians have a right to return, but have a choice of whether they want to or not."

The PLO strategy in negotiations has been to get Israel to accept the principle of the refugee right to choose and to offer the refugees several options including immigration to the new Palestinian state; rehabilitation and permanent homes in the host countries where they already reside; immigration to a third country which offers to accept them; and finally, returning to what is now Israel. The options would be presented with varying degrees of incentives in a compensation package that, although the negotiators do not say so outright, would favor those who choose not to return to Israel. Israel, for its part, rejects the Palestinian claim to a right of return, arguing that it was not the Jewish state that was responsible for creating the refugee problem, but rather the Arab states that went to war against it in 1948.

Buttu, a startlingly attractive and sophisticated Canadian-born Palestinian, came to Ramallah to make her contribution to the national cause after Oslo. She is one of a group that became known as "Abu Mazen's lawyers"—a team of bright, highly educated Palestinians from the diaspora, graduates of the law departments of the best North American universities, who staff the NSU, a department that Abu Mazen headed from the mid-1990s until 2003. Abu Mazen is himself a refugee from Safed in the Galilee, where he was born in 1935.

Given that most of the nostalgic Palestine the refugees carry with them is buried under modern-day Israel, another controversial question has become how many refugees would even want to return if they had the choice. Khalil Shikaki, the respected Ramallah-based strategic analyst and pollster, published a survey in July 2003 indicating that if Israel were to recognize Resolution 194 or the right of return, only 10 percent of refugees in the West Bank, Gaza, Jordan, and Lebanon would choose to return to Israel, as part of a small number allowed back over several years. And if returning required taking Israeli citizenship, only one percent said they would choose that option. The poll was designed in consultation with PLO officials in charge of negotiations and the refugee issue, Shikaki said. The results, he argued, showed that Israel could afford to recognize the right of return without undermining its Jewish character.

Critics of the poll in Israel and abroad countered that its conclusions were flawed, and that it said nothing about laying the refugee issue to rest. On the home front, Shikaki came in for some trouble as well. On the morning that he was due to release the poll results, a mob from the Al-Amari refugee camp on the southern edge of Ramallah stormed and trashed his offices in the center of town and physically assaulted him, fired by rumors that the analyst was about to deny the refugees their rights.

Even two generations on, any debate on the refugee issue is highly charged and suffused with emotion. Yet on the ground, many of the refugees appear to have already returned to reality. I accompanied Muhammad Jaradat, a thin, energetic man with a lush mane of black hair, on a march one May from the entrance of Bethlehem's Deheisheh refugee camp to the Abu Amar Sports City a few blocks away, to mark the anniversary of the 1948 *nakba*. Only some 150 locals joined the ragtag procession. Some of them were boys carrying oversized cardboard keys to signify their parents' and grandparents' lost homes, but when asked where they come from, rather than answering Beit Jibrin or Malhah or Lifta, referring to their ancestral villages inside Israel as the refugees are supposed to do, they replied "Deheisheh." The grown-ups seemed jaded, standing around in the Sports City courtyard listening to the Palestinian anthem and a couple of speeches blared out through loudspeakers. Someone complained that the proceedings had started before everybody had arrived. But no one else arrived, and ten minutes later, the marchers wended their way back to the camp.

Likewise, in Al-Amari camp, near Ramallah, the ideology of return is fading fast. A few weeks after the mob stormed Shikaki's offices, I sat in a coffee shop in the camp—which today looks more like a poor neighborhood on the city's edge—and spoke with a couple of the residents who had participated in the riot. Jamil, 43, called Shikaki a "liar" for his poll findings and said he and his fellow camp residents would only give up on returning to their parents' former homes "if that is imposed on us." Yet moments earlier, the same Jamil had been expounding on the fact that he did not believe in the possibility of return, and that he would not want to go to live in Israel as an Israeli anyway. He also said he had a sister in Florida and a brother with a grocery store in California. Ideally, he said, he would like to join them, but with three wives and 21 children in Al-Amari, that was not an option. A 25-year-old called Ashraf also went to Shikaki's office though he could not quite articulate why. He has two uncles in New Jersey and wished he could go too. Asked about return, he said he was "fed up with hearing about it."

And somewhat incongruously, in the gray alleyways of Al-Arroub refugee camp, rising up an incline by the Jerusalem-Hebron road a few kilometers north of Karmei Tzur, even Sari Nusseibeh's eminently moderate approach has recently been gaining ground. Jamil Rushdie, 39, a member of the leadership council of Nusseibeh's HASHD, the People's Campaign for Peace and Democracy, is a resident of Al-Arroub. Rushdie, who describes himself as a "Fatah man," was elected head of the Council of Labor Unions in the southern West Bank in the summer of 2004. Eleven of the 27 members elected were HASHD people.

The same summer, Rushdie also ran a HASHD "Smarter without Violence" summer camp for about 150 youths from the Hebron area at the Arroub Agricultural College adjacent to the camp, providing three weeks of education through art, sports, and other activities stressing the importance of peace, democratic values, and nonviolence. Though taking place during the intifada, it was a far cry from the notorious Gaza summer camps where children are trained to jump through hoops of fire and practice the mock storming of Jewish settlements. The point, Rushdie told me at the time, was to learn "how to live with the neighbors. Our partners are the people, not the governments," he stated. "We need to remove ourselves from the ideology."

Of the 9,000 residents in Al-Arroub camp, according to Rushdie, 1,100 had already signed on to the HASHD petition supporting the Nusseibeh-Ayalon plan. Altogether, in the first year following the launch of the plan, some 140,000 Palestinians had registered their names in support, compared with 192,000 Israelis.

Jamil Rushdie spent nine years in an Israeli prison for what he calls his "activities against the occupation" and was released in 1992. He believes in "the establishment of two states that would live in peace together." His vision of living with the neighbors would be unlikely to include Karmei Tzur. The Nusseibeh-Ayalon plan calls for an Israeli-Palestinian agreement based on the 1967 lines, with an option for minor border adjustments and equitable land swaps where necessary. The quid pro quo for the Palestinians giving up the right of return to their homes of 1948 is the removal of all the settlements that would fall in the territory of the new Palestinian state.

Rushdie's family hails from Al-Fallujeh, in the Ashkelon area, where the Israeli town of Kiryat Gat now stands. The refugee issue needs to be dealt with "logically," he said, since bringing the refugees back to Israel "would mean no Israeli state. The most important thing for us is to have our own state in the territories of 1967," he noted, adding that a refugee return to the new Palestinian state "would not be such a bad thing."

For most Palestinians, though, the refugee issue cannot be closed and filed away so neatly. Refugeehood remains a cardinal symbol of the national struggle. Some refugees say that although they know they will not return themselves, they still would not be prepared to sign a paper giving up that right for future generations. Other voices, even within the mainstream Fatah, say that if they had to choose between the right of return and an independent state, they would sooner give up on the state.

In the meantime, an increasing number of Palestinians argue, the Jewish settlers are chipping away at the viability of a two-state solution in any case. Badil's Muhammad Jaradat pronounces that soon the settlement enterprise will reach a critical mass with half a million Israeli Jews living across the pre-1967 Green Line in East Jerusalem and the West Bank, areas the Palestinians claim for their state. As a result, he proclaims, "Things will get resolved very nicely. The settlers are creating a binational state all by themselves." Lawyer Diana Buttu, when asked directly where the PLO stands regarding the question of binationalism, told me that "while we are still committed to the two-state solution, the issue cannot be separated from the settlement issue, which is making a two-state solution impossible anyway." Israel's construction of the wall, she added, cutting away at the remainder of the Palestinian land, was just about the final straw.

And in January 2004, the Palestinian Authority prime minister himself, Abu Ala, added his own voice to the debate in the run-up to the hearings in The Hague. He declared that in his personal opinion, given Israel's settlement building and unilateral setting of borders in the territories as defined by the new barrier, the idea of two states was becoming irrelevant. "If this is the situation, then there is no other solution other than a binational state," said the seasoned PLO politician and negotiator who has invested years in trying to shape Palestinian independence. "The idea raised in the past by the Palestinians might be the only possible solution."

It remains something of a mystery how Jalal Abu Toameh's forbears ended up in Baqa al-Gharbiya over a century ago. There are family rumors of a skeleton in the closet, a murder that forced his grandfather to flee his native village of Qaffin, home of the Toameh clan, and seek the protection of a more powerful clan in the village across the valley. In those days there was no Green Line, no West Bank or Jordan or Israel, just the Ottoman Empire.

The Toamehs of Baqa al-Gharbiya (Baqa West) added Abu to their name to give it a more sophisticated ring, and to distance themselves from their humble beginnings. Jalal's father, who was born in 1910, built the house Jalal lives in today. Now expanded into a three-story residence painted a pale lemon and set in a pretty garden, it has a Volvo and an SUV parked in the drive. Jalal recently completed a renovation of the original wood-paneled domed reception room on the ground floor.

Baqa al-Gharbiya, a lively commercial town of 20,000, radiates entrepreneurship and prosperity as well as tradition. Its main street is lined with restaurants and fast-food eateries that offer traditional *shwarma* (strips of roasted lamb or turkey) in either pita or a freshly baked baguette. Boutiques display low-cut puffy ball gowns, though most of the women and teenage girls on the street wear the headscarves of conservative Islam. Toy shops are filled with bright-colored plastic tricycles, baby swings, and slides, and there is a large new mosque with twin minarets and a traffic circle with a fountain outside.

Though the houses of Qaffin are only a couple of kilometers away from Baqa al-Gharbiya as the crow flies, and are even visible from the town's higher points, Jalal, now a distinguished-looking man in his late 50s with graying hair, a smoky voice, and a cultured air, cannot remember the last time he crossed the valley to visit his distant relatives there, including Muhammad Toameh, known to all as Abu Rushdie, the almost toothless weather-beaten farmer and father of 16.

When the armistice lines were drawn up between Israel and Jordan in 1949, Baqa al-Gharbiya fell within the new state of Israel, in the area known as the Triangle, while its sister village of Baqa al-Sharqiya (Baqa East) remained in the Jordanian-held West Bank along with Qaffin. Four years later, Kibbutz Metzer was established to the north. Fear of arrest by the Jordanians kept the populations of the two Baqas apart for nearly 20 years, but the Arab villages of the area were physically reunited when Israel conquered the West Bank in 1967.

A tiny hamlet called Nizlet Issa, which sits between Baqa East and Baqa West, spread out over the next 30 years until the houses started joining up in the middle, straddling the Green Line and fusing Israel and the West Bank into one. On the seam between the two Baqas, the bustling popular market of Nizlet Issa sprung up. Israelis and Palestinians, Jews and Arabs alike would flock from the surrounding towns, villages, and farming communities to shop at the fruit and vegetable stalls and the permanent grocery and household stores, to place orders at the metal and stone workshops, and to bring their cars for repair. In deference to the peaceful culture of commerce, once the intifada broke out in late 2000, the army placed its checkpoint regulating traffic between Israel and the West Bank on the road just beyond the market, about a hundred meters further inside Palestinian Authority territory, leaving Nizlet Issa in purposely ambiguous terrain and accessible to all.

Things started to change in the summer of 2001 when Aharon Obidiyan, a 41-year-old Jew who worked as a kosher-food supervisor in factories in the area, was shot in the head at close range by unknown Palestinian assailants as he loaded shopping into his car. The morning after the killing soldiers came in and dismantled the temporary street stalls, leaving nothing but a few crushed watermelons and rotting vegetables on the dusty ground. Then, as pressure in Israel grew for physical separation from the West Bank, and the construction of the security barrier got underway, a pall of uncertainty fell over the two Baqas. At first, the fence was built to loop around the back of

10. *There can be few more paradoxical existences than that of a Palestinian Arab in Israel: The wall winding between the houses of the Arab Israeli town of Baqa al-Gharbiya and the neighboring Palestinian Authority town of Baqa al-Sharqiya in the West Bank. Credit: Esteban Alterman/The Jerusalem Report*

the PA-controlled Baqa al-Sharqiya, stranding about 6,000 Palestinian residents of the West Bank in a no-man's-land between the steel security-curtain and the Green Line. Later, in February 2004, as a result of internal and international pressure, the army tore down that 8-kilometer section and moved the barrier to between the two Baqas, onto the Green Line itself. Now an 8-meter-high concrete wall snakes its way through the houses of Nizlet Issa for several hundred meters, dividing east from west. An army-manned crossing point in the wall, overlooked by a gray cylindrical watchtower, allows locals with special permits and Jewish settlers from the area to cross 24 hours a day. On the east side, the Nizlet Issa popular market is now a flat, bulldozed wasteland, the stores and workshops having disappeared overnight from the face of the earth. There is nothing ambiguous about that.

Jalal Abu Toameh was born in Baqa al-Gharbiya around the time that Israel was founded and served three times as its mayor. His first term in office was in 1969–70 as a 20-year-old, when the youngsters of the village—the soccer team, as they were known then—decided to mount a rebellion against the rule of the *mukhtars* (traditional chiefs). Jalal also served terms in the late 1970s and 1990s. Now he is chairman of the Arab Farmers' Council and busies himself with maintaining the family's agricultural estate and olive groves opposite Metzer.

There can be few more paradoxical existences than that of a Palestinian Arab in Israel. While some 700,000 fled into exile in 1948, about 150,000 stayed put on the land and were granted citizenship in the new Jewish state. Their steadfastness gained them little standing or respect in the Arab world. Rather, they were treated for many years as objects of suspicion for having chosen to live among the enemy. At the same time, they were considered a potential fifth column by the state and lived under military rule until 1966, requiring a permit from a (Jewish) district governor to travel from one village to another.

The Arab minority in Israel constitutes about a fifth of the population. It has undergone a dual process of "Israelization" and alienation, resulting in a unique, if split, personality. The educational and material standards of the community far surpass those in the West Bank, Jordan, or Syria, setting Israel's Arabs apart from the generally reactionary and lethargic societies of the Middle East. Israel's Arabs fully participate in the country's democratic process and are elected to the Knesset. One of Israel's more radical and controversial politicians, Azmi Bishara of the Arab nationalist Balad Party, briefly stood as a prime ministerial candidate in the campaign of 1999.

(Balad, a Hebrew acronym for National Democratic Alliance, also means "village" in Arabic.) The polls gave him only 2–3 percent before he backed out of the race to help Ehud Barak. Yet the Arabs of Israel have suffered decades of discrimination in areas like state budgets, land allocation, and appointments to positions of influence, preventing any real partnership in the decision-making process.

Though over 90 percent of Arab voters supported Ehud Barak, he disappointed them by failing to appoint an Arab minister to his government, which would have been a first. He did not even engage a single Arab-backed party in his coalition talks to form a government, leaving the Arab sector smarting. In the next prime ministerial ballot, most Arabs did not vote, which contributed to Sharon's victory. On the professional level, even vaguely security-related careers, including in many of the state industries, remain off-limits. Underpinning the Israeli establishment's relationship with the country's Arab citizens is the notion that at heart they remain part of the Palestinian nation.

Israeli Arabs often used to explain their dichotomy as stemming from the fact that "their country was at war with their people." But when peace was on the agenda, from 1993 onwards, their lot did not significantly improve either. Occasionally, the alienation from the state has been so acute as to lead individual Arab citizens to cooperate in the Palestinian campaign of terror. A 26-year-old man from Baqa al-Gharbiya was charged with murder in March 2005 for having knowingly driven a West Bank suicide bomber to a nightclub in Tel Aviv a month earlier, where the bomber blew himself up along with five Israelis, in violation of the unofficial cease-fire in place at the time. There have also been some outbursts of popular rage, as in October 2000, when Arab communities all over Israel came out in solidarity with the Palestinians of the West Bank and Gaza during the first bloody days of the Al-Aqsa intifada. Though the Arab-Israeli protesters and rioters were unarmed, 13 were shot dead by police. Notwithstanding the complexity of the relationship, the Arabs in Israel have proved overwhelmingly loyal to the state for more than 50 years. The trouble, they say, is that they still feel that their loyalty is something they have to constantly prove.

Jalal Abu Toameh lives the paradox, but he is in absolutely no doubt that Israel is where he belongs and where his future lies. One illustration of this is the way he has nurtured ties over the years with Kibbutz Metzer, the Jewish communal farm with which he once ran a gas station as a joint venture, as opposed to the total disconnect with Qaffin. Though I had known of him for years, I first met Jalal in early 2004 when I joined him and his old friend and contemporary, Metzer's Yoav Ben Naftali, for a lunch of hummus and salad in a basic Baqa al-Gharbiya eatery. Another illustration of Jalal's integrationist philosophy is the fact that even when he was the mayor of Baqa, he insisted on sending his three sons and two daughters to a Hebrew-language state school in the Jewish town of Hadera, over 20 kilometers away.

Sitting in the modern reception room on the third floor of the Abu Toameh house, furnished with plush velveteen couches, I ask Jalal how it is possible to integrate and fully belong in a state where the national anthem speaks of the Jewish soul longing to return to Zion and the blue and white flag features a star of David. "I can live with that," he replies confidently, coincidentally dressed in a starched blue-and-white striped financial-district-type shirt as if to prove the point. "You respect my difference and I'll respect yours. If a Jew observes the Sabbath, I have to respect that. And he has to free the Arab worker up to go pray on a Friday. These are mutual values." In Baqa al-Gharbiya, Israel's Independence Day is not celebrated. Nor do the residents mark *Yom al-Nakba*, the anniversary of the Palestinian catastrophe of 1948. Jalal says that when he was a kid, he and his friends would provoke the Jordanian soldiers sitting on the West Bank border because they knew they could. The Jordanians were not allowed to chase them into Israeli territory. Here they were safe.

Israel's Arabs have on the whole expressed satisfaction with the new barrier, believing it to provide the clearest definition yet of their permanent status as citizens of the state. However, the concrete separation wall not far from Jalal's house has not taken away the always-latent anxiety he harbors about what the future may hold. If anything, the Israeli policy of separation has opened up questions of identity and belonging that Jalal had thought were closed. Israeli-Jewish public figures from across the political spectrum have recently been raising the idea of a territorial arrangement in the West Bank based on land swaps of a grander scale than the "minor border adjustments" the Palestinians had envisaged at Camp David. Israel would annex the large settlement blocs in the West Bank and cede to the Palestinians some of its own territory—namely, the heavily Arab-populated towns of the Triangle such as Um al-Fahm and Baqa al-Gharbiya that sit just within the Israeli side of the Green Line, with the aim of strengthening the Jewish majority inside the state. Without drastic action, Israeli projections suggest, the Arab minority within Israel will increase to 25 percent by 2025. Veteran Laborites like Ephraim Sneh have made such proposals in the past, and more recently, far-right politician Avigdor Lieberman added his voice in enthusiastic support.

After half a century of trying to blend in, nothing pains Jalal more than the idea of being considered up for swaps. "I didn't come here as a new immigrant," he starts, "I was sitting in my house. The state came to me. I was given citizenship. That's it. For me, there is nowhere else. I can adapt myself to new rulers and customs and educate my children to fit in, but don't come to talk to me about changing my citizenship. I am not a piece of furniture or merchandise to be haggled over." A friend of Jalal's who has come to join in the conversation, Baqa council member Said Abu Muh, adds, "I told Ephraim Sneh, why don't you go and live there yourself?"

As an Arab-Israeli, Jalal is happy to separate from what he calls the "negative elements" of the West Bank and its population. "They aren't part of this state. They don't have any status here. We, on the other hand, have invested a lot." While on his walls he displays photos of himself meeting the late Yasser Arafat and "cares" what happens to the Palestinians, he has focused all of his life's work on the Israeli side of the Green Line, not on that of the Palestinians. He thinks his children, all university graduates, have probably only ever been into the West Bank twice in their lives.

Jalal is neither in favor of the barrier, nor particularly against it. Ultimately, he does not believe fences and walls can help resolve the conflict. "But if it brings quiet for my friends in Metzer and doesn't harm my friends in Qaffin, then welcome. I can't be for it, though, if it takes their land."

Meanwhile, in Israeli Baqa al-Gharbiya, other than keeping out thieves, the wall has proved something of a disappointment. Before it went up, many Arab-Israelis here had assumed that it would be good for business and for the town's economy, since the Israelis would no longer have access to the cheaper goods of the West Bank. Instead, as in Jewish Israel, Baqa al-Gharbiya has lost the cut-price labor force it used to rely on from the West Bank. Few of the local youth have learned basic trades; there are no builders, plasterers, or olive pickers to hire. Construction has become a much more costly affair, there is a shortage of street cleaners, and Jalal is turning over his groves from traditional methods to mechanization, and promoting the modernization of farming in the Arab sector through the council he heads.

As twilight falls, the green neon lights of the mosque minarets flick on. From the balcony off Jalal's third-floor lounge, Baqa al-Gharbiya begins to twinkle below. The sense of harmony that Jalal has managed to create, the balance between fidelity to the land and fidelity to the state, makes me think of Muhammad Dahleh, the ambitious Arab-Israeli lawyer from the Galilee who is battling to dismantle the barrier through the Supreme Court in Jerusalem and who would just as soon see the dissolution of the Jewish state.

Contrary to Jalal, Muhammad Dahleh does not accept the definition of Israel as a Jewish state. Rather, he wants Israel to be a state for all its citizens. That would mean extending fundamental privileges such as the law of return, which grants unlimited immigration and instant citizenship for Jews, to eligible Arabs as well. The ingathering of exiles is a basic tenet of Zionism. It is no less a matter of principle to the Palestinians. Though Dahleh represents a relatively marginal stream among the Arabs in Israel, his negation of the legitimacy of the Jewish state and its right to exist would resound deep down with many Palestinians, on both sides of the line.

"It drives me crazy to be an unwelcome guest in this exclusive club of the Jewish homeland," says Dahleh, during our conversations in Jerusalem. "I personally can never admit that I live in a Jewish state in my own homeland. I won't accept Israel's continuous attempt to make us immigrants. We are the indigenous population, part of the landscape."

Dahleh's wish, or dream, is to have a binational state in all the land "where two peoples could exercise self-determination. I'm talking Switzerland, or Belgium. I know for Jews this is crazy. They would say that's not what we fought for. But for me, all the other options are frightening."

Few Israeli Jews are likely to buy into Dahleh's utopian vision of a secular Eden out of choice, so his first line of attack is to challenge Israel through its own legal system. The real struggle, he asserts, will take place about ten years from now, in the Knesset, the bedrock of Israeli democracy. At present, all parties and politicians running for the Israeli parliament have to be prepared to swear allegiance to Israel as the Jewish state. Dahleh is confident that that will not always be the case, which will open the door to the struggle for binationalism and a one-state solution from within. "It's going to be very embarrassing for Israel," he continues, assuming that by then, the Palestinian majority between the river and the sea will join his cause. "If there's a call for one man, one vote, what exactly can they say?"

Ten years is about as long as Dahleh gives Abu Mazen, the heirs of Oslo, and the Palestinian struggle for an independent state. "I think Abu Mazen will be the last stop for the two-state solution," he predicts, suggesting that whoever comes next is unlikely to be more moderate or conciliatory than Arafat's successor. "He's going through the motions, but I don't think he'll make it. If he can't pull it off, no one will."

In the meantime, some 60,000–100,000 Jewish settlers are about to find themselves beyond the barrier, while more than a million Arab citizens of Israel, along with over 200,000 Palestinians in East Jerusalem, will for the foreseeable future stay in. Ruthi is right. It's not much of a separation.

By the spring of 2005, there are 12 families living in Tzur Shalem, perched above the deep ravine with a breathtaking view of the mountains. There is a small wooden play-gym for the young children between the trailers, and asphalt or gravel paths leading up to the front doors. The furthest mobile home has a baby stroller parked outside along with a white plastic clotheshorse dotted with colorful pegs, the trappings of domesticity in the wilds of ancient Judea. Beyond that is a khaki-green lookout post raised on stilts, one of several army positions dotting the settlement's perimeter. On the approach-road to Karmei Tzur, there is an army base. It is only the presence of the IDF that makes Jewish life sustainable here. Regardless of the legal status of any given settlement, the army is committed to protecting Israeli civilians wherever they are.

In the four years since Tzur Shalem's foundation, the area between it and the mother settlement of Karmei Tzur has filled up. There are a couple of rows of brand-new red-roofed houses waiting to be inhabited, and a new neighborhood of half a dozen mobile homes. The neighborhood is named "Yonatan" (Jonathan) in honor of Jonathan Pollard, the former U.S. naval intelligence analyst convicted of spying for Israel and now serving a life term in an American prison. Recently, the Defense Ministry confirmed plans to build a "smart" electronic fence around Karmei Tzur. Ruthi notes that approval has been given to include Tzur Shalem within it, imbuing the precariously established outpost with another sign of permanence.

One former settler leader once remarked that the true Zionist response to terrorism is not to build outposts, but to capture the terrorists. As far as

Ruthi knows, Shmuel's killers escaped into the Al-Arroub refugee camp and have never been found. Ruthi says that first of all, the Arabs have to learn not to kill. The task the ideological settlement movement has taken upon itself, in the meantime, is to hold on and build, despite, or because of, the fence.

Ruthi is planning to add another story onto her house to accommodate her growing children. "They talk about us expanding, but I've watched the village out of that window expand several times over," she says. "Why has that man got more right to his house on the opposite hill than I have to this one? Because it's been there longer? He built his three years ago. I saw. There's plenty of place for everyone here. What's needed is place in the heart."

Ruthi believes that if Israel had responded with more massive force at the beginning of this intifada it would have ended much sooner, to the benefit of all. "They've suffered too," she says, nodding toward her neighbors in Beit Umar, where she has never set foot. She also believes that if her own people were more united, "the Arabs wouldn't dare do what they do." The nation of Israel is full of self-hatred, she says, and does not understand its own worth. The governments zigzag and look for quick fixes, like the barrier, devoid of any long-term vision. "Where do we want to be 30 years from now?" she asks. "What is the goal?"

During Shmuel's *shiva*, Ruthi had photocopied one text for those who came to pay their condolences, a text that Shmuel had read out at the bat mitzvah party of his eldest daughter Re'ut, exactly a year before his death. It was a cry for Jewish unity from a book called *Love of Zion and Jerusalem* written in Europe in 1891 by Rabbi Yosef Yaffe, Shmuel's great grandfather. "We are torn from within and scattered about," it read. "Seek peace and unity . . . because peace and unity are a shield against all affliction and distress."

In her own efforts at outreach and unity, Ruthi teaches art at a school for troubled youth in Jerusalem and volunteers once a week at Natal, a Tel Aviv-based hotline for terror victims and soldiers. She formed a close and lasting friendship with a secular Jerusalemite who also lost her husband early on in the intifada, and worked energetically to set up a hospitality corner for soldiers at the Etzion Junction offering free refreshments and a place to relax, built entirely on donations and run by local volunteers.

The efforts have been reciprocated, at least in part. Ruthi was chosen to light one of the 12 torches at the annual state ceremony on the eve of Israel's 57th Independence Day at Jerusalem's Mount Herzl in May, 2005. The lighting of the torches is one of the most emotive, symbolic moments of the national calendar; being chosen to light one is an official gesture of embrace, a clear manifestation of belonging in the Israeli fold. Even on the podium, though, the ambiguity is inherent. Another of the twelve to be honored in 2005 was Arieh (Lova) Eliav, the Tel Aviv octogenarian, veteran politician, diplomat, and special operations man who, among other things, became a lone voice in the Labor establishment after 1967 opposing Jewish settlement in the occupied territories. A former protégé of Golda Meir, the prime minister who once declared that there was no such thing as a Palestinian people, Eliav went on a one-man mission to survey the newly conquered territories after the Six Day War and came back convinced that the Palestinians should be treated as an incipient nation. His principles cost him his political career.

Ruthi's dream is just to be able to live here on this mountain in Judea, without the need for bulletproof cars, armies, and guns in a country with no borders. "Why not?" she asks. "Let them vote for an Arab Knesset, we'll have a Jewish one, and that's it."

She also realizes she may have to wait for the Messiah to come for any such vision to be realized. For that, she states, would be "a sign of the End of Days. That would be true peace."

9

The Gray Line

It is dark and drizzling in Caesarea, the sleepy, flat coastal town built on Roman ruins that spreads out at the feet of the smokestacks of the Hadera power station. Boasting Israel's only 18-hole golf course, the place has the serene and genteel air of a wealthy retirement village. A middle-aged Russian immigrant guards the gate of the Neot Golf apartment complex whose curved buildings seem to have turned their back on the sea. It is off-season; the car lots are almost empty, the windswept pathways deserted. Only a couple of jet skis parked in an open garage hint of the leisurely lifestyle that summer will bring.

Avi Ohion lives alone on the ground floor at the center of one of the curves, in a compact bachelor pad that consists of a lounge and kitchenette and one bedroom. The apartment feels more like a beach chalet or pied-à-terre than a permanent home. A Pooh bear and other soft toys are arranged on top of a cupboard in the salon, and there is a bowl of candy on the coffee table as if the children might drop by. They won't. Three *yartzheit* candles are burning in long, thick glasses—the kind of candle that lasts a week. When they are finished, Avi will light more. There is a series of framed photos on the wall of Revital, Avi's former wife, as an attractive woman in her 30s, laughing in sunglasses on a boat, with their sons Matan, 5, and Noam, 4, two gorgeous boys with long, curly locks. The low music humming from the radio and a vase of flowers that are well into their second week complete the shrine-like atmosphere. It is over two years since Revital, Matan, and Noam were murdered in their little stucco house in Kibbutz Metzer by Sirhan

Sirhan of the Tulkarm refugee camp. I have come to give Avi the message from Sirhan's father, Burhan.

I have my doubts that Avi will react well to Burhan's words of sympathy, doubts that only increase as Avi recounts the events of that night in November 2002. He was at work in Tel Aviv, editing the sports news at Channel Two, and was due to knock off at 11 p.m. A few minutes after 11, his cell phone rang. It was Revital, calling as Avi had asked her to, with an efficiency that made him laugh to himself even a year after their divorce, to remind him about some bureaucratic task he needed to do. When he answered the call, Avi heard the children shouting in the background, in what would prove to be their last moments alive. "I called out 'hello, hello,' but nobody answered. Then there was a loud noise, a crashing sound, and the call got cut off. Revital hadn't managed to say a word. I tried to phone back but there was nothing. It was clear something terrible had happened. I got a friend to drive me to the kibbutz. We flew up the highway. On the way, there was a news flash on the radio that there had been a terrorist infiltration at Metzer. Then I broke down."

Avi is tall and wispily thin, like a hollow reed, his short, dark hair speckled prematurely with gray. He wears black-rimmed, yuppie spectacles, jeans and a casual top, and a Kabbalist bracelet of red thread on his wrist. He sits cross-legged on the beige couch, or with his socked feet up on the large square coffee table which is scattered with at least five remote controls to work the music and TV equipment. On and off, tears stream silently down his face and he reaches for tissues to wipe them away. The pain is dense, solid. It hangs like an extra presence in the close air of the small room offering no relief or refuge from the raw emotion or from the unspoken, inevitable pangs of guilt. No relief, because Avi says he is not yet ready to be cured.

There is no gentle or subtle way of introducing the fact that I have sought out and met with the family of the muderer Sirhan Sirhan, living just 20 kilometers away to the southeast, so I just come straight out with it. It sounds like a confession, blunt and almost sacrilegious, but Avi, until recently an inured TV newsman, does not flinch. He hardly shows any reaction at all, even though the Sirhan family has not yet received any exposure in the media. He sits silently as I plug on, describing my impression of the murderer's parents and relating some of the things they had said. About how Israeli soldiers had killed Palestinian children and about Sirhan Sirhan's obsession with Iman Hijjo, the baby killed by an Israeli shell in Gaza. About the family's past wanderings and the return to Burhan's home in the Tulkarm camp under the auspices of the Oslo accords. About the hardened mother and the grief-stricken father, and about Burhan's conviction that his teenage son had never meant to kill infants, but that, untrained as he was, he had merely fired at random, hitting anybody in his path.

Avi makes no comment and asks no questions. When I tell him that the father has asked me to convey a personal message, he signals for me to go ahead. I start reading out Burhan's words from my notebook, translated into English which Avi understands: how both fathers have lost their children because of this "crazy war," of the need for rationality to stop it, and of the desire to "work together" for "a just peace." I end with Burhan offering his condolences, and requesting that I pass on his phone number in the Tulkarm camp should Avi be willing to talk. When I finish there is a long pause. Avi's eyes swim with confusion. He smokes nervously, and seems to have retreated to a remote place deep inside. A few moments later he abruptly gets up, heads for the kitchenette and says, "Let's move on."

By the time Avi reached Metzer on the night of the attack, the kibbutz was surrounded by security forces. He could not get close to the gate for two hours. "I stood there, I phoned people at the TV and the news, but there were just rumors, that one old woman had been killed, that there were only injuries. Nobody knew anything." Eventually, after speaking with a kibbutz official, Avi was allowed in just as the bodies of Revital, Matan, and Noam were being brought out of the house. "I went into the kids' room. It was covered in blood. It had all happened on Matan's bed. I took the two pacifiers. Later we understood from how they'd been found that Revital had been hugging them both, trying to shield them with her body. If you want to tell his father anything," he says, relating to Burhan Sirhan for the first and only time, "tell him his son didn't fire at random. The shooting was concentrated and precise. He shot Noam in the eye, Matan in the mouth, and Revital in the head. I know, because I saw."

Avi has no desire to communicate with Burhan. In general, he believes, Israelis will not be able to look at the other side at all until they are no longer in mourning or visiting someone in mourning. "We are a small country. It hits everyone," he says of the terror, "if not in your family, then close to it. I don't know anyone who's not been affected somehow." Right now, Avi is for himself, and for his people. He says he would much rather be on "his side" than feel like the betrayed people at Metzer—like Yitzhak Dori, the kibbutz secretary who spent the days before he was killed fretting about the route of the security fence and its effect on the farmers of Qaffin.

Grown men are crying on both sides of the wall. An indelible line has been drawn between the dank alleyways of the Tulkarm refugee camp and the coast. The land of milk and honey is stained with blood. Nearly 40 years after Israel conquered the West Bank, East Jerusalem, and the Gaza Strip, the fate of the territories is as unclear now as it was then. It is a bleak and frightening thought, but perhaps there is no real solution. "Since 1967, left and right governments have had roughly equal time in power in Israel," posits Avi. "Neither has been able to reach a settlement, or at least one that could be implemented."

In the end, he surmises, "there will be a Palestinian state and it will be attached to us. They will remain Arabs, and they won't like us then either. In the meantime the fence has to go up all the way, however brutal it may be, in order to save life. It is doing the same on the other side if you take the loss of Palestinian life this year compared to last, though that interests me less."

However undesirable this curtain of concrete and wire may be, it is impossible to sit before Avi Ohion and not understand the need. It was and is pressure from ordinary Israelis, with the backing of the security establishment, that has driven the process of separation. Ariel Sharon still may not want the barrier, but according to the defense officials responsible for building it, the project is no longer in the prime minister's hands. The army machine has taken over; the bulldozers have taken on a momentum of their own. The officials laud the barrier's role in stopping the march of terror. Shin Bet statistics suggest that in the year since the first third of the fence went up, from August 2003 to July 2004, attacks in Israel by Palestinian terrorist infrastructures based in the northern West Bank declined by approximately 90 percent.

Nevertheless, Israeli officials are also sensitive to the effects of the barrier both on the Palestinians and on Israel's standing in the international community. As a result, there is a conscious effort to turn the image of the barrier from that of a problem between Israel and the Palestinians to part of the solution; to present it as a component of peace, not war. For the reality is that any Israeli government, whether on the right or on the left, would be hard-pressed to push a peace process forward with its civilians under attack. Colonel Dany Tirza insists that even if terror subsides and political negotiations resume, the barrier remains crucial as the last obstacle between peace and the lone perpetrator of a mega-attack who would blow the process up.

At least officially, there has been increased consideration of the negative impact on the Palestinians. To this end, Brigadier General (res.) Baruch Spiegel was recruited by Defense Minister Shaul Mofaz in January 2004 to head an interagency team dealing with Palestinian civilian and humanitarian issues arising from the new barrier. During his army career, Spiegel served as, among other things, commander of the combat Golani Brigades and as coordinator of government activities in the territories. A trim and affable man with sandy-colored hair and a neat beard, Spiegel has in recent years been known for more dovish affiliations, working as a private consultant for the Economic Cooperation Forum, a left-leaning Tel Aviv think tank formulating final status issues for an Israeli-Palestinian settlement, and as a regular participant on the "second track" circuit of unofficial meetings among Israeli, Palestinian, and other Arab academics and experts. The timing of Spiegel's appointment, three weeks before the start of the hearings against the barrier in The Hague, led some Israeli cynics to assume that the fence-mender and humanizer had been brought in as a fig leaf.

Just over a year later, on February 20, 2005, the same day that the cabinet in Jerusalem finally approves the revised route for the rest of the barrier in the wake of The Hague and Israeli Supreme Court rulings, I sit with Spiegel in his office in the Defense Ministry in Tel Aviv as he lays out his vision of how it will work and the benefits it will bring.

Spiegel notes that a combination of factors have influenced and determined the barrier's route, among them U.S. pressure, the courts, and a part played by his team. He is obviously satisfied with the result: 90 percent of the fence, he says, is now on the Green Line, the 1949 armistice line, or has it "as its reference," where the barrier lies not exactly on the line, but close enough. With further alterations, he asserts, that percentage could rise to 95. Spiegel does not belittle the suffering of the Palestinian individuals who are still adversely affected, and on whose land the walls and fences encroach. "Each dunam and each olive tree is somebody's living," he concedes, pointing out that the army has replanted tens of thousands of trees on the eastern, Palestinian side of the barrier. "But in the big picture, in strategic terms, we have a fence on the Green Line."

Moreover, the short-term adjustment for people on both sides should not obscure the benefits of the barrier for Palestinians generally, Spiegel insists. Once the West Bank barrier is completed, he portends, the occupation will loosen its grip as the army will "move to the fence," like in Gaza. In theory, after the four small settlements slated for evacuation from the northern West Bank under Sharon's disengagement plan are removed, and if quiet prevails, internal checkpoints can be dismantled and a quarter of a million Palestinians in the Jenin governorate will no longer interact with Israeli soldiers other than at organized crossing points in the fence. "If today the army is 80 percent inside the West Bank and 20 percent along the seam," Spiegel says, "that balance will be reversed." In short, the army will move away from the day-to-day tensions and turmoil of occupation and return to its classic purpose: defending Israel by preventing incursions and invasions from across the lines.

To what extent that means the separation of the two peoples remains unclear. On Spiegel's desk there is a slick brochure prepared by the Seam Zone Authority presenting the plans for the new Erez terminal that will be located inside Israeli territory at the northern end of the fenced-off Gaza Strip after the Israeli withdrawal. A $40 million construction nicknamed in Israeli defense circles as "Project Spiegel," it will serve as a model for the future movement of people and goods between Israel and the West Bank. There will be some 29 crossing points along the Israel-West Bank seam, in addition to the dozens of agricultural gates for use by Palestinian farmers whose lands lie beyond the fence. Spiegel is spearheading efforts to replace the army at the major terminals with a professional civilian border regime. Advanced technologies and biometric "smart card" systems will be introduced in order to allow those Palestinians who are authorized to cross to do so as efficiently, and with as little friction, as possible. "Since 1994, after the bombs at Beit Lid, Rabin started a system of closure," Spiegel expounds. "Now we are going back to a system of 'normally open' thanks to the fence. It's a paradigm shift. The concept is changing from being normally closed. If there is a security alert, the measures taken will be local. Collective punishment will come to an end."

However, the meaning of "normally open" has changed dramatically from the policy of unhindered passage that Moshe Dayan had envisioned, and from the freewheeling commerce that once flourished between Israel and the West Bank, with its flood of Palestinian laborers into Israel that characterized the pre-intifada years. In the fall of 2004, I visited the first new terminal completed on the Israeli-West Bank seam, at Jalameh, between Afula and Jenin. The buildings have been painted in pink, lemon, and terracotta tones though the aesthetic effect is somewhat spoiled by a concrete military bunker in the middle of the site covered in khaki camouflage netting. Four pedestrian lanes with computerized booths, manned initially by soldiers, have the capacity to process 2,800 Palestinian permit holders per hour crossing between Israel and the West Bank. Above the lanes, armed soldiers keep watch, patrolling on raised metal walkways. Dozens of specially designed parking bays outside provide the infrastructure for a "back-to-back" system of trade, allowing for the transfer of goods between Palestinian and Israeli trucks with neither having to drive across the divide.

The sophisticated terminal was almost deserted. Only a slow trickle of Palestinian day laborers was crossing on foot since hardly any of the local population held work permits at the time. Under the close supervision of two soldiers, crates of dairy products were being offloaded from one forlorn Israeli truck and reloaded onto a Palestinian truck destined for Jenin. When I ask Spiegel later about the huge investment in such an underutilized facility, he explains that the large capacity of the new terminals gives Israel the option of being "normally open." In typical contradiction, the stated policy of the government of Sharon and Mofaz is to phase out all Palestinians working in Israel by 2008.

Spiegel, in a lilac shirt, jeans with the cuffs turned up, and tinted spectacles, occupies an office in one of the older buildings in the compound that houses the Defense Ministry and the army HQ in central Tel Aviv. Touted as the first Hebrew city to rise out of the sand, Tel Aviv's original grid of low, white Bauhaus and International style buildings is being increasingly dwarfed by modern skyscrapers of glass and steel. A block away from Spiegel's office, the gleaming blue-glass Azrieli Towers stand proudly to attention over the traffic-clogged Ayalon highway. Inside the round, square, and triangular buildings executives and office workers beaver away, shoppers browse in expensive boutiques, and thin women work out and then relax at the rooftop health bar, snacking on Cajun-spiced tofu wraps and sipping skinny lattes. Inside the Defense Ministry compound itself, the security hub of the country, the old squat brown office blocks are outshone by the new accommodations, a futuristic structure with a silver helicopter landing dish on the roof and a steel tube running down the middle.

⋯⇒◯⇐⋯

Only 44 kilometers away from Tel Aviv as the crow flies is Ramallah, the PA's administrative capital in the West Bank. While Jerusalem remains the spiritual and historic capital of Israel, and is equally coveted by the Palestinians and the wider Muslim world, the two cities of Tel Aviv and Ramallah are the actual beating hearts, the engines that tick with life in this conjoined land of two nations who stand to be separated, but are nervous about surviving the operation.

During the last months of the Al-Aqsa intifada, in the second half of 2004, as exhaustion and resignation set in, Ramallah had already decided to move on. New commercial projects started going up, a United Colors of Benetton store arrived in the recently opened glass-fronted Plaza shopping mall, and luxury housing projects, one called "Dreams," were springing up. Restaurants like Darna, an elegant eatery with a large outdoor patio offering nouvelle Mideast cuisine, opened for business, as did clubs and bars like Sangria's, whose advertisements promised "siempre fiesta," a nonstop party. Boutiques with foreign-sounding names like Macy's and the Safari shoe store stocked Ralph Lauren and quality Israeli lines, just a block or two away from the rubble-strewn Muqata'a compound where a sallow-looking Yasser Arafat continued his political machinations while slowly rotting inside.

In July 2004, the first Ramallah International Film Festival took place and the $6 million Japanese-funded Ramallah Cultural Palace was inaugurated six years after its inception. In August, its plush, state-of-the-art 740-seat auditorium was the venue for a week-long production of "Fawanees" (Lanterns), the first-ever Palestinian children's musical performed by sixty youngsters from Ramallah, Jerusalem, and Bethlehem and accompanied by the German Youth Forum orchestra. The musical, based on a short story by Palestinian novelist, resistance member, and martyr Ghassan Kanafani, who was killed in a car bomb in Beirut in 1972, played to a full house and got a standing ovation every night from an adoring, mainly Palestinian audience that shed tears of joy and pride.

But not everyone was ready for a fiesta; the four-year intifada had left the overwhelming majority of Palestinians poorer and more radical, and the rage of the militants and the disaffected youth simmered just below the surface. One September lunchtime, as diners chatted quietly on Darna's patio and music played softly in the background, restaurant owner Osama Khalaf described to me how a gang of 60 or 70 young Fatah thugs armed with sticks and stones had recently marched on the place on two consecutive Sunday nights and forced everybody to leave. They were protesting in support of Palestinian prisoners who were hunger-striking inside the Israeli jails, and more specifically, were protesting against what they saw as an unseemly local obsession with the Arab world's "Superstar" singing contest, aired on Lebanese satellite TV, in which a Palestinian crooner from nearby Salfit was facing off in the finals against a Libyan contender. Khalaf's restaurant was not even screening "Superstar," but that did not help. Nor did the PA police, who said they could not afford him any protection against the thugs. (The Libyan won in the end.)

In the spring of 2005, I visit Qadura Fares, a prominent member of Fatah's young guard and a Ramallah representative in the Palestinian Legislative Council. He meets me in his bureau in a smart office building that also houses the PA Interior Ministry in the up-and-coming Balu' district of the city. Until a recent cabinet reshuffle, Fares had been minister of state in the PA government, responsible for the portfolio of "the wall." Since the file had not yet officially passed to anybody else in the new cabinet, Fares was continuing with his activities, liaising between the PA and local authorities on projects for priority areas affected by the barrier, working with grassroots activists involved in the popular resistance campaign, and following the various cases in the Israeli courts. One highlight came with the August 2004 visit of Dr. Arun Gandhi, grandson of Mahatma Gandhi, to the Palestinian territories and Israel to campaign for nonviolence. Addressing a joint Palestinian-Israeli peace rally by the 8-meter-high concrete wall cutting the West Bank village of Abu Dis off from Jerusalem, Gandhi declared that the wall reminded him of the "Bantustans which the Apartheid regime in South Africa tried to create."

Fares, a wiry, thin man in his early 40s, has come to work smartly dressed in a gray suit with a faint pinstripe, a light gray shirt, and a subtle patterned tie. He has dark hair and a moustache, wears tinted steel-framed spectacles a bit like Spiegel's, and speaks in fluent Hebrew in a husky smoker's voice. A royal blue pack of Rothman's International lies before him on the coffee table in his spacious L-shaped office suite furnished with a large wooden desk, a long conference table, and black leather couches. Behind the desk there is an obligatory picture of Arafat, who has by now been five months in the grave. On another wall there is a framed photo that looks like a graduation picture of about a dozen young men, mostly with thick, dark walrus moustaches, seated in two rows. It is a rare photo, taken in an Israeli prison in 1984. Fares is in the front row next to a younger, hairier Jibril Rajub, another grassroots Fatah leader who went on to become a senior PA security official in the West Bank.

While the likes of Spiegel, Shaul Arieli, Dany Tirza, Sharon, Barak, and countless other Israeli professionals and politicians spent their formative years in military uniform, Fares, like most of the young generation of the "insider" Palestinian leadership, spent theirs behind bars. Fares went to prison in 1980, charged with belonging to a Fatah cell that carried out what he calls "military operations." He spent over 14 years in jail, finally being released in the mid-1990s under the auspices of the Oslo accords. It was in jail that he learned Hebrew; studied the politics, mores and literature of his enemy; and garnered the contacts and solid nationalist credentials that led to a career in politics.

Fares was born in the village of Silwad in the district of Ramallah in 1962, when Jordan still controlled the West Bank. The family owned a lot of land and worked in agriculture. Since the start of the Israeli occupation, however, some 90 percent of the land has been confiscated, he says, for the building of the settlement of Ofra and for the Ramallah bypass road that allows settlers to travel around, not through, the city. Silwad has a history of resistance. In March 2002, a 23-year-old sniper from the village perched himself on a hilltop above the Ein Arik army checkpoint between the village and the nearby settlement of Ofra and with an old hunting rifle killed seven soldiers and three Israeli civilians. At the same spot on the old road in the 1930s, two villagers from Silwad ambushed a British officer who had been sent from Egypt to quash the anti-British resistance in the area, and who was said to have boasted that he would tread the Palestinians under his boots. The two villagers killed the officer and stuffed his boots in his mouth, then were captured and publicly hung in Jerusalem. According to Fares, the whole village went on foot to Jerusalem to witness the execution.

A few minutes' drive away from Fares's office, Arafat lies in a tomb that has been encased in a glass mausoleum. Three khaki-clad members of the PA security forces stand watch at the grave, which is covered in fresh flowers and wreaths. Some of the tributes are from foreign dignitaries from places like Chile, Sweden, and Greece. Most are local offerings, though, bearing notes inscribed in Arabic, such as the one from the accountancy department of Nablus's Al-Najah University. At 11 a.m. this weekday morning, a small group of students have come to pay their respects, the girls all dressed in Islamic headscarves and long robes. Next, a couple of bareheaded middle-class women approach, and after them, a father with two children. Outside the glass enclosure a line of young pine trees has been planted to augment the original cypresses, along with a couple of olive trees, their truncated branches sprouting first leaves, symbolizing peace to the Israelis and, to the Palestinians, *sumud*.

Beyond the moribund Muqata'a, the struggle goes on, though it appears constantly to change in form and purpose. Like many of his peers, Fares seems to be expecting a third intifada, perhaps imminently, and is already laying the blame for it at Israel's door. Unless Israel boosts Palestinian confidence in the current PA leadership by removing all the checkpoints, releasing significant numbers of prisoners, and allowing the Palestinians to get to work, he warns, and so long as Israel continues building the barrier and the settlements, the people will turn on Abu Mazen and conclude that there is no partner on the other side. Then, he argues, the spirit of compromise that led the Palestinians to settle for the idea of an independent state on 22 percent of the land may well dissipate altogether in favor of fundamentalist Hamas's goal of a greater Palestine stretching from the Jordan River to the sea.

When it comes to Hamas, Fares speaks from experience. Khaled Masha'al, one of the organization's top leaders in exile, comes from Silwad and belongs to the same clan. He last visited the village in 1975, when Fares was 13. The next time Fares met him was in Damascus in June 2003, when he and two other Fatah envoys went secretly to negotiate a *hudna* (temporary truce) in the intifada. An agreement was reached. That lull lasted 51 days.

As we are speaking, an aide enters Fares's office and hands him a slip of paper with a note informing him of rioting at the barrier construction site in the village of Deir Balut, in the Ramallah district. Seven have been injured. Four weeks later, two youths aged 14 or 15 would be shot dead during another clash along the fence route in the nearby village of Beit Liqya. The anti-wall resistance has failed at the political level. The barrier still protrudes over the Green Line into occupied lands. But for the people on the ground, Fares says, a change of a few hundred meters at least minimizes the damage. Between the fields of confrontation and the courtroom, thousands of dunams of farmland have been saved.

With the reality of separation setting in, though, the appetite of ordinary Palestinians for a state with defined physical borders is waning. Fares, a leading supporter of the Geneva Initiative, still believes in the two-state solution but says his people increasingly ask him where that state will be. "They ask, can you have a state with this barrier? Our answers are not convincing."

The logic of Tel Aviv does not wash in Ramallah, 44 kilometers from the coast. The notion that the security fence will enable a peace process, and eventually enable the division of the land into two states, does not make the distance. I repeat to Fares the point made by Spiegel, that over 90 percent of the barrier is more or less on the Green Line. "We say we're for a Palestinian state in the territories of 1967 *with* Jerusalem," Fares retorts. "Jerusalem is the key to peace and to war." As for Tirza's assertions that the walls and fences will probably have to be moved as the result of negotiations, he responds: "That's how he speaks to journalists. But we know Israel's method of creating facts on the ground. I know the security mentality of Israel. This is a border. I am 100 percent sure that this structure is only the beginning."

Settlements, barriers, poverty, and despair. If these continue, fears Fares, a pinstriped prophet of doom, the days are coming when there will not be anyone left on the Palestinian side ready to talk about compromise, about settling for a state in the 1967 lands. Nor will Israel ever agree to a single, bi-national state, he assumes. So that leaves the option of continuing struggle, which he foresees as evolving from a national one to a religious one between Muslims and the "Chosen People." "There will be a bloody war until God intervenes. Either we give hope," he says of Fatah, the secularist national movement, "or we disappear."

Already, the Palestinian masses are punishing the corruption-ridden, internally splintered Fatah for the woes that have befallen them. In a second round of local city council elections held in May 2005, Hamas chalked up impressive gains in Gaza and the West Bank. In the walled city of Qalqilya, the fundamentalists trounced the Fatah establishment and won all 15 seats. For the time being, Sami Khadar, the veterinarian of the city zoo, will likely have to shelve his dreams of turning the ladies' mosque above the natural history room into a cinema that screens animal movies. A PA reformist, Fares belongs to the camp of Fatah young-guard firebrand Marwan Barghouti and sees him as the future leader of Palestine. But like a symbol of his people's prison mentality nurtured under the lock and key of the occupation, Barghouti, convicted by Israel on terrorism and murder charges for his role as intifada militia chief, sits in jail.

Under any other circumstances, Spiegel and Fares are the kind of reasonable people who ought to be able to agree. Both support a two-state solution based on the old armistice line, with some give and take, and seek a compromise that will lay this hundred-year conflict to rest. But the barrier has come between them; they now find themselves on opposite sides of the divide. While one sees Israel's defensive system of fences and walls as contributing to the peace, the other views it as a source of destruction. Each side's fear of the other is the essence, and the tragedy, of the conflict; distrust and mistiming are the enemies. Now that Prime Minister Sharon has finally come around to the idea of a Palestinian state, those Palestinians who still support it no longer seem to believe it will happen. In the meantime, the idea of living behind fences, walls, and gates is putting them off. As far as many ordinary Palestinians are concerned, if the choice is between an independent state or free movement, open borders, jobs in Israel, the sunset, and the sea, they would sooner pass on the state.

At Israel's state ceremony on the eve of its 57th Independence Day, before an audience of thousands and with millions more watching on TV, Ruthi Gillis, the widow of Shmuel, lit her torch. Standing on the podium at Jerusalem's Mount Herzl, built around the grave of Theodor Herzl, the visionary of the Jewish state, reading the text prepared for her by the officials of state, she dedicated her torch to "the lovers of the Land of Israel, in all its length and breadth." The same morning, the liberal *Ha'aretz* newspaper's editorial pleaded that "there is nothing more optimistic and important to strive for than the repartition of the Land of Israel, by agreement and not through war, into the state of Israel and the state of Palestine," without stinginess, without whining, and without settling of accounts. The same week, the Palestinians marked the *nakba* of 1948. On May 15 they stood still for a minute at midday in streets all over the West Bank and Gaza Strip as sirens wailed in mourning over the establishment of the Jewish state. In a speech before the Palestinian parliament, Prime Minister Abu Ala said the Palestinians' "wound is still bleeding 57 years later," citing Jerusalem under occupation, the daily expansion of the settlements, and "the separation wall strangling our land." Thousands of Palestinians rallied for the refugees' right of return.

Six decades after the creation of Israel, four decades after it conquered the West Bank, and seven decades after the Peel Commission suggested partition for the first time, the fundamental issues and dilemmas remain the same. The Israelis want to maintain the democratic and Jewish state, but have not yet decided in what borders. The Palestinians want a state without the confinement of physical boundaries, but have yet to define where the homeland of this nation of refugees begins and ends.

The Green Line has turned gray—not only because of the 600 kilometers of meandering fences, dirt tracks, walls, and wire, but also because of the lingering ambiguity over the barrier's meaning and purpose. The dust of controversy, the depths of conviction, and the pain and trauma on both sides have all obscured what kind of border it will ultimately be. The political, legal, and diplomatic furor raised by the barrier is as much about the fundamental disconnect between the two peoples as it is about the actual concrete and steel. Whether the divide is between Tel Aviv and Ramallah, two cities striving for modernity and normality, or between Metzer and Qaffin, two communities struggling with the diminished importance of agriculture and the departure of their youth, or between the two Baqas, both Arab yet split between Israel and the West Bank, there are deep psychological, emotional, and historical chasms and great distances to cross.

As Robert Frost wrote in his classic 1915 poem "Mending Wall," "Before I built a wall I'd ask to know / What I was walling in or walling out." Since neither Israel nor the Palestinians seem to know who or what they want in and out, fences have so far not made for good neighbors, and walls have not been mending.

The barrier is both symptomatic and symbolic. It cuts to the core of the questions Israelis and Palestinians confront. It has created a seam, a thin line between peace and war that has the potential of becoming either a melding suture or a stubborn, angry scar. Turning this seam into a juncture of healing and reconciliation, not hostility and confrontation, will take people of goodwill, spirit, courage, and conscience. And of these I have met many—in Israel, in Palestine, and in the vaguer gray areas in between.

Index